*Pitt Series in Russian and East European Studies*

# TROUBLED
# WATERS

◆ ◆ ◆

*The Origins of the 1881
Anti-Jewish Pogroms
in Russia*

## I. MICHAEL ARONSON

*University of Pittsburgh Press*

Series in Russian and East European Studies No. 13

Published by the University of Pittsburgh Press, Pittsburgh Pa. 15260
Copyright © 1990, University of Pittsburgh Press
All rights reserved
Baker & Taylor International, London
Manufactured in the United States of America

**Library of Congress Cataloging-in-Publication Data**

Aronson, Irwin Michael, 1942–
    Troubled waters : the origins of the 1881 anti-Jewish pogroms in
Russia / I. Michael Aronson.
    p.    cm.—(Pitt series in Russian and East European studies :
no. 13)
    Includes bibliographical references.
    ISBN 0-8229-3656-9
    1. Jews—Soviet Union—History—Pogroms, 1881–1882.    2. Soviet
Union—Ethnic relations.    I. Title.    II. Series: Series in Russian
and East European studies : no. 13.
DS135.R9A74    1990
947'.004924—dc20                                    90-33957
                                                        CIP

*I dedicate this book to the memory of my late parents,*
*Minnie (Koss) and Sam Aronson,*
*and my late father-in-law,*
*Jack Israel Flack,*
may their memory be for a blessing.

# CONTENTS

# TABLES AND MAPS

## Tables

## Maps

# ACKNOWLEDGMENTS

I could never have written and completed this book without the loving and able assistance, support, and encouragement, as well as endless patience, of my wife, Alice. She read and typed the manuscript more times than she would probably like to recall. She made innumerable valuable suggestions regarding matters of style, clarity, and sense. Her exertions as housewife, mother, and professional working woman allowed me to have the time and resources I needed in order to devote myself to this work. In a very real sense, she shares its authorship with me. I could never adequately express in words the appreciation I have for her.

I also wish at the outset to indicate my fondest gratitude to my beloved children, Simcha Yisrael, Ayelet Michal, and Adin Yaacov, who tolerated my numerous foibles so well during all the years of my work on this study, and helped me in more ways than they can ever know.

I was introduced to the ambiguities, "dynamic tensions," and profundities of the world of the spirit and the intellect by Rabbi Norman T. Goldberg in Waco, Texas. I was introduced to history as a way of thinking by Professors Ralph Lynn and Rufus B. Spain at Baylor University. Professor Alfred J. Rieber introduced me to the intricacies of Russian history at Northwestern University. Professor David Joravsky gave me further guidance in this field at Northwestern and saw me through to my Ph.D. To them and all my other teachers over the years I extend my deepest appreciation for the valuable intellectual baggage they helped me collect.

Numerous people gave me their encouragement, kind support, and expert guidance over a very long period of time as I worked on this book. I would like to single out Professors Hans Rogger and John Klier and thank them for their valuable and detailed scholarly comments on my manuscript. I owe a special debt of gratitude to Professor Alfred Abraham Greenbaum, who has shared with me during most of my professional life his deep friendship and profound learning in a broad range of disciplines. My colleague Mrs. Ella London was always at my side to urge me on when the going got rough; my particular thanks to her. Professors Edith Frankel, Yonatan Frankel, Shlomo Lambroza, Alexander Orbach, and Steven Zipperstein also deserve special acknowledgment for assistance they gave me at various times.

Librarians at Bar Ilan University, Columbia University, Haifa University, the Hoover Institution and Stanford University, the Jewish National and University Library of Jerusalem, the Library of Congress, Northwestern University, and the Slavonic and Jewish Divisions of the New York Public Library helped me gather the sources for this book. I would especially like to mention Mr. Yaacov David Aronson, head of the Bar Ilan University Library, and the staff at the Bar-Ilan University Interlibrary Loan Department for the cheerful and willing assistance they always extended to me as my work was nearing its completion.

My gratitude to Professor A. A. Greenbaum, Mr. Zvi Shier, and the late Mr. Moshe Springer, may his memory be for a blessing, for help in translating works in Yiddish.

I would also like to express my appreciation to the staff of the University of Pittsburgh Press for their patience, professionalism, and unflagging interest in this work.

Finally, I am grateful for permission to use (in revised form) material from my article, "Geographical and Socioeconomic Factors in the 1881 Anti-Jewish Pogroms in Russia," *The Russian Review* 39, no. 1 (January 1980): 18–31.

# NOTE ON DATES

Unless otherwise indicated, all dates are given according to the Old Style calendar in use in Russia prior to the 1917 revolution. During the nineteenth century the Old Style calendar was twelve days behind the New Style.

# TROUBLED
# WATERS

# INTRODUCTION

◆ ◆ ◆

THIS BOOK IS ABOUT A CONSPIRACY, OR, MORE PRECISELY, ABOUT THE absence of a conspiracy. It sets out to disprove the widely held assumption that the Russian government, or elements within it or close to it, supported the pogroms of 1881. As I argue the case, the focus will shift back and forth between the Jewish and Russian aspects of the problem. In the process the book becomes essentially a study of Russian history, even though it was occasioned by an episode usually placed within the context of Jewish history.

The events in question had an immense impact on the future development of Russian Jewry and world Jewry as well; they were perhaps much less significant from the perspective of the Russian Empire as a whole. However, these considerations must not be allowed to obscure the wider Russian context if we are to deepen our understanding of what happened. For the pogroms of 1881 had implications not only for Russian Jews and Jewish-gentile relations; they also offer important insights into the functioning of the Russian state, official attitudes toward popular violence, the relations between the central government and the provinces, and the nature and effectiveness of the mechanisms of state control.

Since the beginning of the Christian era, if not earlier, a polluted current of anti-Jewish sentiment has flowed through European life. All too often this current swelled into torrents of physical violence. In the eighteenth century many Europeans felt that their world had entered an "Age of Enlightenment." However, the anti-Jewish attitudes persisted. A political struggle for Jewish emancipation was waged, but it was a difficult and prolonged campaign. Meanwhile, popular violence against Jews continued, as, for example, in the "Hep, Hep" rioting that occurred in a number of German principalities in 1819.

In the nineteenth century many educated Russians and many in Russia's ruling circles prided themselves on the idea that their country had become an important member of the European community. Yet the struggle for Jewish emancipation was nowhere more prolonged and difficult than in the empire of the tsars; and anti-Jewish violence was nowhere

3

more consequential. Indeed, after the major anti-Jewish rioting of 1881–84, the Russian word pogrom ("massacre," "devastation") came to be commonly used throughout the Western world to designate mob violence against Jews, no matter where it occurred and, even more broadly, mob attacks made against any minority group.

Following the first pogroms of 1881–84, even more destructive large-scale anti-Jewish violence occurred in Russia in 1903–06 and 1918–21, in conjunction with the revolutionary upheavals that racked the country. These disasters were followed by World War II and the Holocaust, which overwhelmed many of the same places.

Major questions in regard to the anti-Jewish pogroms of 1881 are: Were they planned, or were they a spontaneous outburst? Did the Russian government, or influential persons close to it, sponsor the eruptions of mass violence, aiding and abetting them, or were the violent attacks the culmination of diverse political, social, economic, and cultural currents flowing together in an unplanned and hardly foreseen cataclysmic floodtide over which individuals or groups had almost no control? The answers that have been given to these questions, and the way in which those answers were arrived at, have important implications from the point of view of both historical methodology and the content (and lessons) of the historical analysis produced.

The upheavals and transformations the world has undergone during the past century are well known. Historical conditions and world views have changed accordingly, often drastically. Yet the events of 1881 retain their significance as marking the beginning of a new era of tremendous suffering and physical violence—as well as achievements and triumphs of the human spirit.

Soon after the assassination of Alexander II and the pogroms of 1881, the Russian imperial government abandoned the tentative steps it had recently taken toward the liberalization of Russian society and Jewish emancipation and began adopting reactionary and repressive policies, which would eventually contribute to its own violent destruction.

More and more Jews began to feel an urgent need to find a way out of the troubles plaguing their people. Increasingly large numbers embarked upon emigration to the United States, Palestine, and other places. The internationalist ideology of socialism continued to attract Jewish youths, while many other Jews now turned to Zionism, the nascent modern political form of Jewish nationalism. The socialists for the most part devoted themselves to the revolutionary movement within the empire; the Zionists sought a solution outside Russia. There were also Zionists who dreamed of a socialist Jewish homeland and Zionists who supported the revolutionary movement in Russia, hoping that a more liberal regime would aid them in the realization of their nationalist goals.

The mass emigration movement laid the foundations for the flourishing and populous American Jewish community of today. The socialist movement eventually brought about the establishment of the Soviet Communist state on the territory of the old Russian Empire, after the horrors and destruction of World War I, the revolution, and the civil war. Modern political Zionism eventually brought about the establishment of the State of Israel, after the horrors and destruction of World War II and the Holocaust. The supporters of each of these two new states hailed its emergence as a triumph of humanity and as a promise of a better future. The struggle to bring these promises to complete fruition continues today. Meanwhile, the Soviet Union and Israel remain major centers of international political and moral concern, as they have been since their inception.

The pogroms of 1881, because they stand out as an influential prelude to these momentous developments and as an important turning point at the beginning of the present era, are of enduring interest. Any reevaluation of them must have implications for our understanding of all that followed—in both the Russian and the Jewish contexts.

The interpretation of the pogroms given immediately after their occurrence and by historians some years later are no longer adequate. One interpretation—the idea that the pogroms were planned, which for the sake of convenience I call the conspiracy theory—seemed to be confirmed by analogy to subsequent events, and it became standard for almost all writers until very recently.

In 1971, Hans Rogger raised a series of telling questions against the conspiracy theory, which should have put serious students on the alert.[1] However, his pioneering study has had almost no repercussions in secondary works touching upon the history of the Jews in Russia during the late nineteenth century. Here are several examples taken from reputable scholars.

The widely respected *Encyclopaedia Judaica* which appeared in 1972, soon after Rogger's article, sets the scene.

> The year 1881 was a turning point in the history of the Jews of Russia. In March 1881 revolutionaries assassinated Alexander II. Confusion reigned throughout the country. The revolutionaries called on the people to rebel. The regime was compelled to protect itself, and the Russian government found a scapegoat: the notion was encouraged that the Jews were responsible

for the misfortunes of the nation. Anti-Jewish riots (pogroms) broke out in a number of towns and townlets of southern Russia, including Yelizavetgrad (Kirovograd) and Kiev.[2]

According to the late Shmuel Ettinger, "the very fact that the pogroms spread so rapidly seems to indicate that there was some guiding hand involved. It is possible that this was the work of a clandestine group of courtiers (the Holy Brotherhood, as they were called), who had set themselves the task of combatting revolutionary terror." Ettinger went on to discuss the influence of local conditions, but his emphasis remained on the willful negligence of the authorities, the desire of the "ruling clique . . . to make anti-Jewish feeling the basis of its policy of *rapprochement* between the authorities and the people," and "the use of mobs to implement policy."[3]

Ettinger's words are from a 1976 translation of a text published in 1969 and left unrevised. But here is what Benjamin Pincus, a scholar writing in 1988, had to say:

[An] outstanding characteristic of the pogroms was their lack of spontaneity. The regions where they were carried out, and the fact that they were so widespread—in 1881 alone there were pogroms in 215 places—constituted proof that there was a directing hand. Besides this circumstantial evidence, a body of reliable evidence exists testifying to the presence of emissaries from Moscow who spread rumours and incited riots in the pogrom towns, and also to the existence of bands of rioters who went openly from town to town to take part in the pogroms. Who had an interest in the eruption of the pogroms and who was behind their organizers? The central authorities, headed by the tsar himself, were apparently not against "clean" pogroms of the "accepted" kind: it was hinted authoritatively both by word of mouth and in writing that, in the event of a pogrom, the reaction should be permissive and tolerant, and use should not be made of fire-arms. The difference of opinion between those openly advocating pogroms and their opponents sprang mainly from the fear that it would be difficult to control the pogroms if they got out of hand and went beyond the "accepted" bounds; furthermore, they were liable to make a bad impression abroad, with all that this entailed economically and politically. Against the background of this confused policy of the central authorities, the local authorities could do a great deal either to encourage the rioters or else to suppress them firmly. A semi-official body that had a considerable role in organizing pogroms was the "Sacred Society", founded on 12 March 1882, which numbered among its leaders the Minister of Interior, Ignatyev. . . .

The official explanations for the pogroms . . . [could not mask] the direct responsibility of the authorities for the atrocities that were committed.[4]

The interested student may choose at random any recent text, whether devoted to Russian Jewry in particular, or modern Jewish history more broadly, or late imperial Russia in general, and it is almost certain that, if the pogroms of 1881 are mentioned, they are interpreted according to the conspiracy theory.

This study rejects the conspiracy explanation and sets out to revise our understanding of the events of 1881 in light of all the evidence now available and in accord with a rigorous and critical approach.

A surprisingly large amount of material from people on the spot is available in printed sources—statements, memoranda, reports, analyses, diaries, letters, and memoirs—from non-Jews and Jews, victims and observers, officials on all levels, soldiers and civilians. Occasionally one even gets to hear from the common people, participants in the pogroms or onlookers, though such eyewitness testimonies are not as available as one might have liked. As a result, one is forced to rely mainly on outsiders in trying to understand the mind-set of the common people, with all the complications this entails. Everyone had a particular explanation and interpretation of what happened. People with an anti-Jewish perspective did not necessarily agree with one another, nor did those with a Jewish or Judaeophile perspective.

I have attempted to engage these sources in a dialogue on two levels. One is the level of interpretation. I asked how the sources explained the pogroms and whether such an explanation was legitimate. The other level is that of information. I searched for the facts and data in the sources and compared them with what is known from other sources.

Almost all the sources used in this study, both those close to the events and those farther away, including the historians who wrote about 1881 during the next half-century and more, had rather pronounced biases. On the one hand, their answers to the question of how the pogroms originated reflected their own basic assumptions, attitudes, and aspirations. On the other hand, insofar as they were active in public affairs, their answers were meant to be used as guides in formulating policy and practical political, economic, social, and cultural programs. Keeping this in mind, one can critically analyze the old interpretations and try, as far as possible, to see through them in the quest to elicit whatever reliable information they have to give.[5] Often it is possible to learn things that the informants themselves would have had no idea they were revealing. Readers will see this for themselves over and over in the pages that follow.

I do not assume that anyone has a monopoly on the truth, not even myself. My advantage, I hope, over my sources is mainly that I have the luxury of hindsight and the perspective of distance, which they could not have had. I have tried to guard against allowing the position taken by any particular author on the Jewish question to be the only (or even the main) factor in determining the value I ascribed to his testimony. Jewish and Judaeophile sources could err in their evaluation of the events as badly as anti-Jewish sources; and the latter sometimes offered insights that the former were far from perceiving. This point will frequently find illustration in the text below.

Unfortunately, two important avenues of research were closed to me. I was not able to read the Russian periodical press of the period firsthand, nor have I had the opportunity to investigate Soviet archives. However, I hope these deficiencies have been remedied by my reliance upon the excellent research and scholarship carried out in recent years by other scholars. My debt to them will become clear in the following pages.

New insight in reevaluating what happened in 1881 may be gained if we can discern why the conspiracy theory was so widely accepted and why it persisted for so long, particularly among Jewish historians and writers. Several recent scholars of Russian Jewish history have made observations that draw our attention to an important aspect of this problem: what we might call the manpower aspect. They have noted that scholarly literature devoted to Russian Jewish history "dates to the prerevolutionary period and is largely the creation of Russian Jewish historians." The Russian revolution, the Communist dictatorship over the history profession in the Soviet Union, especially under Stalin, two world wars, the Holocaust, and various cultural purges—all combined to destroy Russian Jewish life and Jewish lives, including at least two generations of native scholars. As for scholars abroad, they were totally denied access to original historical documents in the Soviet archives. According to one author: "in a less tragic age [the study of Russian Jewry] would have given rise to reassessments and qualifications. This normal progression failed to occur in the discipline of Russian Jewish history, for the reasons listed above. Consequently, the judgements of these early pioneers and partisans have become securely established in the secondary literature. . . . Bibliographies devoted to Russian Jewry are dominated by the names of men who wrote their most important works almost a century ago."[6]

The manpower considerations help explain the longevity of the conspiracy theory, but they do not account for its popularity. Nor do they exhaust the catalogue of influences at work in the failure to reexamine this explanation for such a long time. After all, not all historical research into the pogroms ended in 1914, or even in 1930 or 1940; and for the most part, later scholars continued stubbornly to cling to the view that the Russian government, or certain elements within it or close to it, sponsored or supported the 1881 anti-Jewish violence.[7] As for general studies and textbooks on the history of Russian Jewry, they are almost unanimous in presenting the conspiracy explanation (examples are quoted above). What accounts for this persistence?

In Jewish consciousness three biblical images are deeply ingrained as archetypes of Jewish oppression. First is that of Pharaoh, who enslaved the Children of Israel in Egypt. Next are the treacherous and murderous Amalekites, who attacked the Children of Israel in Sinai after their exodus from Egypt and became the symbol of causeless hatred. And third is the archetypical murderer Haman (by tradition a descendent of Amalek), who tried to destroy all the Jews in the Persian Empire during their dispersion after the destruction of the first Jewish commonwealth. For the most part, Jews understood the biblical stories as showing that the fate of the Jewish people in exile was decided almost exclusively by the ruler. The native population was merely his instrument, even if willingly so. In this view the popular masses may have been backward, brutal, and mean, in general, and nurtured one degree or another of hostility to Jews, in particular, but primarily they acted at the instigation of their ruler.

From the very beginning of the anti-Jewish outbreaks in 1881, the biblical images must have sprung to people's minds and influenced their interpretation of the events. Indeed, these images were invoked repeatedly in both journalistic and historical literature on the pogroms written by Russian Jews, as well as others.[8]

Paradoxically, perhaps, the biblical paradigm also fitted in well with a certain understanding of the antireligious Enlightenment view of historical and social development, which became widely accepted among Jews with the popularization of the Haskalah (Jewish Enlightenment) movement in Russia from the middle of the nineteenth century. According to this conception, the history of mankind is marked by continuous progress, in both the moral and the material spheres. This progress comes about with the advancement of knowledge. Just as modern science was succeeding in revealing the laws operative in nature and matter, so modern rationalist thinkers could expect to discover more and more of the natural laws operative in history and society. Using this knowledge, the state and society could be restructured, and mankind's happiness assured.

There was one important difference between the laws of nature operative in the world of matter and those operative in the world of humankind: the former operated independently of the will of people, whereas the latter would take effect only if people applied their intelligence and will. Followers of the Enlightenment did not always show an awareness of the implications of this distinction between *descriptive* scientific reasoning and *prescriptive* rationalistic thinking. Furthermore, they imagined that the rational laws of nature operative in society were beneficent, while scientists placed no moral judgements on the laws of matter. In any case, the important point for my purpose is the emphasis that rationalistic, humanistic thinkers placed upon human thought and will.

If these thinkers felt that there was so much room for optimism, how did they explain the abundance of evil—the cruelty, the misery, the inequality, the lack of freedom—in history and society? They found the explanation in the reign of ignorance and superstition, unnatural established custom and irrational ancient laws. This situation endured because those in power, a limited circle of privileged persons organized in the church and state, profited from it. It would change with the application of human reason and intelligence.

Human beings are infinitely perfectible, in this view. Their character, morals, and values are largely determined by their environment and their institutions. Improve these, and people will improve. Make good laws, and good, prosperous, and happy people will be the result. This was thought to be not too difficult, nor was the process imagined to be a very lengthy one, since humankind had already progressed so far in knowledge and wisdom. In short, enlightened government—or perhaps even an "enlightened despot" of some sort—was thought to be able to bring all good things to the people at large. By the same token, society's ills could be blamed primarily on the ruler or ruling circles.

The historians who have written the history of Russian Jewry during the last one hundred years have, for the most part, been liberal, rationalistic humanists in orientation who adopted Enlightenment views to a greater or lesser degree. In particular, they tended to believe that enlightened government could be instituted rather mechanically, the main problem being one of education, and that such a government would foster a liberal and tolerant populace. Conversely, if the population was unenlightened and brutal, then the system of government must be to blame. These historians carried on a feud with Russia's rulers much more than with the people of the Russian Empire, so, when mass violence struck the Jews, liberal historians naturally looked for the culprit in the government. They were impressed by the facade of strength and control displayed by the Russian autocracy. They could not believe that any large-scale popular movement in the empire could take place without the assistance and approval, or at least the tacit consent, of the authorities.

Liberal historians have also tended to look upon the Jewish people mainly as victims, often of benighted rulers pursuing unenlightened policies. Hostility to Jews was thought to be mainly the work of outside agitators. If the local population and the Jews had been left to themselves, so the argument ran, then their relations would have developed amicably. But when outsiders intervened, Jewish-gentile relations were distorted and aggravated. This approach to Jewish history is another avenue conducive to belief in conspiracy theories.

To illustrate the accuracy of this portrayal, let us take just two of the most important writers on the pogroms of 1881, Emmanuil B. Levin and Simon M. Dubnow. The works of both of these men deeply influenced all subsequent interpreters. Levin investigated the events on the spot, whereas Dubnow wrote about them as scholar and historian.

Levin was born in Minsk in 1820 and died in St. Petersburg in 1913. He was a well-known writer and public figure, active mostly in the Russian capital. Beginning in the 1840s, he became an early and ardent supporter of the Haskalah and of spreading secular education among Russian Jews. He was among those who took the position that "enlightened" Jewish leaders must guide their people to modernize themselves and become culturally more like their neighbors, as a prerequisite for being granted emancipation by the state. Levin took an active role in the establishment of the paternalistic Society for the Promotion of Culture among the Jews of Russia, drafting its constitution and serving as its first secretary. The purpose of the society, established in 1863 in St. Petersburg, was to teach Jews the Russian language and encourage Jewish youth to study secular subjects and the sciences.

Levin's patron was Baron H. O. Guenzburg, who commissioned him to write a number of works on Russia's discriminatory and restrictive Jewish legislation. The aim of these works was to promote the campaign for Jewish emancipation and equality. In short, E. B. Levin was an important and typical figure in the Russian Haskalah movement.

He was also an important figure in introducing the conspiracy theory of the 1881 pogroms. Toward the end of 1882, Levin put the final touches on a 250-page book entitled *Evreiskii vopros i anti-Evreiskoe dvizhenie v Rossii v 1881 i 1882 g.* (*The Jewish Question and the Anti-Jewish Movement in Russia in 1881 and 1882*). The book was never made public. It was produced on a hectograph machine, without the author's name, and intended for submission to the High Commission for the Review of Existing Laws Concerning the Jews in the Empire (later known as the Pahlen Commission) established by Alexander III.[9]

In a forceful and seemingly well-informed manner, Levin asserted that the pogroms were the result of a well-thought-out plan, prepared in advance, and carried out with the complicity of government officials both in the capital and in the provinces. He outlined many of the ideas that were later used by all writers who accepted the conspiracy theory. Several points made by Levin are quite revealing when one tries to understand his worldview and its influence on his interpretation of the events.

For example:

> Many representatives of the regime in the provinces, even high-ranking ones, must have been personally involved in the anti-Jewish movement, for this is the only way to explain the otherwise unthinkable fact that *in a well-organized {blagoustroennoe} state,* for such a long period of time, the authorities, knowing each time about the disorders being prepared, allowed themselves to be caught napping and did not take any preventive measures in advance. This idea finds confirmation in the contrary fact, that in the northwest guberniias, where there are so many Jews, *not one pogrom took place, because of the firm, energetic declaration of the governor-general to the authorities in the guberniia, that he would not tolerate any disorders in the region under his jurisdiction.*[10]

In short, the Russian government had it in its power to control events and chose not to do so, in conformity with the anti-Jewish plot.

Elsewhere, Levin says:

> In a word, with few exceptions, complete freedom to beat the Jews, to injure and mutilate them, to violate their wives and daughters, and to steal their property was granted [by the authorities]. Meanwhile, apart from a few rare exceptions, the rioters did not allow themselves any improper pranks against the authorities, or even against the lowest ranking officials. On the contrary, they often listened to the *admonitions of private persons, . . . . Christians not from the official ranks.* Only thanks to this, several Jewish homes and shops with goods were left untouched. *Many Christians themselves saved Jewish moveable property from destruction.*[11]

Levin was referring here to events of 1882 in the town of Balta in particular, but he affirmed that the situation was similar in 1881 in other places. The important point is the implication of Levin's words, that the government was bad and the people basically good.

Here is another highly revealing statement:

Thus, all the facts enumerated above bring us to the conclusion that the anti-Jewish movement was not engendered and did not arise among the people, but on the contrary, the people was deceived, confused, led into error, by inspirers and leaders who have not been exposed till now and will probably never become known. If, after what has already been said, still more confirmation is needed that the *anti-Jewish movement* was not spontaneous or incapable of being overcome, and that it *could easily and quickly have been suppressed and taken care of by orders from above,* then one can refer to the remarkable fact that when the Austrian government, concerned about the influx of Jewish refugees, made representations to our government, then the pogroms, without any apparent special efforts by the administrative authorities, were momentarily stopped.[12]

Levin's Enlightenment worldview did not allow him to entertain the possibility of any other explanation than the one he gave, which placed all its emphasis on the will of the government and its powerful ability to control events. The people, while being basically good, were merely instruments of the government's policies.

The famous historian and Jewish thinker S. M. Dubnow was born in Mstislavl, Belorussia, in 1860 and died a victim of the Nazis in Riga in 1941. Dubnow accepted the accuracy of Levin's portrayal of the 1881 pogroms and went on to write his own highly influential works on Russian Jewish history using the same interpretation.

Dubnow, like Levin, was a follower of the Haskalah. He advocated a Jewish renaissance in which the individual would be liberated and Jewish life would be built on secular principles. During the present period of emancipation in European Jewish history, Dubnow felt, there was no need for the discipline of religion. This was to be an era of cooperation with the nations of the world. Jews would be active in the civic and political life of their countries and enjoy all the rights of citizens. But in addition to individual rights, they would have special rights as members of their own national group. The Jews would continue to exist, as a European people with a secular culture, and as a permanent minority enjoying communal autonomy within the framework of multinational states. Such was Dubnow's dream.

This dream received a rude shock during the pogroms of 1905, and in response to these events, Dubnow penned a highly emotional essay that gives us much insight into his worldview and, incidentally, into his interpretation of anti-Jewish violence in Russia. Dubnow read his essay before a memorial meeting in Vilna on 17 November 1905 dedicated to the victims of the bloody pogroms of October. It was reprinted as the tenth letter of his *Letters on Old and New Judaism,* under the title, "The Moral of Stormy Days."[13] The first section of the essay has the revealing title "What Has Amalek Done to Us?"

According to Dubnow: "The massacres of October 1905 were brought about not only as a result of the recent unrest [the revolutionary events of 1905]. They came about as a result of the entire political system of Russia." Dubnow spoke about the "political apathy" of the *"ignorant masses" whom Russia's rulers wished to keep ignorant.* The government's approach was, "Let us . . . explain to the 'native' inhabitants that the Jews are outside the pale of the law, and if this influence is effective and leads to pogroms, *let us not hasten to suppress the mobsters."*[14]

Accusing the government of organizing the pogroms, Dubnow went on to ask:

> And what did the people do? Did *the savage mob* . . . only carry out the bidding of its leaders? . . . Not at all! They were doing what their fathers and brothers had done in years gone by, they will do it again in the future if conditions permit, and they *will* command their children and grandchildren to *do the same until civilization has reached a higher level and has changed the wild beasts . . . into human beings.* It will take a long time to effect such a change, *to re-educate the masses in the spirit of a state based on law* and to eradicate the law of the fist which is so deeply rooted in Russian life."
>
> The terrible experiences of the recent past implanted in Russian Jewry a mortal hatred against an oppressive regime whose cruelty surpasses the Spanish Inquisition. . . . *The latest pogroms,* unparalleled in their cruelty, *through which the government tried to extinguish the fire of freedom* that burns in us, will not achieve their purpose. . . . We shall never forget the moral of these stormy days. "Remember what Amalek did unto thee by the way as ye came forth out of Egypt!" . . .
>
> *Who is the Amalek of our times? Not only the officials of the old despised order but also the ignorant masses who follow their lead.*[15]

Dubnow expressed the pain, outrage, and frustration of his people. He called for Jewish self-renewal and self-defense and a struggle to achieve the recognition of Jewish national rights. While coming close to giving up his faith in the possibility that the Russian people would progress and eventually become enlightened and civilized, he did not do so entirely. "We know perfectly well that, even after we have defeated the anti-Semitism of the government, we will still have to fight against social anti-Semitism, and we do not minimize this struggle. However, we see a strong basis for this struggle only in the road to freedom provided by democracy."[16]

These passages indicate that Dubnow believed in the leading role of the Russian government in the anti-Jewish manifestations, that he viewed the masses as ignorant and subject to manipulation, and that he thought the only chance for bringing enlightened education and civilized manners to the people lay in a change of government. He remained devoted to his optimistic Enlightenment assumptions and worldview in spite of the blow inflicted upon them by the brutality of the Russian masses toward the Jews in 1905. Furthermore, like other writers of that period and later, he was undoubtedly influenced to interpret the events of 1881 in the light of the traumatic experiences of 1905—when the government's support of the pogroms seemed even more indisputable than earlier.

Leaving aside Levin and Dubnow and the Enlightenment worldview, one may add that conspiracies hold a certain fascination for many people.[17] They are a neat way of tying up loose ends in the complex fabric of historical events. They provide "an integrated and self-sustaining system of explanation," an approach that may be particularly tempting to certain writers of history textbooks. Intricate issues can be dealt with in a few sentences rather than the many pages they deserve in order to indicate all their implications. Conspiracy theories also help to maintain the belief, which many people find comforting, that complicated topics can be defined in simple terms of black and white, good and evil.

Belief in a conspiracy theory may also be connected with paranoia. In their dealings with the Russian government, Jews surely had solid reasons for being particularly sensitive to persecution and for viewing the government as the main villain in their national tragedy. This was bound to affect Jewish historiography. To put it abstractly: If one hates a certain government, which seems to be in firm control of its subjects and which is admittedly repressive and hostile to Jews, and if within the borders of that government large-scale anti-Jewish violence takes place, under circumstances when it would seem convenient for the government to find a scapegoat for popular unrest and discontent, then one has the perfect ingredients for a conspiracy, with the government in the role of villain.

Thus far I have identified four factors that help explain the popularity and longevity of the conspiracy theory regarding the origins of the 1881 pogroms: human psychology; the projection by scholars and other interpreters of their understanding of later experiences—for example, the major anti-Jewish violence of 1905 and later the Holocaust, in which the role of planning was obvious—back onto the earlier events;[18] the conformity of the conspiracy theory to the assumptions of the sort of rationalistic

humanism described above, as well as to the biblical paradigm so familiar
to Jews; and the tragic destruction of whole generations of historians who
might have reevaluated earlier approaches.

There is also a fifth factor: the conspiracy theory took into account the
outward features of the Russian government and Jewish-gentile relations—but those outward features were misleading. When I began the
research that led to the present study, I found that the position of the
Jews in the Russian Empire was much more complicated than commonly
portrayed. The attitudes toward the Jews on the part of the men in
Russia's governing circles were also much more complex than commonly
supposed.[19]

It is true that the Russian regime was autocratic; but it was not
monolithic. Various interest groups and political tendencies were represented within the government. Even on the rather narrow question of the
Jews, there was no uniformity of attitudes. In fact, officials held extremely
divergent views running the whole gamut from favoring complete emancipation to favoring the imposition of unprecedented restrictions. Would
such a government, so divided against itself, have dared foster anti-Jewish
violence in the streets?

A whole cluster of other questions also arose: Could the government
have planned such a large-scale movement as the 1881 pogroms even if it
had wanted to? What part do outside manipulation, environment, and
free choice play in the actions of large groups of people? Do populations
act as the blind instruments of their rulers? To what extent are they
responsible for their behavior? How well must a government be organized
and how well must the ground be prepared before rulers can succeed in
harvesting the fruits they desire? Did the nineteenth-century tsarist regime
even begin to approach the sweeping scope of organization and manipulation of masses of people witnessed in the twentieth century?

With these questions in mind, I set out to study the 1881 pogroms.
As my research progressed I became more and more convinced that the
pogroms were not planned. I submitted the evidence to the analysis
presented in the following pages. It is for the reader to judge whether I
have been fair to those who wrote on the topic before me.

In order to reevaluate the origins of the pogroms in depth, it was
necessary to deal with many issues surrounding the violence, such as: the
character of the Russian state and society, the state's treatment of the
problem of nationalities and of Jews in particular, Christian-Jewish relations, traditional anti-Semitism and anti-Semitic violence, and mob violence in general. Jewish emancipation and assimilation and the nature of

Jewish existence in the Diaspora are other matters touched upon. In the course of the study, light is also thrown upon the broad historical questions of whether anti-Semitism in nineteenth-century Russia was disseminated from the top to the bottom of society, or vice-versa; and of what roles were played by human decision and control (the subjective dimension), on the one hand, and external structures and relationships in Russian society (the objective dimension), on the other hand.

A whole different set of attitudes, concerns, and assumptions must be attributed to Russia's ruling circles if one determines that the pogroms were spontaneous rather than planned. Governmental policy in regard to the Jews, the peasant masses, and townspeople must be defined differently. How well the government and its bureaucracy operated in the field, the identity of their personnel, the nature and effectiveness of their methods and lines of communication—these matters take on greater significance. So do questions about the character and social structure of Russian towns, the way they were policed, and their relationships with the surrounding countryside. One's interpretation of the origin of the pogroms will also have implications for one's understanding of the relations between Jews and non-Jews, and the effects on these relations of the social structure and economic role of the Jewish communities in the context of the larger community.

All of these issues are addressed in the pages that follow. My procedure has been first of all to reexamine the older interpretations, pointing out their shortcomings and reflecting the "real" situation largely by implication. Then in my conclusion I attempt to present a straightforward and comprehensive picture by going back and drawing together all the threads that are revealed in the first part of the study.

# I

# THE HISTORICAL
# BACKGROUND

# Chapter 1

# THE RUSSIAN CONTEXT

◆ ◆ ◆

THE REIGN OF ALEXANDER II (1855–81) WAS MARKED BY MOMENTOUS changes in Russian life initiated by the liberation of the serfs. Like a logjam breaking up, at first slowly and laboriously, then more and more rapidly, Russian society began to be transformed. The Russian economy entered the age of capitalism, industrialization, and urbanization. Dislocations and discontent were experienced by every social stratum. The former serfs especially found the terms of their emancipation highly unsatisfactory.

Alexander II's reign began with high expectations. It ended with almost universal disappointment. A small but active and organized revolutionary movement made up of members of the intelligentsia had set out to foment a peasant revolt and to murder the tsar. In the latter it finally succeeded, on 1 March 1881, using a recent invention—homemade bombs.

For a number of years at the beginning of his reign, Alexander II instituted important reforms from above. Peasant life, the legal system, local government, and the army were reorganized; the educational system was modernized; police supervision over society was relaxed. Then a period of reaction set in, during which the government's main concern was to block demands for further reform and preserve the established order. Indeed, the main aim of the reforms that had been instituted was not to liberalize the regime but rather to make it possible for the autocracy to survive under modern conditions. Reforms were legislated, then followed by harshly reactionary measures. New centers of power, influence, and creative activity were given encouragement or emerged on their own, while the autocracy continued to exert itself in efforts to retain the state's control over virtually every facet of national life.

This attempt to square the circle, to institute or make way for change without changing, was the central and fatal weakness of the Russian autocracy. It influenced all aspects of Russia's historical development up to the revolution of 1917. But the gathering momentum of the changes taking place in Russian life could not be stopped, even if occasionally some of them could be temporarily obstructed.

Foremost among the changes occurring were those affecting the economy. With the liberation of the serfs, Russian agriculture became more capitalist, and industry expanded rapidly.

Agriculture presented a mixed picture.[1] The Russian peasant before and after emancipation was generally ignorant, backward, and bound to traditional ways. The continued existence of the peasant communes with legal authority over their members hampered modernization as well as peasant mobility. Peasants could get permission to leave their villages, but not always, and if they did, their legal and financial obligations remained in force. The communes in many places allotted land in scattered strips (in order to equalize access to lands of varied quality) so that each peasant's portion was intermingled with that of his fellows, and many communes periodically redistributed the land. These practices tended to hinder the development of capitalist agriculture and even to discourage investment in improving the land held at any particular time, since the long-term benefits might not accrue to the one responsible for them. However, strip farming and periodic redistribution were not universally employed, and even when they were, it was often in a way beneficial to the economically stronger individuals in the commune. Called kulaks (meaning "fists" in Russian) by their envious fellows, these men were the more enterprising, energetic, and shrewd peasants—or perhaps they were just luckier or more ruthless. They managed to accumulate capital, livestock, and surplus produce. They loaned money and seed to their neighbors, often at exorbitant rates of interest, and thereby gained power and status in the villages. Thus class differentiation in the rural areas and a capitalist mode of production tended to grow constantly, with the rich getting richer and the poor poorer.

It once was thought that, on the whole, the standard of living of the Russian peasantry declined after the Emancipation. The peasants received less land than they had had at their disposal previously and were required to pay dearly for it. They were heavily taxed, being especially hard hit by the government's extensive use of indirect taxation on articles of everyday necessity. Peasant indebtedness—mainly to kulaks and petty merchants for loans and to the government for redemption dues and taxes—increased constantly after 1861. The villagers were forced by economic circumstances to enter the capitalist market and sell their produce, often at unfavorable prices. Thus peasants had to sell their surplus produce during the autumn, when prices were lowest, in order to pay their redemption dues, direct taxes, and other debts; later in the year, when prices were higher, they often found they had to take loans. Many, as I shall show, were forced off the land altogether, to become wage laborers in agriculture and industry. A very large proportion of the peasants' grain was exported to Western Europe as part of the government's plan to pay for industrialization. Consequently, it used to be thought, the great majority of the peasants suffered from chronic hunger, especially when struck by crop failure, which was not an infrequent phenomenon.

Recent scholarship has raised questions about this view. Did Russian agricultural production really not grow rapidly enough to feed the expanding population and also to supply an export surplus? Were Russian peasants really being "squeezed in order to boost Russian export earnings"? According to Peter Gatrell, citing research by Paul Gregory and others, data is available indicating that from the 1860s, Russian agricultural production and labor productivity in agriculture expanded almost continuously, partly as a result of new lands being brought under cultivation and, to a greater extent, because higher yields were achieved.[2] Gregory's research shows that from 1885 to 1913, while the Russian population was increasing rapidly, the output of grain calculated in per capita terms was also increasing. Gregory also demonstrated that from 1885 to 1913, the average annual growth rate of food grains not sent to market was over twice as high as the average annual growth rate of population. In other words, in statistical terms, the per capita amount of grain available in Russia's villages to feed both humans and livestock was growing faster than the population.[3] Furthermore, "the volume of retained cereal crops *increased,* both in absolute terms and as a proportion of net output, between 1885–9 and 1897–1901. In this, the key period of rapid industrialization, village consumption of grain increased at the same rate as Net National Product, . . . although total retail sales in town and country grew faster still."[4] Scholars studying the 1890s have also argued that the fiscal policies pursued during that period of accelerated industrialization did not have a harmful effect on peasant incomes and purchasing power.[5] In particular, in the territories where the pogroms of 1881 occurred, it is generally acknowledged that the peasants were rather better off than those in central Russia. (This does not mean, however, that they were necessarily more satisfied with their circumstances or felt less dislocated by the economic and social changes taking place around them. I will return to this point below.)

In sum, the research published in recent years by Gregory and others does not support a totally negative evaluation of the impact of grain marketings and government taxation policies on rural households.

However, Gatrell warned:

> One ought not to jump to conclusions about the implications of this research for the hypothesis about rural living standards—it says nothing about the distribution of food within the village, or about the consumption of other items—but it is sufficiently impressive to make one pause before accepting at face value the pessimistic verdict about peasant impoverishment during the late nineteenth century. Peasants may have been poor, some of them desperately so, but it is not certain that they became poorer during the 1890s, still less that this happened because of government fiscal policy.[6]

I cite this research, which relates mostly to the period following the pogroms of 1881, in case anyone might be inclined to apply its conclusions to the earlier years, using a fortiori reasoning. However, such an inference may not be entirely warranted. The positive features noted in peasant agriculture may not have made their appearance before 1880.

Two points seem fairly certain: First, while the tsarist economy was growing in the late nineteenth century, Russia remained backward in terms of per capita production and income, infant mortality rates, and standards of literacy, when compared with Western Europe. Second, income and wealth were distributed very unevenly in Russia, with most Russians suffering from poverty and want.

Furthermore, the data cited, in addition to calling for the words of caution expressed by Gatrell, do not take into account the imponderable factor of human perception, which may not conform to external reality yet is a most important consideration when trying to understand the origins of an episode such as the pogroms of 1881. Russian peasants, like many contemporary educated outside observers, felt that the rural population as a whole was getting poorer, even if it can now be shown that this was in some ways not true statistically. The perception of poverty and falling behind was especially strong when peasants saw some of their fellows becoming increasingly richer and when they felt themselves being subjected to the dislocations and disintegrative influence of changing economic circumstances.

> Many [Russian] peasants were poorly endowed with land and other assets. This feature . . . was neatly captured in the words of a peasant from Novgorod, speaking in 1900: "We have been living for almost half a century at the same level, and if this same standard applied to the army, then soldiers would still be carrying flintlocks and the navy would still be using sailing ships,

equipped with iron cannon." These sentiments are typical of the lament about the "crisis" in peasant agriculture at the turn of the century. But, . . . to continue the image created by the peasant from Novgorod: if the majority of peasants were foot-soldiers, there was a corresponding officer class of peasants—and they were wealthier still by 1914.[7]

Russian peasants endured a hunger not only for food. They suffered from land hunger as well. The population in the Russian Empire was growing before the Emancipation and continued to grow rapidly afterward—from about 73 million in 1861 to about 98 million in 1880 and approximately 126 million in 1897. (Peasant society encouraged early and virtually universal marriage.)[8] This growth of over 70 percent took place mainly in the countryside and at a rate faster than new land could be put under cultivation. As a result, there was increasing rural overpopulation along with the ever deepening impoverishment, or perception of impoverishment. As a rule, individual peasant holdings kept getting smaller; fertility tended to decline on the small holdings, since the soil was exhausted by the failure to adopt more advanced agricultural techniques; and periodic crop failures occurred, affecting more and more people. Meanwhile, the price of land more than doubled between 1860 and 1905, as peasants felt compelled to buy or rent more land, mainly from gentry landlords, sometimes from kulaks, and even from each other. Quite often this was a deceptive solution, since the yield of the land acquired, under the prevailing conditions, would not equal the value paid for it. Many observers at the time argued that the Russian peasants' land hunger and feelings of congestion were altogether illusory and that the real problem was a shortage not of land but of technical knowledge and skill.

The peasants responded to their plight in other ways as well. More and more of those who stayed in the villages became involved in home or cottage industry (*kustar*). This included peasants who produced goods in their homes on a part-time basis as well as those involved full-time, peasants who worked for themselves and sold their own wares as well as those who worked for middlemen or directly for factories. Peasant craftsmen produced a wide range of goods, for use in peasant households, in the homes of the well-to-do, and in construction and factories. They often relied on factories for materials used in their work. With industry in many cases thus serving as a source of supplies as well as a ready market, the level of *kustar* production in Russia tended to parallel the level of industrial production. For example, during the early 1870s both branches experienced a period of boom, whereas toward the end of the decade the activity of both slackened.[9]

The picture for Russian cottage industry was not all bright. Production costs tended to rise during the 1870s and 1880s, and competition from mechanization spread to more and more crafts. This happened in the course of a few years around 1880 in the important *kustar* trades of cotton and woolen cloth weaving, flax spinning, and the making of nails and felt boots. Meanwhile, the number of peasant craftsmen constantly increased. Desperately striving to remain in business, they were forced to keep costs and profits down as much as possible.[10]

At the same time, many peasants were migrating to less settled areas, especially to the southern and southeastern regions, Ekaterinoslav, Kherson, and Tavrida *guberniias* (provinces), and western Siberia and the Don and North Caucasus regions. At harvest time, tens of thousands of workhands—men, women, and children—flowed into these areas. Most of them returned to their villages after the harvest; rarely did large estate owners retain workers for lengthy periods. There was also a redistribution of population within the different *guberniias* of the Russian Empire, a process that had begun before the Emancipation Decree. In spite of this movement, however, the greatest concentration of population remained in the ever more crowded older areas.

Many peasants became wage laborers for landlords or their fellow peasants, and frequently they were willing to travel long distances to find employment. So were those peasants who turned to employment in industry, construction, and transportation (with the number of workers on the railroads showing the most marked increase).[11] Indeed, the peasant population was the only available source of factory and other industry-related labor. Working conditions were wretched and the pay was poor, but industrial workers earned more than wage laborers in the countryside. Consequently, peasants responded quickly to the demand for factory hands, sometimes in such numbers that many were left unable to find employment.

The number of workers in agriculture increased at a faster rate than the number engaged in industry-related employment, reflecting "the rapid commercialization of agriculture in the post-reform period."[12] Still, Russia's urban industrial working class grew steadily. Between 1867 and 1897 the population in the towns of European Russia nearly doubled, increasing from about 10 to 13 percent of the total population.[13] Meanwhile, from 1861 on into the 1900s, the members of the industrial working class were never far removed from their peasant origins. For several decades most of the empire's workers were born in the villages and came to the towns from there. Often they remained members of the village commune, left their families in the countryside (being unable to support them in the relatively expensive towns), received food from them and sent them money (which they struggled to save), and themselves spent some time in the village each year. For many, the village continued to be "home," while the distant factory, mill, construction site, or capitalist farm was just a novel way to earn ready cash.[14] And even when the major ties to rural life were severed, the new "industrial proletarians" retained much of their peasant mentality and outlook. But at the same time they were forced to confront and adopt new modes of behavior, attitudes, and values. This situation of upheaval and dislocation was a fertile breeding ground for frustration, alienation, and discontent.

Initially the Emancipation had a depressing effect on the growth of factory industry, which until then had relied on bonded serf labor. It now had to adjust to new conditions wherein workers were free and had to be hired on terms that offered some inducement. But the readjustment was made very quickly, and Russia witnessed the rapid development of "bourgeois" capitalist industry. As I have noted, after 1861 the urban population increased almost twice as fast as the rural. It concentrated especially in Moscow, St. Petersburg, and several other industrial and commercial cities, such as Khar'kov and Odessa. Numerous new towns and industrial villages also appeared. In the southern and southwestern regions alone, where the anti-Jewish pogroms of 1881 were concentrated, between the 1860s and the 1890s the number of industrial enterprises more than doubled and the value of their output increased more than six times.[15]

Russia's industrialists relied heavily on foreign investments and state loans, contracts, and protectionism. A strikingly high percentage of the new enterprises were large-scale operations employing many workers. They started out big rather than developing gradually from small beginnings.

The railroad system in the Russian Empire developed especially rapidly during the reign of Alexander II. In 1861, Russia had only one thousand miles of railroad track. By 1881, thirteen thousand more miles had been constructed. Water transport also developed. The grain-producing areas, the most important being in the southern and southwestern regions, were linked with the major population centers in the interior and with the ports. For a time the Ukraine, New Russia (the Odessa region), and the southwest region became the granary of Europe, the leading exporter of wheat and barley.[16]

The railroad boom encouraged the development of Russia's heavy industry—coal, steel, iron, and oil—and this in turn gave further impetus to the expansion of the railroads. The cotton and woolen industries also expanded. Although the growth of an internal market was inhibited by the peasants' poverty, as time went on more and more money came into circulation, and more and more manufactured goods were purchased.

Retail trade in Russia was dominated by itinerant merchants on into the 1900s. Only very gradually did larger and more permanent shops and stores appear in the towns and villages. As more railroads were built, thousands of new petty tradesmen appeared. They had only modest amounts of capital with which to work, and very often they kept on the move, going from place to place to peddle their wares. To survive, they kept profits low and tried to maintain a large turnover of goods. Jews tended to dominate this branch of the economy in the areas where they were concentrated.

In the regions struck by the pogroms of 1881, economic growth was most marked in coal and iron ore mining, sugar refining, flour milling, and the manufacture of agricultural machinery. As elsewhere in Russia, much of the industry here was financed by Western European capital. The food industry, however, was a striking exception. It was financed entirely by local banks, landowners, better-off peasants (kulaks), and Jews. On the whole, the southern and southwestern regions, with their large Jewish population, were major participants in the economic and social changes rocking the Russian Empire.[17]

*Chapter 2*

# THE JEWS IN 1881

◆ ◆ ◆

LARGE NUMBERS OF JEWS BECAME SUBJECTS OF THE RUSSIAN TSAR ONLY
with the partitions of Poland and Russian expansion westward at the end
of the eighteenth century. Eventually the so-called Jewish question became
one of the most widely discussed and thorny issues confronting the multinational Russian Empire.

By Russian law the Jews were confined more or less to the territories
where they had been found in the late 1700s and adjacent sparsely settled
areas into which they were allowed to move. This whole region came to
be known as the Pale of Jewish Settlement. However, in spite of this
generic name used so facilely and so widely, the region was not uniform
either geographically, ethnically, or culturally.[1] This will become clear
in the pages that follow, and some of the most salient points will be
summarized in the Conclusion.

Table 1 shows the composition of the Pale by *guberniia* (province) and
indicates those that experienced pogroms in 1881. Table 2 shows the
composition of the Pale by ethnic majority.

Most of these *guberniias*, with their large Jewish populations, came
under Russian domination as a result of the partitions of Poland at the
end of the eighteenth century. New Russia was also taken over during the
late eighteenth century from Turkey, as was Bessarabia during the early
1800s. Chernigov and Poltava had come under Russian sovereignty during
the seventeenth century. Since these two *guberniias*, together with New
Russia and Bessarabia, were very sparsely settled, Jews were allowed to
colonize them, along with many Great Russians (people belonging to the
dominant ethnic group in the empire who came from the core provinces
of the center and northeast) who moved in during the course of the
nineteenth century. The ten provinces of Poland proper were not officially
part of the Pale, but Jews were able to move freely between the two
regions.

By long tradition the Russian government and people nurtured an
intense animosity toward the Jews, on religious and moral grounds. Once

29

NORWAY

SWEDEN

FINLAND

St. Petersburg

BALTIC
SEA

Moscow

PRUSSIA

KOVNO

VITEBSK

VILNA

KINGDOM
OF
POLAND

GRODNO

MINSK

MOGILEV

AUSTRIA

VOLYNIA

CHERNIGOV

KIEV

POLTAVA

PODOLIA

KHAR'KOV

KHERSON

EKATERINOSLAV

TAVRIDA

BESSARABIA
(AFTER 1881)

OTTOMAN EMPIRE

━━━ Boundary of the Pale
─── Boundary of Governor-generalships
─── Boundary of Guberniias

BLACK SEA

MAP 1. *Western Russia and the Boundary of the Pale*

TABLE 1
COMPOSITION OF THE PALE, 1881, BY *GUBERNIIA*

| Region and Guberniia | Pogrom |
|---|---|
| Northwest or Vilna | |
| Grodno | no |
| Kovno | no |
| Vilna | no |
| Southwest or Kiev | |
| Kiev | yes |
| Podolia | yes |
| Volynia | yes |
| Ukraine or Khar'kov | |
| Chernigov | yes |
| Khar'kov (outside the Pale) | no |
| Poltava | yes |
| New Russia (*Novorossiisk*) or Odessa | |
| Ekaterinoslav | yes |
| Kherson | yes |
| Tavrida | yes |
| Belorussia | |
| Minsk | no |
| Mogilev | no |
| Vitebsk | no |
| Other | |
| Bessarabia (later part of New Russia) | no |

large masses of Jews became Russian subjects, this hostility gradually acquired more sophisticated and "modern" dimensions involving ethnic, economic, administrative, and political considerations. In time the Jews found themselves the objects of severe legal discrimination, which singled them out even in comparison with other non-Russians in the empire. To be sure, other minorities were persecuted in Russia. For example, almost 200,000 Tatars from the Crimea and southern Ukraine were "encouraged" to emigrate to Turkey in the late 1850s, and the adherents of the Old Believers religious denomination were subjected to a double rate of taxation that went back to the seventeenth century. The Poles and the Ukrainians also suffered, and the list could be extended. But no minority was discriminated against so extensively and persistently as the Jews.[2]

Apart from the various regulations adopted from time to time defining the Jews' residential rights, which eventuated in the establishment of the

TABLE 2
COMPOSITION OF THE PALE, 1881, BY ETHNIC MAJORITY

| Ethnic Majority and Guberniia | Pogrom |
|---|---|
| Belorussian (White Russian) | |
|     Minsk | no |
|     Mogilev | no |
|     Vitebsk | no |
| Lithuanian | |
|     Grodno | no |
|     Kovno | no |
|     Vilna | no |
| Ukrainian | |
|     Chernigov | yes |
|     Khar'kov (outside the Pale) | no |
|     Kiev | yes |
|     Podolia | yes |
|     Poltava | yes |
|     Volynia | yes |
| Mixed (Great Russian, Ukrainian, Jewish, and other) population of New Russia | |
|     Ekaterinoslav | yes |
|     Kherson | yes |
|     Tavrida | yes |
|     Bessarabia | no |

Pale of Jewish Settlement, Jews were barred from certain occupations and had only limited access to others. Their right to own or control land was restricted. Several times during the nineteenth century, efforts were made to remove them from the rural areas within the Pale itself. Jews had to pay special taxes. Their traditional educational institutions and curricula were interfered with, and their opportunities for entering general educational institutions were often subject to restrictions.

On the one hand, the autocracy discriminated against the Jews and kept them perceptibly separate from their neighbors. This could only heighten the awareness of mutual differences. On the other hand, a policy of encouraging fusion (*sliianie*) of the Jews with the non-Jewish population was pursued. It involved, for example, the establishment of agricultural colonies in unpopulated areas of southern Russia and Siberia, attacks on Jewish styles of dress and grooming, recruitment of youths into the army with the intention of forcing them to convert to Christianity, the abolition of the official status of the *kahal*—the traditional governing body existing in each Jewish community—and attempts to control Jewish educational establishments. These measures characterized the reigns of Alexander I (1801–25) and especially Nicholas I (1825–55), who was brutal and ruthless in their implementation.

The *kahal* (from the Hebrew *kehillah,* meaning "community"—*kagal* in Russian) deserves special mention because it was the focus of so much anti-Semitic attention. *Kahals,* elected committees in charge of administering Jewish communal affairs, existed in each locality where there was a Jewish community. Dating far back into the period of Polish rule over the territory of the Pale, the *kahals* had officially recognized taxation, police, and judicial powers. Their rabbinical courts dealt with all matters involving Jewish law, that is, practically all matters involving Jews.

The *kahals* were officially abolished by a law of December 1844 and their powers handed over to the police and the institutions of municipal self-government. However, the Jewish community retained collective responsibility for tax apportionment, and it elected its own representatives to collect funds for charitable and communal services. Under Nicholas I special officials were also elected to enforce the conscription laws. By law, all the Jews' official representatives were subject to the authority of the local government institutions.

As one student summarized the situation after 1844:

> While the juridical basis of [Jewish communal] autonomy—the recognition of the corporate right to self-rule—was abrogated, the coherence of the community as a self-regulating tax entity remained intact, although its officials were now tied more closely to the state's supervision. Most important, the new law did not address the fundamental aspect of Jewish self-rule, the independence of the rabbinical courts and the integrity of Jewish law in the jurisprudence of civil and even criminal cases involving Jews.
>
> While the essential structure of the kahal remained intact even after its formal abolition, its function and status within Russian-Jewish society were significantly altered after 1844. . . . Both Russian Jews and their Western European sympathizers believed that the kahal and rabbinical courts had been substantially, perhaps fatally, debilitated by the new legislation.[3]

"This perceived diminution of the authority of the kahal was of important historical consequence." On the one hand, "centrifugal forces" were now more easily able to weaken the loyalty of many Jews to traditional Jewish society and advance the cause of secularization and Russification. On the other hand, masses of Jews came to the defense of the Torah, traditional learning, ritual, and custom in new, "modernized" ways.[4]

Meanwhile, anti-Semitic propagandists and, consequently, popular opinion exaggerated the powers of the *kahal*. They believed it to be more than a local agency. In their view it constituted a broad, perhaps even international, secret organization having immense control over all Jews.

Nicholas I's successor, Alexander II, for a while tried using the carrot rather than the stick to promote Jewish assimilation. The special regulations from the time of Nicholas I governing military conscription of Jews, which were especially harsh and hateful, were eased as soon as Alexander II ascended the throne and were abolished in the summer of 1856. From then on, the Jews were made equal to the tsar's other subjects insofar as military service was concerned. As I have already noted, residence restrictions were relaxed for Jews who presumably could contribute something positive to the empire. These included retired soldiers, the wealthiest class of merchants (that is, those who paid the highest taxes and consequently had the most privileges—called first guild merchants in Russian usage), artisans, mechanics, and liquor distillers, their families, and in some cases their servants and apprentices. Russian schools and higher educational institutions were opened wide to Jews, and Jewish university graduates not only acquired the right to leave the Pale but also could enter government employment. Alexander II's judicial reforms made no exceptions for Jews, who were allowed to join the legal profession equally with non-Jews. Jews were also allowed to participate in the newly created *zemstvo* (local administrative assembly) and municipal government institutions.

The vast majority of Jews, to a certain extent paralleling the peasants, maintained a traditional way of life, tenaciously holding on to age-old Jewish practices. They had special dietary laws, unusual clothing, distinctive holidays, and a different Sabbath. They spoke the Yiddish language among themselves; as a rule, they knew just enough Russian, Polish, Ukrainian, Belorussian, or Lithuanian to communicate with their neighbors. Classical Jewish learning was almost universally respected, if not always shared by the Jewish masses.[5] The Jews jealously guarded the autonomy of their educational, charitable, and communal institutions. They were a highly visible, well-knit community, in spite of some sectarian discord—the struggle over the proper approach to Jewish tradition between the *Hasidim* and the *misnagdim,* and later the *maskilim.* The *Hasidim* were members of a pietistic, mystical movement that emphasized inwardness, spontaneity, and the guidance of a *rebbe-tsadik,* a saintly leader and teacher. The *misnagdim* were those who opposed the *Hasidim* and favored a more intellectual, staid, and somber style of religion. (The *maskilim* will be dealt with below.) Partly by choice and partly because of the circumstances created by anti-Jewish legislation, the Jews tended to keep aloof from the surrounding population.

During the reign of Alexander II, the "Jewish Enlightenment," called the Haskalah in Hebrew, flowered in Russia. It had begun to find some individual supporters and tiny circles of enthusiasts as early as the 1820s, but only after the death of Nicholas I did it really begin to expand and affect significant numbers of Jews (known as *maskilim*), some of them quite influential. At first it seemed that Alexander would take a genuinely liberal course in regard to the Jews. This encouraged many to adopt the position that the Jews must modernize their social, cultural, and religious lives; they must begin to engage in productive occupations in greater numbers; they must learn Russian, get a secular education, and draw closer to their gentile neighbors. Some argued that the Jews must do this in order to make themselves worthy of emancipation and civic equality; others thought these steps were necessary simply as a matter of maintaining Jewish dignity.

Apart from the *maskilim,* who advocated the calculated entry of Jews into Russian life, and in spite of the Jews' generally segregated condition, the momentous economic and social changes taking place as a result of the Emancipation of the peasants inevitably affected the Russian Jewish community.

Most Jews lived in towns and small trading centers (*mestechki* in Russian, *shtetlach* in Yiddish). Only a small percentage actually lived in villages along with peasants. As a result they constituted a large proportion—anywhere from one-fourth to over one-half—of the urban population of the Pale, but only a small percentage of the rural population. According to the 1897 census there were 5 million Jews in Russia, 48.84 percent of them living in towns, 33.05 percent in townlets, and 18.11 percent in villages.[6]

The *shtetl* (the term *townlet* is used elsewhere in this book) was the typical economic and social link between the Jews and the peasants in the Pale of Jewish Settlement. These settlements varied in size from several hundred people to over twenty thousand, with Jews the vast majority. The style of living to a large extent resembled that of the villages. For Jews it was marked by cultural homogeneity, close-knit family and community life, warmth, and intimacy. Jewish life centered on the synagogue, the home, and the marketplace.

The marketplace is of special concern in the present study, for it was a major meeting ground for Jews and non-Jews. It was usually in the center of the *shtetl,* and around it were small shops and stalls selling all kinds of merchandise, workshops where artisans plied their trades, and taverns and inns where liquor or tea was sold. The Jewish businesses were generally on a very small scale, involving little capital. The majority of the *shtetl* population lived in poverty, and the whole family was usually involved in the struggle to make a living. The neighboring villagers came to the *shtetl* marketplace to buy and sell and have needed repairs made. On market days in particular the *shtetl* came alive with activity.

The *shtetl* was also home for large numbers of Jews who sought their living on the road, peddling goods or working as itinerant craftsmen— cobblers, tailors, smiths, and so on—in the villages. In many cases these men were away from Sunday to Friday, returning to their families only for the Jewish Sabbath, when all mundane activity in the *shtetl* came to a halt.

Most Jews were tradesmen of one sort or another. Often there were more Jews than non-Jews engaged in trade in the towns of the Pale, and in the countryside as well, which, as I have noted above, they would visit daily or periodically from the towns and townlets. Large numbers of Jews were artisans, again often outnumbering non-Jews. The Jewish tradesmen and artisans dealt mainly with consumer rather than capital goods. Many Jews were industrial laborers, domestics, and unskilled day laborers; very few were agriculturalists. A significant number were involved in spiritual professions (rabbis, elementary school Hebrew teachers, teachers of advanced Jewish studies, scribes).

One estimate of the Jews' occupational distribution at the beginning of the nineteenth century gave the following breakdown:

| | |
|---|---|
| Innkeeping and leases | 30% |
| Trade and brokering | 30 |
| No fixed occupation | 21 |
| Crafts | 15 |
| Religious officials | 3 |
| Agriculture | 1 |

The 1897 census gave the following breakdown:

| | |
|---|---|
| Commerce | 38.65% |
| Crafts and industry | 35.43 |
| Domestics and daily workers | 6.61 |
| No fixed occupation | 5.49 |
| Liberal professions and administration | 5.22 |

| Transport    | 3.98 |
|--------------|------|
| Agriculture  | 3.55 |
| Army         | 1.07 |

Also according to the 1897 census, Jews in the Pale made up 72.8 percent of tradesmen, 31.4 percent of craftsmen and industrialists, and 20.9 percent of those involved in transportation.[7] As one scholar has stated:

> The occupational distribution of the Jewish population in the Pale of Settlement reported by the Population Census of 1897 represents a society in flux. Some of the occupations were typical for a traditional, preindustrial society with its preponderance of nonspecialized general services (e.g., unspecified trading activities, a huge labor supply of unskilled labor—domestic servants, day laborers, etc.) with emphasis on trade in foodstuffs and beverages. Other occupations arose in order to meet the needs of an industrializing society for ready-to-wear clothing, for housing, for new forms of distribution of goods, etc.[8]

Jewish tradesmen served as middlemen for both rural clients and the lower classes in the urban areas. Their activities concentrated heavily on foodstuffs and agricultural products, and as such they were a major factor in the economy of the Pale. There were fewer Jews who traded in manufactured consumer goods; these people were concentrated mostly in the large cities. The Jewish tradesmen in the towns bought and sold local products on the spot. They also exported local products and imported cheap foreign goods to supply the local market. Many were involved in the liquor trade.

Jewish artisans engaged in a broad spectrum of occupations. However, they faced fierce competition from one another in the small trading centers where they mostly lived. They generally produced cheap goods for local consumption.

Many Jews managed the estates of absentee landlords, who had neither the interest nor the ability necessary to manage their estates themselves. By establishing or leasing distilleries, breweries, and mills, and by leasing dairies and ponds, Jews were intimately involved in the agricultural products market. Large numbers of them acted as middlemen traders in these commodities. "Within the Pale of Settlement, most of the grain trade (measured in terms of actively employed individuals engaged in the trade) was heavily concentrated in the hands of the Jewish merchants."[9] They also engaged extensively in the exploitation of forests. Jews were thus very important intermediaries between the peasants and the market. They took part in almost all the peasants' commercial dealings in the Pale and generally excluded non-Jewish competitors from this field of activity.

For grain they exchanged money, salt, household utensils, agricultural tools, and also liquor.

Indeed, most Jews in the villages probably combined their other activities with trading in liquor and tavern keeping. This was a heritage of previous times, when ownership of taverns was a feudal privilege of the nobility, who leased their rights to Jews. By the nineteenth century, Jewish involvement in the manufacture and sale of liquor (often on credit) was massive. Intoxicating the peasants was one of the most widespread charges leveled against Jews having dealings in the countryside, along with the related allegations that they granted usurious loans and engaged in deceitful business transactions. These "sins" lay at the very center of the charge (probably largely unjustified, as I shall demonstrate below) that the Jews "exploited" the peasantry.

In general, the Jews were known for being satisfied with low wages and profits, for reducing the costs of trading and craft production, and for being able to limit their physical needs. Over all, their activities generally led to lower prices for consumers, who may not necessarily have been aware of this.

Many Jews served as bankers and moneylenders, since they generally disposed of more liquid wealth than the local nobility or peasantry, and since public credit facilities were scarce.

Some Jews had become quite wealthy by 1881. They had earned large fortunes as lessees of the state liquor monopoly, railroad builders, financiers, and subcontractors supplying the railroad industry, government contractors (roads, fortresses, army provisions), industrialists (especially foods, textiles, tanneries, and distilleries), exporters (especially grain and timber), and finance bankers. Some were successful lawyers, doctors, and writers. These were the Jews able to take advantage of the educational opportunities and residential privileges granted during the reign of Alexander II, as well as the growing commercial and industrial opportunities offered by developing capitalism and industrialization.

On the other hand, the mass of the Jewish population was becoming increasingly impoverished. These Jews were caught by the population squeeze within the Pale, which was intensified by the sluggish development of commerce and industry.

A significant feature in the life of the traditionalist Jewish masses was the institution of early marriages. Youths generally married between the ages of thirteen and sixteen. They were encouraged by communal pressures to have many children, in spite of the prevailing poverty. The high birth rate combined with a relatively low child mortality rate, thanks to medical advances and the concern Jewish parents and Jewish community organizations showed for the welfare of their children. The result was that between 1800 and 1900 the Jewish population grew from about 1 million to about 5 million.[10] Unfortunately, in spite of the various concessions made by Alexander II's government allowing Jews to leave the Pale for the Russian interior, none was extensive enough to relieve the congestion. Nor did Russia's newly emerging industrialization process proceed rapidly enough to absorb all the additional hands entering the labor market.

Although the pace of capitalist and industrial development was quickening in Russia by the 1880s, thus creating new employment opportunities, the process was still relatively slow-moving. And, as in all countries entering upon industrialization, it initially benefited only a relatively few persons and often intensified the poverty of the masses. Thus the local consumers' market expanded relatively slowly. As a result, the growing Jewish population became crowded into urban-commercial occupations in excess of the demand existing in the underdeveloped Pale, while at the same time part of the industrial labor market was closed to them. Jewish workers tended to be excluded from the larger and more modern factories. They would not work on Saturday, their Sabbath, and Christian factory owners often considered them unfit for the work in general. Gentile laborers, newly arrived from the villages with their traditional anti-Jewish prejudices intact, also deterred Jews from seeking jobs alongside them.

The two groups had deep-seated suspicions of each other as well as basic difficulties in communicating, because of both their cultural differences and the different languages they spoke. Non-Jews, who were generally the first to be employed since they tended already to have needed skills, did not want Jewish competition. Very often the confrontation took place in Jewish-owned factories, where the non-Jews were perhaps hostile to Jewish workers because they feared a "Jewish plot" to oust them.[11]

Meanwhile, Jewish laborers accused Jewish factory owners of discriminating against them in hiring. They attributed this "to the employers' preference for hiring a labor force that was less 'class-conscious,' less easily organized, less radical in demanding higher wages and more humane treatment. Some Jewish industrialists retorted by pointing out their unwillingness to force Jewish workers to transgress the laws of the Sabbath, since factories with a mixed labor force had to be closed on Sunday." Other factors at work here may have been the gentile workers' willingness to work for lower salaries; the owners' unwillingness to antagonize them by hiring Jews; the owners' apprehension that Jews, once trained, might leave to open competing enterprises; and the owners' concern that Jewish laborers might have a radicalizing impact on the labor force. In sum, hiring Jewish workers was in fact or seemed to be more expensive for Jewish employers than hiring non-Jews, which naturally acted to deter them from taking this step.[12]

After the abolition of serfdom, many Jewish middlemen and estate managers lost their jobs because landlords were no longer able to afford their services. The landlords had to begin managing their estates themselves. Many Jewish innkeepers, coachmen, and wagoners were also put out of business when the developing railroads took away their customers. Jews were almost completely excluded from employment in railroad transportation because of governmental discriminatory policies. So those Jews who remained engaged in the transportation field were "concentrated in the most backward sector, that of short-haul services for freight and passengers."[13] Meanwhile, competition from Christian businessmen and professionals intensified markedly in all sectors of the economy as capitalism and industrialization advanced.

The large class of Jewish artisans had the right to leave the economically overcrowded Pale. But even those willing to abandon the Jewish communal framework and seek homes in unfamiliar places more in need of their services were generally deterred from doing so; the complex legal technicalities surrounding their departure blocked them. Numerous Jewish artisans and tradesmen sought a way out by entering the interior *guberniias* illegally, but not enough did this to relieve the overcrowding.

The number of Jewish factory owners in western and southwestern Russia, according to official statistics, was far below the Jews' proportion in the population. Their establishments were usually no better than artisan workshops, with small capital investments, simple machinery, and few workers. This was the best Jews could do, as a rule, because they lacked capital and know-how, and they felt legally insecure.[14]

According to some estimates, perhaps one-half to three-quarters of all Jews had no definite occupations. They lived as petty brokers, hucksters, and odd-jobmen, earning what little they could, however they could. The figures listed above for the percentage of Jews with no fixed occupation are probably so low because the Jews, fearing government reprisals, preferred not to be listed in this category.[15]

Large masses of Jews lived in crowded housing of very poor quality. Their food was of poor quality as well. Consequently their health record was often worse than that of the neighboring gentiles. Many observers reported the Jews to be generally more frail, more unfit for hard physical labor, and more unfit for military duty than non-Jews.[16]

There is strong evidence to show, on the other hand, that though the peasants in the Pale were about as impoverished as the Jews, they were in a relatively better economic position than peasants in the interior *guberniias*. The Jews, being urban residents, provided the peasants with a large local market for their surplus produce. The greater demand thus created led to higher prices and bigger profits for the peasants. In addition, the Jews as middlemen helped the peasants sell their surplus produce, whether locally or abroad or in Poland and the Baltic area. Also, as the century progressed, more and more Jews became engaged in the grain trade and the degree of competition intensified, thus providing another impetus for higher prices paid to producers. Competition forced Jewish dealers in agricultural products to make excursions into outlying areas. Places that previously had had nothing to do with the market were opened up for trade. In some places Jews managed to put an end to long-established monopolies held by village kulaks (peasant entrepreneurs) or non-Jewish wholesale merchants. As a whole these activities led to an increase in the marketable portion of grain production.[17]

It was characteristic of Jewish artisans and industrialists to produce for the widest possible market. This meant concentrating on cheaper varieties of goods that the peasants, and others, with their limited purchasing power, could afford. Jewish producers thus helped non-Jewish consumers, as well as Jewish consumers and tradesmen, by expanding the clientele who could be reached.[18]

As is well known, Jews were heavily engaged in the liquor trade. However, there are statistics that show that drunkenness was less widespread among peasants in the Pale than among those in the interior *guberniias*. There are similar statistics for crimes such as murder, looting, robbery, and extortion.[19]

These commendable features of life in the Pale were largely ignored in nineteenth-century Russia. The Jews were concentrated in middleman occupations, trade, and small-scale manufacturing, in a society whose worldview valued agriculture as a productive occupation and considered middleman activities to be almost worthless and even exploitative by their very nature. Furthermore, the idea was widespread that the "parasitic and unproductive" Jews acquired their resources by illegal or unjust means at the expense of their neighbors. Frequently even the peasants whom Jewish tradesmen were benefiting directly remained suspicious and felt that they were somehow being cheated. In addition it was widely assumed that there was a fixed amount of capital in the economy. Thus the more capital the Jews held, the worse it was thought to be for non-Jews. Ironically, often at the same time as these views were expressed, Jewish poverty was also indicated as a sign of the Jews' unproductiveness and parasitism.[20] Many in Russia's ruling circles and the Russian masses as a whole were so blinded by these strongly held prejudices and by deeply ingrained, age-old religious and ethnic hostilities that they could not see any positive contribution the Jews might have made to Russian life.

Anti-Jewish sentiments intensified noticeably during the 1870s. They found candid expression in government circles and in the press, where more and more anti-Jewish articles appeared, especially after 1878. They also found expression in a pogrom in Odessa (1871) and a trial, in Kutais in the Caucasus mountains (1879), in which Jews were accused of using Christian blood in religious ceremonies. The increased anti-Jewish feelings may be accounted for by a number of wide-ranging factors: Chauvinistic Russian (and Ukrainian) nationalism grew during the 1860s and 1870s and advocated taking a firm hand with the empire's national minorities. The infamous *Book of the Kahal (Kniga Kagala,* 1st ed. 1869; 2d ed. 1871, subsidized by a Russian government department), written by the Jewish apostate Jacob Brafman, made its appearance and seemed to document the already well-known accusation that the Jews constituted "a state within the state" whose main aim was to subjugate and exploit the non-Jewish population. The book became an object of heated discussions in the Russian press. On another front, competition between Jewish and Christian businessmen, craftsmen, and manufacturers intensified. Many of the Christians were ambitious newcomers who particularly resented having to contend with Jews, especially since the latter often had much more business experience. Many non-Jews were highly critical of the rapid increase in the number of Jewish students in general institutions of learning—which meant more competition for non-Jews, not only in the educational institutions themselves but also in the professions (medicine, law, teaching, and so on). The increasingly prominent role being played by educated Jews in Russian culture and public life also evoked warnings and condemnations. During 1877–78 and thereafter, the Russo-Turkish War fanned nationalist feelings very strongly and resulted in numerous newspaper articles attacking Jewish contractors who supplied the army. These purveyors allegedly robbed the government and harmed Russia's military might by their various chicaneries. Finally, the 1879 Kutais "blood libel" trial led many press organs to discuss seriously whether Jews actually did use Christian blood for religious purposes—even though the accused Jews were acquitted.

All these attitudes and developments underlay the pogroms of 1881. But it was a host of exceptional circumstances that crystallized early in the year that precipitated the crisis. The Russian and Ukrainian masses joined in large-scale anti-Jewish violence for the first time in over a hundred years; and Russian Jewry suffered a terrible tragedy that was to have major implications for the future.

*Chapter 3*

# THE COMING OF THE POGROMS
◆ ◆ ◆

THE TERRORIST BOMB THAT SHATTERED ALEXANDER II'S LEGS AND quickly led to his death on 1 March 1881 was soon followed by violent eruptions of another sort. In mid March, the anti-Semitic Odessa newspaper *Novorossiiskii Telegraf* began reporting rumors that attacks upon Jews would be perpetrated during the coming Easter holidays. These rumors quickly reached nearby Elizavetgrad.

Called Elizavetgrad until 1924 and Kirovograd since 1939, this town is located on the Ingul River, a tributary of the Bug. The place was originally settled in 1754 as a fort, soon after the Russians took over the region. It quickly developed into a major trade center of the steppe zone of the Ukraine. In the 1880s it was within Kherson *guberniia* (province). Grain, cattle, and wool were traded at its fairs. From its merchants' offices and warehouses rural products were shipped to Moscow—through Kremenchug, Khar'kov, and Kursk—and abroad—through the ports of Nikolaev and Odessa. A railroad line to Odessa was established in the 1860s, through the town of Balta.

Jews began to settle in Elizavetgrad at the end of the eighteenth century, when they were allowed to move from the northern *guberniias* of the Pale to New Russia (the Odessa region). At the time of the 1881 pogrom, the town's population numbered about forty-five thousand, one-third of whom were Jews. The most widespread occupation among the Jews was the making of clothing. In addition, most of the town's flour mills, distilleries, and tobacco factories belonged to Jews, and the trade in grain was also concentrated in their hands.[1]

Some of the townspeople were able to read for themselves the newspaper items reporting rumors of impending attacks on the Jews. Others heard them read aloud and discussed in the town's marketplaces. It was a common practice during this period in Russia for periodical publications to be read aloud before several people, partly because newspapers and journals were rather expensive and partly because so many people were illiterate.[2]

Conventional wisdom teaches that the common man views the printed word as authoritative; this was undoubtedly true in nineteenth-century Russia. "Imperial proclamations and sacred texts had long commanded the obedient trust and faith of Russian subjects and had thereby lent a certain mystique and strong authority to words imprinted on paper."[3] Since as a rule the publications reaching them were carefully censored, Russian subjects tended to believe that what was printed in the press must be both true and sanctioned by the government.

Thus in March 1881 many people drew the conclusion that legal sanction and encouragement were being given to assaults upon the alien and despised Jews. This impression received reinforcement when word spread that several Jews were leading members of the organization responsible for the murder of Alexander II. Fantastic beliefs came easily to a population already extremely agitated and uncertain about the future as the new tsar, Alexander III, an unknown quantity, ascended the throne.[4]

Before proceeding, I must take note of the organization of the Russian Empire. Administratively it was divided into *guberniias* (*gubernii,* "provinces"), which were subdivided into *uezds* (*uezdy,* "districts"). Then there were towns, townlets (*shtetlach*—see above) and villages. In many places *volosts* (*volosti,* "cantons") were organized as administrative units below the *uezds* by grouping together a number of peasant villages (perhaps as many as twenty). In certain areas of the empire several *guberniias* were grouped into regions, called governor-generalships.

*Guberniias* were ruled by governors appointed by the minister of the interior, with the approval of the tsar. The governors were formally subordinate to the minister of the interior, but they frequently wielded independent influence at court, especially when they came from a military background. Indeed, military men were tsarist favorites as appointees to this post. Governors were entrusted with a vast array of responsibilities. It was their job to supervise the organs and officials dealing with such matters as peasant welfare, recruits for the army, sanitation and health, education, roads and other means of communication, commerce, politics, security, and so on. The governors exercised broad authority over practically all the people involved in local government, including certain local activities of central government agencies and the activities of the *zemstvos* (organs of local self-government on the *uezd* and *guberniia* levels established by Alexander II and composed of representatives elected by all classes). Above all, governors oversaw the maintenance of law and order by everyone under their jurisdiction, including their own subordinates, elected officials, and ordinary citizens.

In the *uezds* of each *guberniia,* the chief of police was the central government's highest-ranking official. He was the governor's right arm and representative on the local level, and he also had a wide range of powers and duties, especially in regard to preserving law and order, tax collecting, and overseeing the execution of official decrees. During the period under discussion the lament was often heard that existing legislation failed to define sufficiently his duties and, in particular, his obligations to his superiors and to the judicial authorities. In general, the local police suffered from being understaffed, underpaid, and undertrained. The police chiefs also found it difficult to work directly with peasant society, since the territory over which they had authority was so extensive. Sitting in the capital of the *uezd,* they were quite distant from the villages. Yet they were practically the only agents of the central government ever to make an appearance there.

Towns, townlets, and villages each had their locally elected officials and organs over whom, as I have noted, the governor and his staff had extensive supervisory and veto powers. In towns there were the all-class, elected *dumas* (established by Alexander II), with a limited mandate to handle local affairs. Each peasant village, acting through its assembly of heads of households, elected a village elder and a clerk. Where *volosts* existed, the villages involved sent representatives to *volost* assemblies, which elected officials responsible to the government organs of the *uezds* for, among other things, maintaining order and tranquility.

Powerful governors-general ruled those *guberniias* subsumed under governor-generalships. Both officially and in practice the governors-general were equal to central government ministers in rank and status and had direct access to the tsar.

They and the governors under them had complete and undisputed control over all matters in the territories under their jurisdiction. Lower down the administrative hierarchy, however, lines of authority among different officials were not always clear. Such was the case in regard to civilian officials' relations among themselves, and especially in civilian-military relations. Furthermore, even when formal lines of authority, powers, and functions were clear and well defined, they could be set at naught: lower-ranking officials might with impunity ignore directives issued by their superiors. They could claim as justification their superiors' lack of information on local conditions, shortages of personnel, misunderstandings, and so on.[5]

The Jews of Elizavetgrad became very worried by the atmosphere of foreboding that emerged in their town in March 1881. They repeatedly turned to the police chief to request special protection. The police chief, I. P. Bogdanovich, enjoyed a reputation as an honorable and conscientious official who treated non-Orthodox Christians and non-Russians very humanely. He assured the Jews that all necessary measures had been taken and that there was no need to fear any disruption of public order. Bogdanovich had, in fact, called in extra troops to augment the poorly manned local police contingent.

The Russian Orthodox Easter is celebrated for a full week. In 1881 the popular entertainments characteristic of the season had been canceled by tsarist decree, in mourning for Alexander II. This was misunderstood by the common people, who thought the Jews had bribed the police to limit Easter festivities as a safeguard against public disorders. Certain incautious, even mocking, remarks allegedly made by Jews to their Christian neighbors may have strengthened this impression. So, though there were no violent incidents in Elizavetgrad from Easter Sunday, 12 April, until Wednesday, 15 April (see tables 3 and 4) provocative rumors about imminent anti-Jewish riots continued to be heard.[6]

In spite of this talk, Chief of Police Bogdanovich felt that life had more or less returned to normal, so he relaxed some of the precautionary measures. On the morning of 15 April, taverns were allowed to open, and the military reinforcements were sent back to their base camp.

At 4:00 P.M. an argument broke out in a Jewish tavern. The owner and one of his customers, a retarded townsman well known for his foolishness, quarreled, and the half-wit ran out shouting that the tavern keeper had hit him. Soon the cry was heard all around, "The Yids [*zhidy*] are beating Christians." The police intervened immediately, trying to disperse the crowd, but they failed. People ran through the streets breaking windows of Jewish homes and shops; taverns were a favorite target. The police called upon the local garrison to help them as rioters began looting and destroying Jewish property. The presence of many curious spectators on the streets hindered the activities of the authorities. Still, twenty of the drunkest and most violent rioters were arrested.

Meanwhile, Bogdanovich sent word to recall the soldiers he had dismissed that morning. They arrived at 6:00 P.M. and helped disperse the mobs in the center of the town and the main marketplace. This, however, did not end the disorders, for the rioters simply spread out to the suburbs. Using hit and run methods and the cover of darkness, they continued to cause damage sporadically. A potentially murderous incident occurred early in the evening. The Jews were accused of firing revolvers at the rioters from their synagogue, and the mood of the mob became highly

## TABLE 3
### Calendar of Pogroms, 1881
#### APRIL 1881

| Sunday | Monday | Tuesday | Wednesday | Thursday | Friday | Saturday |
|---|---|---|---|---|---|---|
| | | | 1 | 2 | 3 | 4 |
| 5 | 6 | 7 | 8 | 9 | 10 | 11 |
| 12[a] | 13 | 14 | 15[b] | 16 | 17 | 18 |
| 19 | 20 | 21 | 22 | 23 | 24 | 25 |
| 26[c] | 27 | 28 | 29 | 30 | | |

#### MAY 1881

| Sunday | Monday | Tuesday | Wednesday | Thursday | Friday | Saturday |
|---|---|---|---|---|---|---|
| | | | | | 1 | 2 |
| 3[d] | 4 | 5 | 6 | 7 | 8 | 9 |
| 10 | 11 | 12 | 13 | 14 | 15 | 16 |
| 17 | 18 | 19 | 20 | 21 | 22 | 23 |
| 24 | 25 | 26 | 27 | 28 | 29 | 30 |
| 31 | | | | | | |

#### JUNE 1881

| Sunday | Monday | Tuesday | Wednesday | Thursday | Friday | Saturday |
|---|---|---|---|---|---|---|
| | 1 | 2 | 3 | 4 | 5 | 6 |
| 7 | 8 | 9 | 10 | 11 | 12 | 13 |
| 14 | 15 | 16 | 17 | 18 | 19 | 20 |
| 21 | 22 | 23 | 24 | 25 | 26 | 27 |
| 28 | 29 | 30 | | | | |

#### JULY 1881

| Sunday | Monday | Tuesday | Wednesday | Thursday | Friday | Saturday |
|---|---|---|---|---|---|---|
| | | | 1 | 2 | 3 | 4 |
| 5 | 6 | 7 | 8 | 9 | 10 | 11 |
| 12 | 13 | 14 | 15 | 16 | 17 | 18 |
| 19 | 20 | 21 | 22 | 23 | 24 | 25 |
| 26 | 27 | 28 | 29 | 30 | 31 | |

TABLE 3 *(Continued)*

AUGUST 1881

| Sunday | Monday | Tuesday | Wednesday | Thursday | Friday | Saturday |
|--------|--------|---------|-----------|----------|--------|----------|
|        |        |         |           |          |        | 1        |
| 2      | 3      | 4       | 5         | 6        | 7      | 8        |
| 9      | 10     | 11      | 12        | 13       | 14     | 15       |
| 16     | 17     | 18      | 19        | 20       | 21     | 22       |
| 23     | 24     | 25      | 26        | 27       | 28     | 29       |
| 30     | 31     |         |           |          |        |          |

Notes:
a. Easter Sunday.
b. Elizavetgrad pogrom.
c. Kiev pogrom.
d. Odessa pogrom.

inflamed. Troops immediately surrounded the building. It was pointed out that the windows in the synagogue were too high for anyone to shoot out of, but only with some difficulty were the incensed townspeople finally persuaded to disperse.

As the night of 15–16 April passed, no comprehensive measures to prevent rioting the next day were undertaken by either civilian or military officials on the spot. They also failed to provide for the coordination of their activities.

Sometime during the night of 15–16 April, the governor-general of the Odessa region, A. M. Dondukov-Korsakov, received news of the Elizavetgrad pogrom. He immediately sent instructions to Governor Erdeli of the Kherson *guberniia* to hasten to the stricken town. In addition, he sent the following telegram to the military commander on the spot, Major-General Kosich: "I have received reports about the disorders. I charge Your Excellency, until the arrival of the Governor, with giving all instructions and taking all measures you think necessary to stop the riots. If they continue, I permit you to close all taverns until they end." This message arrived at 6:00 A.M. on 16 April. It seemed to give Kosich authority over both the available troops and the local police.

The major-general, however—apart from issuing a general order giving the troops permission to use force, including firearms—remained inert. He issued no instructions for the police, and he gave no specific orders to the troops. He seemed to be waiting for the civilian authorities

## TABLE 4
### Towns and Villages in Which Pogroms Occurred, 1881

| Number of Days from 15 April 1881 | Date Pogrom Began | Guberniia | Uezd | Town or Village |
|---|---|---|---|---|
| 1 | 15 April | Kherson | Elizavetgrad | Elizavetgrad |
| 2/3 | 16/17 April (night) | Kherson | Aleksandriia | Malaia Mamaika |
| 2/3 | 16/17 April (night) | Kherson | Elizavetgrad | Cherniakovka |
| 2–7? | Sometime during 16–21 April | Kherson | Elizavetgrad | Semenovka |
| 3 | 17 April | Kherson | Aleksandriia | Adzhamka |
| 3 | 17 April | Kherson | Aleksandriia | Aleksandrievka |
| 3 | 17 April | Kherson | Aleksandriia | Aleksandrovka |
| 3 | 17 April | Kherson | Aleksandriia | Kalinovka |
| 3 | 17 April | Kherson | Aleksandriia | Klintsy |
| 3 | 17 April | Kherson | Aleksandriia | Krasnyi Iar |
| 3 | 17 April | Kherson | Aleksandriia | Mar'evka |
| 3 | 17 April | Kherson | Aleksandriia | Pokrovskoe |
| 3 | 17 April | Kherson | Aleksandriia | Subbottsy |
| 3 | 17 April | Kherson | Aleksandriia | Vysokie Bueraki |
| 3 | 17 April | Kherson | Aleksandriia | Znamenka (station) |
| 3 | 17 April | Kherson | Anan'ev | Golta |
| 3 | 17 April | Kherson | Elizavetgrad | Gruzskoe |
| 3 | 17 April | Kherson | Elizavetgrad | Lelekovka |
| 3 | 17 April | Kherson | Elizavetgrad | Poklitarovka |
| 3 | 17 April | Kherson | Elizavetgrad | Sasovka |
| 3 | 17 April | Kherson | Elizavetgrad | Sazonovka |
| 4 | 18 April | Kherson | Aleksandriia | Dolina-Kamenka (or Donina-Kalilika, or Dolika-Kamenka, or Donina-Kamenka) |
| 4 | 18 April | Kherson | Aleksandriia | Gubovka |
| 4 | 18 April | Kherson | Elizavetgrad | Egorovka |
| 4 | 18 April | Kherson | Elizavetgrad | Grigor'evka |
| 4 | 18 April | Kherson | Elizavetgrad | Zelenovka |
| 5 | 19 April | Kherson | Aleksandriia | Aleksandriia (nipped in the bud) |
| 5 | 19 April | Kherson | Aleksandriia | Plosskoe |
| 5 | 19 April | Kherson | Elizavetgrad | Pustopol'e |
| 5 | 19 April | Kherson | Elizavetgrad | Rostvovka |
| 6 | 20 April | Bessarabia | Kishinev | Kishinev town (nipped in the bud) |
| 6 | 20 April | Kherson | Elizavetgrad | Miroliubovka |
| 6 | 20 April | Kherson | Elizavetgrad | Petrovka |
| 7 | 21 April | Kherson | Anan'ev | Romanovka |
| 7 | 21 April | Kherson | Elizavetgrad | Antonopol |
| 7 | 21 April | Kherson | Elizavetgrad | Gavrilenkov |
| 7 | 21 April | Kherson | Elizavetgrad | Kamenovodka (or Kamenovatka) |

TABLE 4 *(Continued)*

| Number of Days from 15 April 1881 | Date Pogrom Began | Guberniia | Uezd | Town or Village |
|---|---|---|---|---|
| 7 | 21 April | Kherson | Elizavetgrad | Katerinovka |
| 7 | 21 April | Kherson | Elizavetgrad | Viatiazevka |
| 12 | 26 April | Kherson | Anan'ev | Anan'ev |
| 12 | 26 April | Kherson | Anan'ev | Berezovka |
| 12 | 26 April | Kherson | Anan'ev | 5 villages (possibly Gandrabury, Zavadovka, Sirotinka, Strukovo, Teftulovo, listed for 27–28 April) |
| 12 | 26 April (27 April?) | Kherson | Tiraspol' | Bernardovka |
| 12 | 26 April (27 April?) | Kherson | Tiraspol' | Demidovo |
| 12 | 26 April | Kiev[a] | Kiev | Kiev |
| 13 | 27 April | Chernigov | ? | Brovary |
| 13 | 27 April | Chernigov | Konotop | Konotop |
| 13 | 27 April | Kherson | Anan'ev | Gandrabury (or Gadrabury, or Gaidrabury) |
| 13 | 27 April | Kherson | Anan'ev | Zavadovka |
| 13 | 27 April (26 April?) | Kherson | Tiraspol' | Bernardovka |
| 13 | 27 April (26 April?) | Kherson | Tiraspol' | Demidovo |
| 13 | 27 April | Kiev | Kiev | Fasovka (or Fasova) |
| 13 | 27 April | Kiev | Kiev | Makarov |
| 13 | 27 April | Kiev | Vasil'kov | Fastov (station) |
| 13 | 27 April | Kiev | ? | Kanev |
| 13 | 27 April | Podolia | ? | Zhmerinka (station) |
| 13/14 | 27/28 April (night) | Chernigov | Konotop | Konotop |
| 13/14 | 27/28 April (night) | Kiev | Vasil'kov | Vasil'kov |
| 14 | 28 April | Chernigov | (The *uezd* surrounding Konotop) | |
| 14 | 28 April | Kherson | Anan'ev | Sirotinka |
| 14 | 28 April | Kherson | Anan'ev | Strukovo (or Strunovo) |
| 14 | 28 April | Kherson | Anan'ev | Teftulovo |
| 15 | 29 April | Kiev | Cherkasy | Ol'shanovka |
| 15 | 29 April | Kiev | Cherkasy | Peregonovka |
| 15 | 29 April | Kiev | Charkasy | Vasil'evo |
| 15 | 29 April | Kiev | ? | Along the road from Kiev to Vasil'kov and Zhitomir |
| 16 | 30 April | Kiev | Kiev | Liudvinovka |
| — | (April or May) | Chernigov | ? | Cheriko |

TABLE 4 *(Continued)*

| Number of Days from 15 April 1881 | Date Pogrom Began | Guberniia | Uezd | Town or Village |
|---|---|---|---|---|
| 17 | 1 May | Ekaterinoslav | Aleksandrovsk | Aleksandrovsk |
| 17 | 1 May | Ekaterinoslav | Aleksandrovsk | Andreevka |
| 17 | 1 May | Ekaterinoslav | Aleksandrovsk | Grigor'evka |
| 17 | 1 May | Ekaterinoslav | Aleksandrovsk | Natal'evka |
| 17 | 1 May | Ekaterinoslav | Aleksandrovsk | Nikopol |
| 17 | 1 May | Ekaterinoslav | Aleksandrovsk | Petrovsk |
| 17 | 1 May | Ekaterinoslav | Novomoskovsk | Elizavetovka |
| 17 | 1 May | Ekaterinoslav | Novomoskovsk | Manuilovka |
| 17 | 1 May | Kherson | ? | Nikolaev (small, quickly suppressed) |
| 17 | 1 May (2, 3, 4 May?) | Tavrida | Orekhov | Orekhov (town and *volost*) |
| 19 | 3 May | Ekaterinoslav | Aleksandrovsk | Kamyshevka (or Kamyshevatka) |
| 19 | 3 May | Ekaterinoslav | Aleksandrovsk | Voznesensk |
| 19 | 3 May | Ekaterinoslav | Pavlograd | Lozovaia (station) |
| 19 or 26 | 3 or 10 May | Kherson | Odessa | Ianovka |
| 19 | 3 May | Kherson | Odessa | Maiaki |
| 19 | 3 May | Kherson | Odessa | Odessa (not serious, thanks to actions of officials) |
| 19 or 26 | 3 or 10 May | Kherson | Odessa | Varvarovka |
| 19 | 3 May | Kiev | Cherkasy | Smela |
| 19 | 3 May | Poltava | Romny | Romny |
| 19 | 3 May (4/5 May; night?) | Volynia | Starokonstantinov | Volochisk (station) |
| 19/20 | 3/4 May (night) | Volynia | Starokonstantinov | Fridrikhovka |
| 20 | 4 May | Kherson | Odessa | Shpaier |
| 20 | 4 May | Kiev | Near Smela | Balakleia |
| 20 | 4 May | Kiev | Near Smela | Berezniaki |
| 20 | 4 May | Kiev | Near Smela | Budki |
| 20 | 4 May | Kiev | Near Smela | Dubievka |
| 20 | 4 May | Kiev | Near Smela | Grechkovo |
| 20 | 4 May | Kiev | Near Smela | Iablonovka |
| 20 | 4 May | Kiev | Near Smela | Konstantinovka |
| 20 | 4 May | Kiev | Near Smela | Malaia Smelianka |
| 20 | 4 May | Kiev | Near Smela | Malo-Starosel' |
| 20 | 4 May | Kiev | Near Smela | Pleskachevka |
| 20 | 4 May | Kiev | Near Smela | Pleskal'ko |
| 20 | 4 May | Kiev | Near Smela | Smelianka |
| 20 | 4 May | Kiev | Near Smela | Starosel'e |
| 20 | 4 May | Kiev | Near Smela | Stepanovka |
| 20 | 4 May | Kiev | Near Smela | Zalevki |
| 20 | 4 May | Tavrida | Berdiansk | Villages near Berdiansk |

TABLE 4 *(Continued)*

| Number of Days from 15 April 1881 | Date Pogrom Began | Guberniia | Uezd | Town or Village |
|---|---|---|---|---|
| 20 | 4 May | Tavrida | Melitopol' | Malye Tokmachi and other villages near Melitopol' |
| 20 | 4 May (1, 2, 3 May?) | Tavrida | Orekhov | Orekhov (town and *volost*) |
| 20 | 4 May | Volynia | Starokonstantinov | Golokhvasta |
| 20 | 4 May | Volynia | Starokonstantinov | Kopachevka |
| 20 | 4 May | Volynia | Starokonstantinov | Nemirovets |
| 20 | 4 May | Volynia | Starokonstantinov | Poliana |
| 20 | 4 May | Volynia | Starokonstantinov | Volchkovets |
| 20/21 | 4/5 May (night) | Ekaterinoslav | Novomoskovsk | Imenie Vasinovka |
| 20/21 | 4/5 May (night) | Ekaterinoslav | Novomoskovsk | Konskie Razdory |
| 20/21 | 4/5 May (night) (3 May?) | Volynia | Starokonstantinov | Volochisk (station) |
| 21 | 5 May | Ekaterinoslav | Novomoskovsk | Gaigula |
| 21 | 5 May | Ekaterinoslav | Novomoskovsk | Preobrazhenka |
| 21 | 5 May | Ekaterinoslav | Novomoskovsk | Voskresensk |
| 21 | 5 May | Tavrida | Berdiansk | Villages near Berdiansk |
| 21 | 5 May | Tavrida | Melitopol' | Villages near Melitopol' |
| 22 | 6 May | Ekaterinoslav | Aleksandrovsk | Alekseevka |
| 22 | 6 May | Ekaterinoslav | Aleksandrovsk | Belomanka |
| 22 | 6 May | Ekaterinoslav | Aleksandrovsk | Blagoveshchensk |
| 22 | 6 May | Ekaterinoslav | Aleksandrovsk | Krutoe |
| 22 | 6 May | Ekaterinoslav | Aleksandrovsk | Mezherich (Jewish colony) |
| 22 | 6 May | Ekaterinoslav | Aleksandrovsk | Novoselovka |
| 22 | 6 May | Ekaterinoslav | Aleksandrovsk | Sofievka |
| 22 | 6 May | Ekaterinoslav | Aleksandrovsk | Tsarekonstantinovka |
| 22 | 6 May | Poltava | Romny | Bobrik |
| 22 | 6 May | Tavrida | Berdiansk | Villages near Berdiansk |
| 22 | 6 May | Tavrida | Melitopol' | Imenie Belogor'e |
| 22/23 | 6/7 May (night) | Ekaterinoslav | Aleksandrovsk | Nechaevka (Jewish colony) |
| 22/23 | 6/7 May (night) | Ekaterinoslav | Aleksandrovsk | Trudoliubovka (Jewish colony) |
| 23 | 7 May | Ekaterinoslav | Mariupol' | Grafskaia (Jewish colony) |
| 23 | 7 May | Ekaterinoslav | Mariupol' | Sladkovodnaia (Jewish colony) |
| 24 | 8 May | Ekaterinoslav | Aleksandrovsk | Gavrilovka |
| 24 | 8 May | Ekaterinoslav | Aleksandrovsk | Pokrovskoe |
| 24 | 8 May | Ekaterinoslav | Aleksandrovsk | Verbovo |
| 26 | 10 May | Kherson | Kherson | Kherson town (small, quickly suppressed) |
| 26 | 10 May | Kherson | Odessa | Egorovka |

TABLE 4 (Continued)

| Number of Days from 15 April 1881 | Date Pogrom Began | Guberniia | Uezd | Town or Village |
|---|---|---|---|---|
| 26 | 10 May | Kherson | Odessa | Mikhailovka |
| 77 | 30 June | Poltava | Pereiaslav | Pereiaslav |
| 78 | 1 July | Poltava | ? | Andrushi |
| 78 | 1 July | Poltava | ? | Korony Khutor (or Koropy Khutor) |
| 89 | 12 July | Poltava | Pereiaslav | Berezan' |
| 89 | 12 July | Poltava | Pereiaslav | Borispol' |
| 90 | 13 July | Poltava | Pereiaslav | Gorodishche |
| 90 | 13 July | Poltava | Pereiaslav | Ivanovka |
| 90 | 13 July | Poltava | Pereiaslav | Lemanovka (or Lemana) |
| 90 | 13 July | Poltava | Pereiaslav | Liubartsy (or Liubortsy) |
| 90 | 13 July | Poltava | Pereiaslav | Martosovka |
| 90 | 13 July | Poltava | Pereiaslav | Semenovka (or Semenovna) |
| 90 | 13 July | Poltava | Pereiaslav | Skoptsy |
| 91 | 14 July | Poltava | Pereiaslav | Voron'kovo |
| 97 | 20 July | Chernigov | Nezhin | 4 villages |
| 97 | 20 July | Chernigov | Nezhin | Nezhin |
| 97 | 20 July (13 July?) | Chernigov | Oster | 9 villages |
| 99 | 22 July | Chernigov | Borzna | Dremailovka |
| 100 | 23 July | Chernigov | Borzna | Kirillovka |
| 100 | 23 July | Chernigov | Borzna | Pashkovka |
| 100 | 23 July | Chernigov | Borzna | Tarashevo Khutor |
| 104 | 27 July | Poltava | ? | Lubny |
| 105 | 28 July | Poltava | ? | Kononovka |
| 105 | 28 July | Poltava | ? | Ol'shanka |
| 114 | 6 August | Chernigov | Borzna | Borzna |
| 114 | 6 August | Chernigov | Borzna | Pustovoitov Khutor |
| 114 | 6 August | Chernigov | Borzna | Shapovalovka |
| 114 | 6 August | Chernigov | Borzna | Vysokoe |
| 116 | 8 August | Chernigov | Borzna | Kozinets |
| 117 | 9 August | Chernigov | Borzna | Alenovka |
| 117 | 9 August | Chernigov | Borzna | Ivangorod |
| 124 | 16 August | Chernigov | Borzna | Ichnia |
| 214 | 14 November | Kherson | Odessa | Odessa (small, insignificant disturbances) |
| 255 | 25 December | Poland | — | Warsaw and nearby settlements |
| ? | ? | Chernigov | Kozelets | All over |
| ? | ? | Chernigov | ? | Zholdaki |

TABLE 4 *(Continued)*

| Number of Days from 15 April 1881 | Date Pogrom Began | Guberniia | Uezd | Town or Village |
|---|---|---|---|---|
| ? | ? | Ekaterinoslav | ? | Rostov-on-Don (attempt at pogrom only; police suppressed it) |
| ? | ? | Kiev[a] | ? | Berdichev (insignificant incidents) |
| ? | ? | Kiev | ? | Belaia Tserkov |
| ? | ? | Kiev | Cherkasy | Bykovo |
| ? | ? | Kiev | Kiev | Belgorodka |
| ? | ? | Kiev | Kiev | Borshchagovka |
| ? | ? | Kiev | Kiev | Buzovaia |
| ? | ? | Kiev | Kiev | Germanovo |
| ? | ? | Kiev | Kiev | Glevakhskoi Volost |
| ? | ? | Kiev | Kiev | Gorelichka |
| ? | ? | Kiev | Kiev | Gruzskoe |
| ? | ? | Kiev | Kiev | Gvozdovo |
| ? | ? | Kiev | Kiev | Iankovichi |
| ? | ? | Kiev | Kiev | Ignatovka |
| ? | ? | Kiev | Kiev | Iurovka |
| ? | ? | Kiev | Kiev | Kholen'e |
| ? | ? | Kiev | Kiev | Khotavy |
| ? | ? | Kiev | Kiev | Krasnoe |
| ? | ? | Kiev | Kiev | Kriukovshchina |
| ? | ? | Kiev | Kiev | Litovskaia |
| ? | ? | Kiev | Kiev | Liutensk |
| ? | ? | Kiev | Kiev | Manovishche |
| ? | ? | Kiev | Kiev | Mikhailovskaia |
| ? | ? | Kiev | Kiev | Mostishche |
| ? | ? | Kiev | Kiev | Motyzhino |
| ? | ? | Kiev | Kiev | Myshelovka |
| ? | ? | Kiev | Kiev | Nepryshi |
| ? | ? | Kiev | Kiev | Novosel'e |
| ? | ? | Kiev | Kiev | Novoselki |
| ? | ? | Kiev | Kiev | Novye Petrovtsy |
| ? | ? | Kiev | Kiev | Obukhovo |
| ? | ? | Kiev | Kiev | Petrovskaia |
| ? | ? | Kiev | Kiev | Petruchiki |
| ? | ? | Kiev | Kiev | Pirnov |
| ? | ? | Kiev | Kiev | Pochtovaia |
| ? | ? | Kiev | Kiev | Polynovo |
| ? | ? | Kiev | Kiev | Roslavichi |
| ? | ? | Kiev | Kiev | Rubensovka |
| ? | ? | Kiev | Kiev | Shcherbinovo |
| ? | ? | Kiev | Kiev | Shchikhrovshchina |
| ? | ? | Kiev | Kiev | Shpitki |
| ? | ? | Kiev | Kiev | Starye Petrovtsy |

TABLE 4 (Continued)

| Number of Days from 15 April 1881 | Date Pogrom Began | Guberniia | Uezd | Town or Village |
|---|---|---|---|---|
| ? | ? | Kiev | Kiev | Vity |
| ? | ? | Kiev | Kiev | Vyshegorod |
| ? | ? | Kiev | Kiev | Zabuzh'e |
| ? | ? | Kiev | Kiev | Zhilimy |
| ? | ? | Kiev | Kiev | Zhukovtsy |
| ? | ? | Kiev | Kiev | Zlodeevka |
| ? | ? | Poltava | ? | Greblia Khutor |
| ? | ? | Tavrida | Berdiansk | Andreevka |
| ? | ? | Tavrida | Berdiansk | Danilovka |
| ? | ? | Tavrida | Berdiansk | Novo-Andreevka |
| ? | ? | Tavrida | Berdiansk | Petropavlovsk |
| ? | ? | Tavrida | Berdiansk | Popovka |
| ? | ? | Tavrida | Berdiansk | Shcherbaki |
| ? | ? | Tavrida | Berdiansk | Tokmak |
| ? | ? | Tavrida | Berdiansk | Verbovo |
| ? | ? | Tavrida | Melitopol' | Ianchekrak |
| ? | ? | Tavrida | Melitopol' | Khitrovka |
| ? | ? | Tavrida | Melitopol' | Kopani |
| ? | ? | Tavrida | Melitopol' | Melitopol' |
| ? | ? | Tavrida | Melitopol' | Prishib |
| ? | ? | Tavrida | Melitopol' | Sladkaia Balka |
| ? | ? | Tavrida | Melitopol' | Troitskoe |
| ? | ? | Tavrida | Melitopol' | Tsaritsyn-Kur |
| ? | ? | Tavrida | Melitopol' | Veselianka |

Notes:

The above list may *not* be complete. Every effort has been made to ensure its accuracy and correct spelling. However, I often had to rely on sources which did not give complete information or which were not entirely clear about the correct spelling or nominative endings of the locations cited, or the precise dates on which pogroms occurred.

The table is arranged chronologically, then alphabetically, in the order: *guberniia, uezd,* town or village.

In Kherson *guberniia*, pogroms spread from Elizavetgrad town to the villages of Elizavetgrad and Aleksandriia *uezds*, and from there to Anan'ev and Tiraspol' *uezds*, and then to Odessa *uezd*, as will be seen from the table.

Pogroms occurred from 7 to 10 May along a square formed by the Odessa-Kiev, Elizavetgrad-Khar'kov, and Fastov railroads.

To a certain extent, the waves of pogroms can be divided into three periods: 15–21 April (days 1–7); 26 April–10 May (days 12–26); 30 June–16 August (days 77–124).

a. After the Kiev pogrom began (26 April), about forty-eight near-by localities suffered pogroms, starting from 27 April.

to call the soldiers to action. The police, meanwhile, practically all retired from the scene, as if they considered their job done once troops appeared on the streets.

Some contemporaries explained Major-General Kosich's inaction by saying that the telegrammed instructions he received were not specific enough. According to Russian law, troops brought in to suppress riots automatically came under the authority of the civilian administration. Consequently, in this view, Kosich interpreted the governor-general's telegram as giving him authority only over the troop reinforcements that were yet to arrive or that Kosich might yet call in.

On the morning of 16 April, peasants from nearby villages joined the rioters. Jewish property continued to be destroyed or thrown into the streets. From there it was carried away by passers-by, sometimes in peasant carts. With no clear instructions about how to suppress the rioting, both soldiers and police refrained from acting. The police, in fact, were conspicuous by their almost total absence. When yet another house or shop was attacked, the troops on the spot waited for specific orders before moving in to disperse the rioters. Eyewitnesses reported a case of soldiers refusing to stop two men who were casually walking along the street and breaking windows. The officer in charge explained that this was a police matter and, anyway, they could not arrest everyone.

The absence of definite instructions about how to handle the disorders was only one problem. The situation was compounded by the division of the soldiers, in a vain effort to cover the whole town, into quite small patrols, acting independently and without coordination. Often because their units were so small and the rioters so numerous, the soldiers were pushed aside and forced to stand idly by as Jewish property was destroyed. Crowds of spectators from the educated and well-to-do classes, including women and children, also clogged the scenes of destruction, as they had the day before. In general, military officers refused to use force with so many "innocent" bystanders present. Still, the blunt ends of lances and the flat edges of sabres were occasionally employed. In one case soldiers shot their rifles into the air, after Major-General Kosich issued a general order on the morning of 16 April giving permission to use force, including firearms. The mobs rarely manifested active resistance. When confronted by energetic opposition from soldiers, they interpreted it to mean that, while rioting was no longer permitted in that particular place, it was allowed elsewhere. So, without dispersing, they moved along to another Jewish home or tavern or shop.

In a few instances soldiers drank liquor with rioters in plundered

Jewish taverns or accepted gifts of looted clothing and household items. But even more than such criminal behavior, the obvious inertia, hesitancy, and lack of forcefulness on the part of the representatives of the government became major factors in reinforcing the common people's belief that the regime approved of anti-Jewish violence.

By the evening of 16 April, the crowds in the streets had grown quite large and the looting quite extensive. Many feared that the mob might start attacking the authorities and well-to-do non-Jews. Only now was the more promising tactic tried of dividing the town into sections and assigning a certain number of troops to each one. The rioting died down almost entirely between 8:00 and 11:00 P.M. with the arrival of rain, a cold wind, and fresh troops. Still more troops arrived on the morning of 17 April, and an end was put to the disturbances within the town. By then six hundred rioters had been arrested.

Governor Erdeli also arrived that morning and set about taking measures to calm the population and restore life to normal. He ordered the municipal government (*duma*) to increase its budget in order to strengthen the police force, to make provisions for the disposal of looted goods that might be turned in to the authorities, to undertake an investigation into the amount of property losses, and to decide whether or not the forthcoming trade fair should be postponed. Two other actions taken by the governor as soon as he arrived in Elizavetgrad are particularly noteworthy for the intriguing inconsistency that they reveal.

On the one hand, Erdeli instructed the *duma* to oversee the establishment of a Jewish committee that would provide charity for poor Jews who had suffered the destruction of their property. The *duma* immediately assigned 1,000 rubles to this committee to be used for food. Ultimately, over 160,000 rubles were received from donations and distributed to local pogrom victims. On the other hand, Erdeli allowed the *duma* to establish a committee to assist the families of indigent persons arrested on suspicion of having participated in the rioting. Public announcements were made about the formation of this committee, and prominent citizens were active in it. When, after a short time, most of the arrested were released, the committee was abolished. Its existence did, however, lead to the rumor that not only would the accused go unpunished, but rewards were being given to their families.

Elizavetgrad was finally quiet. But this was only the beginning of the massive anti-Jewish rioting that was to strike in 1881.[7] Villagers returning from the town spread word about what they had seen in ways that could only encourage further violence. The initial inertia of the authorities made a particularly strong impression: the people saw it as a sign of approval of their behavior. The actions finally taken to end the violence did little to dispel this impression. Soldiers had arrested rioters, but this was thought to be the result of Jewish bribes or just to show that the authorities were still in control. During the evening of 16 April, troops had been stationed at the entrances to Elizavetgrad for the purpose, it was announced, of preventing new arrivals from joining the rioting. Nevertheless this led to the rumor that soldiers had surrounded the town in order to prevent Jews from leaving it.

From 16 to 21 April rioting spread to eighteen villages and one townlet in the vicinity of Elizavetgrad, and to fourteen villages and one railroad station (Znamenka) in the nearby district of Aleksandriia. An attempt to start a riot in Aleksandriia itself was nipped in the bud by military forces. On 17 April a pogrom began in Golta, a large village in the Anan'ev district, connected with Elizavetgrad by railroad.

During the first week of massive anti-Jewish rioting, over thirty settlements in the northern section of Kherson *guberniia* suffered attacks on Jewish homes, shops, and especially taverns. On 20 April a scuffle between Christians and Jews occurred in the marketplace of Kishinev, in Bessarabia *guberniia,* but no pogrom took place.

From 22 to 25 April no rioting was reported. This calm was followed by two weeks of extensive pogroms ranging over eight *guberniias* of the southwest, New Russia (*Novorossiisk*), and the Ukraine. The violence began on 26 April, when a district seat, Anan'ev, the townlet Berezovka, five villages in Anan'ev district, and two villages in Tiraspol' district experienced outbreaks. These settlements were all located in southwest Kherson *guberniia.*

Pogroms also began on 26 April in the major town of Kiev and its suburbs. They continued until 28 April, spreading to fifty villages in the Kiev and Vasil'kov districts. On 3–4 May sugar factory and railroad workers led a pogrom in the large industrial town of Smela, located in the south of Kiev *guberniia* on the road to Elizavetgrad. This rioting spread to fifteen nearby villages. After four Jews were killed in this violence, the army resorted to firing on the rioters; several dozen people were wounded, and two were killed.

On 27 and 28 April railroad workers led a pogrom in the railroad terminal town of Zhmerinka, located on the line running from Kiev to the southwest. This was the only case of a pogrom in Podolia *guberniia.*

On 27–28 April anti-Jewish rioting broke out in Konotop, a district seat which lay east of the town of Kiev, in southern Chernigov *guberniia,* on the Kiev-Kursk railroad line. The disturbances were begun by railroad workers, some of whom had just arrived from riot-torn Kiev. On 3 May violence occurred in Romny, another district seat, and nearby villages. These settlements were located not far from Konotop in northern Poltava *guberniia*.

On 1 May a new part of southern Ukraine was struck by rioting: a district seat, Aleksandrovsk, on the Dnieper River in southern Ekaterinoslav *guberniia,* then seven nearby villages and the town of Orekhov in northern Tavrida *guberniia.* Railroad workers were among the initiators here too. On 4 May the violence spread to settlements in the Berdiansk and Melitopol' districts, located in northern Tavrida on the border with Ekaterinoslav.

On 3 May the railroad towns Lozovaia, in northern Ekaterinoslav *guberniia,* and Volochisk, in Volynia *guberniia* on the border with Austrian Galicia, experienced pogroms. From Volochisk they spread to six nearby villages on 4 and 5 May. These were the only cases of rioting in Volynia.

On 3–7 May disturbances occurred in Odessa, Kherson *guberniia,* and several nearby villages. More neighboring villages were hit on 10 May. In Odessa itself, thanks to actions taken by local officials, the disturbances were sporadic and relatively insignificant. The rioting of 7–10 May occurred along a square formed by the Odessa-Kiev, Elizavetgrad-Khar'kov, and Fastov railroad lines.

A tense but quiet period ensued for more than seven weeks. Then on 30 June Pereiaslav, a district seat in Poltava *guberniia,* erupted in violence. All the pogroms that occurred thereafter during the summer of 1881 were contained within a contiguous area in northern Poltava and southern Chernigov *guberniias.*

The rioting in Pereiaslav occurred on 30 June and 2 July. Here we can discern an immediate and conscious motive: the Christian residents were protesting the influx of Jewish refugees from Kiev, which caused an inflation of food prices. From Pereiaslav rioting spread to nine nearby villages.

A pogrom that broke out on 12 July in the townlet of Borispol' ended, after the perpetration of extensive damage, when troops fired and killed five rioters. On 20–21 July Nezhin, a district seat in southern Chernigov, experienced anti-Jewish rioting, and the army killed nine rioters. The violence spread to thirteen villages in the Nezhin and Oster districts. On 27 July the army suppressed rioting in Lubny, a district seat in Poltava *guberniia,* and in two nearby villages. On 6 August, Borzna, a district seat in Chernigov *guberniia,* and five neighboring villages suffered pogroms. The last significant anti-Jewish violence of 1881, except for that in Warsaw, Poland, on Christmas Day (13 December, Old Style), occurred on 16 August in Ichnia, a commercial center in Chernigov *guberniia*.

The several waves of anti-Jewish pogroms during 1881 engulfed 8 *guberniias* out of the Pale's 15 and over 240 communities in southwestern Russia. A number of pogroms took place in 1882, and a few swelled up in 1883 and 1884. Property losses were extensive, and many Jews were beaten during the violence of this period. The number of cases on record of rape and murder (one of the highest estimates refers to 40 deaths and 225 rapes in 1881)[8] seem relatively low by twentieth-century standards. But this did not prevent the stormy events of 1881–84 from having a deeply shocking and long-lasting impact on contemporaries. In the aftermath of the pogroms, the Russian government became noticeably more repressive in its Jewish policy; and, for the first time, large numbers of Jews turned to Zionism or simply fled the empire, going mostly to the United States.[9]

From 1884 until 1903 no significant anti-Jewish violence occurred. Then vicious pogroms erupted in Kishinev and Gomel in 1903, in Smela, Rovno, and elsewhere in 1904, and all over the Pale in 1905–06, in the aftermath of the 1905 Russian revolution. *The conclusions arrived at in the present study have no application to these later, immensely more sanguinary and destructive events,* which took place in significantly changed historical circumstances. Russia's government, society, and economy after 1900 were vastly different from the government, society, and economy of 1881–84.

As I have noted in the Introduction, until quite recently almost every specialist who wrote about the 1881 anti-Jewish pogroms in Russia concluded that they took place as the result of purposeful planning, according to a program worked out beforehand, and with the approval of the government or powerful factions within the ruling circles. These specialists were echoed by the popularizers and authors of more general works. Historians who will be cited throughout this study[10] built up a case for their thesis that at first seems quite convincing. In outline it reads as follows:

The plot began with an anti-Semitic newspaper campaign. It continued as rumors were systematically spread, by word of mouth, handbills, and wall posters, that the new tsar commanded beating the Jews. On the eve of the outbreak of violence, secret emissaries from St. Petersburg and Moscow traveled from place to place to inform local officials about what was soon to happen and about how they were expected to behave. When rioting actually occurred, officials refrained from acting or, in some cases, aided, abetted, and even joined the rioters, thereby testifying to the effectiveness of the secret messengers in delivering their communications. The simultaneous occurrence in different locations or the rapid spread of the pogroms seem to offer more evidence of planning, as does the fact that the violence appeared to follow the same pattern everywhere. The tsar and his government made no public protest against the outrages, and convicted rioters received only light punishments.

In this view the planners' intentions included, on the one hand, harming the Jews and, on the other hand, turning the discontent and confusion of the population after the murder of Alexander II away from the government, the agency really guilty of causing the people's ills, onto a convenient scapegoat, and in the process perhaps even generating popular patriotic and nationalistic support. Not everyone in the government agreed with such a policy, so the conspirators had to act secretly, using the claim that the pogroms were a spontaneous outburst of popular anger against the Jews' ceaseless and merciless exploitation of the Christian population. According to this line of thinking, in the spring of 1882 those who opposed the popular violence gained the upper hand within the government, and the rioting soon subsided.

Three candidates have been suggested as possible organizers of the pogroms: the conspiratorial revolutionary socialist (*narodnik*) circles that were active already in the period prior to the assassination of Alexander II, the government itself, and the Holy Brotherhood, an aristocratic counterrevolutionary society formed soon after the assassination of Alexander II in order to fight the radicals with their own conspiratorial and terrorist methods. Insofar as is known, these are the only organizations of that period that were capable of undertaking so large and ramified a project and might have been inclined to do so.[11]

Perhaps some small group, purely local in character, allied with one of the local anti-Semitic newspapers but leaving no trace of itself in the historical records, was responsible for setting off the waves of pogroms. However, even if this were established as fact (and it has not been), it would not constitute an adequate explanation of the broad sweep of the rioting. Only if the conspiracy was on a grand scale is there any sense in talking about it.

Historians who have believed in the existence of a conspiracy have tacitly accepted the proposition that no local organization or group was capable on its own of setting off and sustaining widespread rioting; to do so, it would have had to have powerful assistance from one of the bodies named above. If these are ruled out, however, the interpretation that I call the conspiracy theory falls, and any local organizers fit in as merely one part of the total picture of *objective circumstances*. In such a case it is not inaccurate to talk about the "spontaneous" occurrence of the pogroms. *Spontaneous occurrence* here does not mean an uncaused effect but rather an outcome unplanned and hardly foreseen and over which individuals or groups had almost no control.

Hans Rogger has defined the problem thus: "How the disorders started, to what degree they were spontaneous or organized or a mixture of both and who, if any, were the organizers, still remain a mystery."[12] The present study will attempt to solve that mystery by placing the pogroms in their larger regional and imperial context. The arguments supporting the notion that planning was involved will be challenged. I will try to show that the conspiracy theory is based upon an inaccurate understanding or outright distortion of the evidence used to support the theory, that it ignores a mass of evidence that would seem to disprove the theory, and finally, that it prevents us from understanding both what was really happening on the spot in southern and southwestern Russia (the real origins of the pogroms) and the actual situation within the Russian government in regard to the Jewish question and internal security and stability.

The defenders of the conspiracy theory admit that no documentary evidence is available to prove their case.[13] Even the police archives, which were opened after 1917 and published in full, offer no explicit indications of conscious planning or connivance.[14] Only hints and vague references at best are to be found there. Undaunted, one ingenious student of this material came up with what must be one of the most bold and fascinating, yet flimsy, interpretations a historian could ever hope to find. Insisting on the existence of a conspiracy, he concluded that we are "forced" to suppose "that there was, along with the intimate correspondence, a still more intimate one. And perhaps this most intimate was not committed to paper."[15]

In order to maintain the conspiracy theory, one must also assume that the mass of documents—528 large, closely printed pages in the main source alone, including the correspondence of provincial governors, governors-general, the successive ministers of the interior, policemen, military officers, and local officials of different ranks, as well as the reports of various individuals, including Count P. I. Kutaisov, the tsarist emissary specially sent in the summer of 1881 to investigate the causes of the riots—that all this material was written in some elaborate code, according to which much of what was said signified exactly the opposite of its literal meaning.

Rare was the defender of the conspiracy theory who was so bold as to take up that view, at least not openly. Most simply resorted to the use of indirect evidence and to the elaboration of those hints and vague references that peeked out now and then from the documents. Such an approach is acceptable, provided it takes into consideration all relevant circumstances and evidence. This, however, conspiracy theorists have not done. The present study will attempt to prove that alternative explanations are available that fit the case of the 1881 pogroms much better than the conspiracy theory.

# II

## THE GOVERNMENT

*Chapter 4*

# THE PRESS, THE GOVERNMENT, AND THE POGROMS

◆ ◆ ◆

WHEN THE ANTI-JEWISH VIOLENCE OF 1881 FIRST ERUPTED, AND FOR a few months thereafter, government officials and others suspected the revolutionary socialists of being responsible. This notion was rather quickly abandoned, never to be revived. Everyone agrees that the *narodniki* had practically nothing to do with causing the pogroms. For this reason the discussion of their role may conveniently be left aside until later in the study.

After the revolutionary socialists, the government itself and the Holy Brotherhood remain as possible instigators of the pogroms. Most of the evidence for a conspiracy theory allows a choice between these two candidates. In either case, according to conspiracy theory historians, the pogroms were intended to strengthen the reactionary autocratic regime. In this view, the imperial government welcomed the riots. If it was not itself the organizing hand behind them, then its officials, both central and local, were, at the least, guilty of conniving with the organizers of the riots and in some cases even of rendering them active assistance.

Rogger has modified this interpretation: "The belief that the government had a hand in initiating the pogroms was widespread and seemed plausible. But that hand, if indeed present, was uncertain, unsteady and unsystematic."[1] A full review of the facts will show how well founded Rogger's suspicion was that the government had no part in promoting the riots.

Chronologically the pogrom movement began with an anti-Semitic press campaign. Most often mentioned for their hostility to the Jews were the St. Petersburg *Novoe Vremia*, the *Kievlianin*, the *Vilenskii Vestnik*, and the Odessa *Novorossiiskii Telegraf*. The first two reportedly received government subsidies.[2] Officially, all were subject to censorship.[3] Their anti-Semitic campaign had begun toward the end of the 1870s and seemed to many at the time and later to have intensified after the assassination of Alexander II.[4]

In article after article these newspapers accused the Jews within the Pale of Jewish Settlement of being merciless exploiters of the Russian laboring classes and the major source of their impoverishment and suffering. Certain reforms of Alexander II had allowed some categories of Jews to move beyond the Pale into the interior of the Russian Empire. These were accused of having brought their exploitative skills with them; they now threatened to conquer new domains. Measures must be taken immediately, the press cried, to place new restrictions on the Jews in order to ensure their removal from positions of economic superiority.[5]

Jews were also accused of participating in the revolutionary movement in inordinate numbers. After 1 March hints and near accusations were published, implying a large share of Jewish responsibility for the assassination of Alexander II. *Novorossiiskii Telegraf,* for example, transparently implied Jewish guilt by reporting cases of Christians beating Jews because they believed that the circle of St. Petersburg assassins included many Jews.[6] *Novoe Vremia* described one of the assassins as having an "Eastern demeanor and a crooked nose." Immediately after the assassination, on 2 March, *Vilenskii Vestnik* said, "This [the assassination] is their [the Jews'] affair."[7] These are evidently the most direct accusations one can find in the Russian press during the period before the outbreak of the pogroms; while slanderous, they are a far cry from being "open calls for the murder of Jews."[8]

The anti-Semitic press also stressed the case of the Jewish woman Gessia Gelfman. As a member of the executive committee of the *narodnik* terrorist organization, People's Will, Gelfman was in the inner circle of assassins. Though her role had been confined to maintaining a home used as a meeting place, she was nevertheless arrested, tried, and condemned to death along with five other executive committee members. When informed that Gelfman was pregnant, the court postponed her execution until forty days after she gave birth. According to Avrahm Yarmolinsky, the prosecutor in the trial of the assassins (26–29 March 1881) displayed no anti-Semitic tendencies and placed no emphasis on Gelfman's being Jewish. If the government had wanted to prepare a pogrom atmosphere, it certainly missed a good opportunity. The anti-Semitic press was more "astute." Here was a wonderful occasion to claim Jewish trickery and bribery, and the press took full advantage of it. Alexander III, chiefly to placate European public opinion, commuted Gelfman's sentence to hard labor for life. He did this in July—after the pogroms were well underway. Gelfman and the daughter born to her both died some months later in prison.[9]

Gelfman's name frequently figured in the spring riots. In Kiev the workers and peasants thought they perceived the Jews' legendary ability to avoid punishment for any crime whatsoever in the fact that Gelfman was not executed along with the other five condemned. The mob members did not bother to ask why this had happened or else they were skeptical about the officially announced reason. In their view the Jews' craftiness lay behind the whole affair, and they, the people, must avenge the tsar's murder. In the small town (*mestechko, shtetl*) of Zhmerinka, in Podolia *guberniia,* the mob reportedly shouted, "The Jews killed the tsar; the fat-bellied Jewess [pregnant Gessia Gelfman] is guilty. She was not hanged; the Jews will free her. So we, the people, must settle accounts with the Jews." The same attitude was heard expressed in Rostov-on-the-Don.[10]

According to those who support the conspiracy theory, the anti-Semitic press set out intentionally to create a hostile atmosphere that would eventually lead to rioting in the streets.[11] To hasten the process, during the middle of March 1881, the anti-Semitic *Novorossiiskii Telegraf* published an account of rumors allegedly being spread among the people to the effect that anti-Jewish rioting would take place in Odessa during Easter as a protest and act of revenge against the Jews' exploitative economic activity and their participation in the assassination of Alexander II. Similar rumors were soon reported in the press as occurring in Elizavet-grad, located only 146 miles from Odessa.[12]

A more careful reading of the evidence reveals a somewhat different picture. As Easter 1881 approached, people in Odessa began to talk about celebrating the tenth anniversary of the pogrom that had occurred there in 1871 by renewed attacks upon the Jews.[13] Such chatter, sometimes accompanied by minor clashes, was common during the Easter season every year, and not only in Odessa. It may have been more persistent in 1881 because of the tenth anniversary. In any case, the gossip was reported in the *Novorossiiskii Telegraf* on 20 March as "rumors of impending anti-Jewish rioting." The newspaper was read in neighboring Elizavetgrad, and people there also began to talk about beating the Jews. This talk too was picked up by the press, and matters snowballed, until the outbreak of 15 April.[14]

Some conspiracy theorists maintain that the rumors were purely an invention of the press. A few go so far as to accuse the editor of the *Novorossiiskii Telegraf* of hiring a team of agents to fabricate and spread anti-Jewish rumors in Odessa. His supposed aim was to frighten the Jews, incite the non-Jews, and in general create an air of anger in which any insignificant quarrel might be turned into mob rioting.[15] Other supporters of the conspiracy theory note the existence of rumors before the press picked them up but accuse the newspapers of encouraging their dissemination and belief in them. In this view, it seemed as if the papers were indicating to the mob what was expected of it.[16]

At this point the government's alleged role in the conspiracy becomes important. Article 1036 of the Criminal Code (*Ulozhenie o Nakazaniiakh*) of 1866 explicitly prohibited inciting one part of the population against another.[17] Nevertheless, the censorship authorities remained passive in the face of the anti-Semitic press campaign. Conspiracy theorists interpret this inaction as a clear sign of government connivance in and approval of what was being written.[18]

Would the Russian masses understand this sign? Those who see a plot assume that in the troubled and uncertain atmosphere prevailing after the assassination of the tsar, it was easy enough to convince the masses not only that plans were being made to attack the Jews but also that the government approved of this action. After all, if the press could publish with impunity articles accusing Jews of economic exploitation and regicide and report rumors of impending anti-Jewish riots, then in the popular mind this must surely have implied governmental approval for, if not insistence upon, both the appearance of the articles and the coming violence.[19]

The evidence does in fact indicate that the government's tolerance of the Jew-baiting press was popularly interpreted as official approval; the prevailing anti-Jewish prejudices of the Russian masses were reinforced, especially since the Jews had almost no opportunity to refute the charges made against them in a forum as public as that enjoyed by the anti-Semitic newspapers.[20]

What is probably an accurate assessment of the situation is found in the observations made on this topic by Court Kutaisov, the tsar's special emissary to investigate the pogroms. He charged that the press had acted "very tactlessly" by spreading "ridiculous" rumors of impending riots. It had thereby contributed to the mob's already agitated mood and to its belief in the lawfulness of popular violence against Jews. Still, claimed Kutaisov, the newspapers achieved this result unintentionally. And their role in the emergence of the anti-Jewish violence should not be exaggerated. They were not influential enough by themselves to cause the riots. Nor were they responsible for the initial emergence of the rumors, especially the one alleging that permission had been granted officially to attack the Jews. The riots were a spontaneous outburst of hostility against the

Jews' exploitative activities, concluded Kutaisov, who firmly believed in the Jews' guilt.[21]

On 11 July 1881 a group of Elizavetgrad Jews handed Kutaisov a report outlining their explanation of the pogrom that had taken place in their town. They asserted that the March report in *Novorossiiskii Telegraf* had indeed made an impact. It was eagerly read in the marketplace by crowds of people, who concluded that to attack the Jews was lawful. Apparently the editorial staff of the newspaper did not approve of the proposal to beat Jews, but it expressed this idea so vaguely and displayed such hostility to the Jews in general that the people were misled.[22]

Kutaisov and the Elizavetgrad Jews, then, agreed that there was no intentional effort on the part of the anti-Semitic press to promote pogroms. On another point, however, the Jews disagreed with Kutaisov. They asserted that the press reports were responsible for setting in motion, at least in Elizavetgrad, the rumors about impending anti-Jewish rioting.[23]

Thanks to the efforts of John D. Klier, it is possible to reproduce the response of *Novorossiiskii Telegraf* to the charges that it instigated the pogroms or created a climate conducive to their outbreak.[24]

On 25 April 1881 the newspaper quoted in its own defense two articles that had appeared previously in its pages. The first was from the issue of 18 December 1880. A leader of the local Jewish community had asked the paper if it supported violence against Jews. Its answer was, "No and a hundred times no! . . . Our anti-Jewish line has the goal of reducing the Jews' national boastfulness, of paralyzing their aspirations to exploit the Russian people, . . .—and all this is done to convince them to take measures toward rapprochement [*sblizhenie*] with the native population, towards the abolition of age-old hatred, and so to avoid a catastrophe like the assaults on Jews in Berlin," where a number of Jews had recently been beaten as a result of agitation by the anti-Semitic Christian Socialist Workingmen's Union led by the court preacher Adolf Stoecker.

*Novorossiiskii Telegraf* thought that it had had some success in its aims, since the Jews were already losing some of their boastfulness, arrogance, and passion to enslave. "After all that has been said, it is clear, it seems, that we stand for the peaceful resolution of the Jewish question and first of all will exert all the strength of the printed word against the manifestation of wild physical [*kulachnaia,* "using the fists"] reprisal upon the whole race [or tribe, *plemia*]." The paper then went on to quote the all-important article from its issue of 20 March 1881, which asserted that rumors had appeared in the town several times recently to the effect that at Easter the

Jews would be beaten. There was no foundation to this rumor, the paper
noted, yet it kept reappearing. "To stir up the passions of the crowd is
never hard; this is especially easy at the present time when, after the events
of the first of March, the people are insulted, bitter, and eager in some
way to tear out the evil. But at such a time the obligation of every citizen
is to withstand base instincts, to pacify the popular fury, and by all
measures to oppose any initiative to physical reprisals."

The spread of such rumors could only have been the work of shady
characters, eager to fish in troubled waters. "*Novorossiiskii Telegraf* has
more than once declared that it considers Jewish exploitation an evil,
especially for our area, and it is ready to fight this evil by all force. But
it understands this to mean a struggle by words, even by deeds, if
you want—but by deeds is meant economic measures, administrative
measures, but under no circumstances wild, physical reprisals." An instance had recently occurred when certain Odessa butchers assaulted some
Jews and shouted to other Christians to assist them since "there are many
Yids [male and female, *zhidov i zhidovok*] among the troublemakers in
Petersburg." *Novorossiiskii Telegraf*'s answer to this assertion was that,
while all Russia wanted to punish the guilty parties, it must not be
forgotten that Russians provided a higher percentage of the culprits:

> The Jews are guilty of much, but their guilt is only economic; they beat us
> with the ruble, sucking the juice from the inhabitants among whom they
> live. So it is not necessary to fight their exploitation with the fist, or to
> defend against them by violence, but rather by the pressure of the ruble, by
> blocking the paths of exploitation, and by all possible diminution of the field
> of their endeavor. For such a struggle we Russians ought to join tightly
> together, to support each other, as the Jews support each other; but any
> honorable person and true patriot should stand against physical reprisals, for
> such reprisals only serve the interests of the anarchists, for whom there is one
> goal—to sow confusion wherever possible.

Having cited these articles, the editors of *Novorossiiskii Telegraf* went on
to claim that anyone who, after reading these excerpts, still claimed that
the paper advocated attacks upon Jews, must be in the pay of the *kahal*,
the officially defunct, semi-legendary organ of Jewish self-government.
What really impassioned the Christian populace against the Jews was not
newspapers like *Novorossiiskii Telegraf* but those papers that, neglecting
historical shortcomings, defended the Jews and attacked Christians. *Novorossiiskii Telegraf* could not be accused of stirring up Christians because it
never preached hatred. Furthermore, the "little brothers" primarily read
the "cheap press," not *Novorossiiskii Telegraf*.

Another issue of *Novorossiisksii Telegraf* is also very revealing. On 3 May 1881 disturbances began to occur in Odessa. The local authorities contained these and reduced them to relative insignificance by energetic and efficient action. On 8 May, *Novorossiiskii Telegraf* noted the effectiveness of prompt and forceful measures against the rioting. Yet it expressed concern about the threat of continuing disorder. A "single decisive blow" was necessary to put an end to the unfortunate situation where a gang of rioters could strike fear into the *whole* population of the city.

> Nobody is at ease, each fears for his property. The Jews do not fear alone; Christians are afraid as well. Trade activities have ceased; offices have closed. There remains no doubt that among the rioters there is almost no workingman element. Bums who reside in stone quarries and flop-houses, riff-raff never engaged in any work and easily influenced by the Nihilists to seek easy gain, predominate. And because of this riff-raff the whole city is in fear. It is necessary therefore for the good of all peaceful and hard-working inhabitants of Odessa to carry out a decisive blow against the rioting rabble and, we repeat, not to refrain from the most extreme measures.

In *Novorossiiskii Telegraf's* view it was acceptable to sacrifice a few rioters in order to quiet the city and free the troops from such dangerous and burdensome work.

The articles just reviewed reveal clearly the inflammatory character of the writing in *Novorossiiskii Telegraf.* The editors were obviously irresponsible journalists. While denying that they taught hatred, they did just that. While condemning violence, they encouraged it. Their primary intention was, of course, to sell newspapers. If one can fathom their aims beyond this, it was evidently to stir up passions, or generate excitement, without too much expectation of people acting. After all, as the remark about the "little brothers" indicates, the editors thought that in general, persons from the upper classes constituted their reading public—people not likely to go out and riot. It must have seemed rather safe to the editors to appear to say more than they did in fact: Fight the evil of Jewish exploitation—but not by violence; beat the Jews—but not with fists.

It seems, then, that the press initially had no idea that its anti-Semitic campaign might lead to rioting in the streets. Still, as Easter approached, some newspapers, even such anti-Semitic ones as *Novoe Vremia* and, as we have just seen, *Novorossiiskii Telegraf,* began to show concern, and statements condemning physical attacks on Jews appeared. Then, when the first wave of pogroms broke, the press manifested great surprise, disarray (publishing all kinds of rumors about what was happening and sticking to descriptions of the events, with no attempt at analysis), and even dismay (such as we just saw in the case of *Novorossiiskii Telegraf*).[25]

As with the *Novorossiiskii Telegraf* articles, Klier found no instance elsewhere in which the press called openly for anti-Jewish violence.[26] Though less direct in character, other evidence, for example, the statement of the Elizavetgrad Jews cited above, supports this conclusion.

Some Odessa Jews also wrote a report for Kutaisov (10 July 1881). Evidently referring to the notorious pre-Easter article in the *Novorossiiskii Telegraf*, they asserted that it ended with the exhortation to strike out at the Jews because they were such a terrible evil, sucking the people's blood, and so on, but the blow should be by means of rubles only. The newspaper also pointed out that many Jewish men and women were among the regicides. This account was received enthusiastically, according to the Odessa Jews, especially by the simple people, who were happy to see in print what they considered to be confirmation of the current rumors about forthcoming anti-Jewish acts. They looked forward to striking out at the Jews, with rubles or otherwise.[27]

E. B. Levin, a Jewish lawyer and an early and firm believer in the conspiracy theory, in a report prepared in 1882 for the enlightenment of high government officials, could speak of "badgering" in the press and "bitter attacks, baseless accusations, insinuations, gibes, and forebodings of bloody violence." He could not, evidently, find any direct calls for violence against the Jews.[28] S. L. Shvabakher, the officially recognized municipal rabbi of Odessa, argued in his 1881 book on the causes of the pogroms that the anti-Semitic press had worked for a whole year to create an atmosphere conducive to pogroms. But when riots were actually about to occur, and then after they occurred, this press, in order to protect itself, gave "hypocritical counsels" to the effect that the people should not physically beat the Jews, even though their harmful exploitation deserved all possible punishment.[29] None of the historical studies written by conspiracy theorists has revealed any instance of direct appeals for violence. No such direct appeals were mentioned even in the article on "Anti-Semitism in Russia" in the *Evreiskaia Entsiklopediia*, which discussed at some length the anti-Semitic press of 1880–81.[30]

The notion that the Jews as a whole were responsible for the assassination of Alexander II was also advanced by insinuation rather than by outright accusations. A number of conspiracy theory historians indicate that they investigated the anti-Semitic press. One would assume that, given their overall thesis, they would have been quite eager to mention outright assertions of the Jews' collective guilt. Yet each speaks only of "insinuations" and "allusions."[31]

Shvabakher spoke of the anti-Semitic press's desire to protect itself by feigning opposition to violence in the streets. But he was not clear about whom the press had to protect itself from. Could it have been that the editors had no assurance that the government would support mass violence, or even more significantly, that they feared the government's wrath for having contributed to the provocation of such a potentially dangerous movement?[32] Or perhaps the editors of the anti-Semitic papers, at least initially, never really expected rioting to take place at all. Perhaps they were simply playing with fire without realizing how ready the fuel was to burst into flames beyond anyone's control. After all, no major anti-Jewish rioting had occurred in the Ukraine area for over one hundred years. The latest pogrom of any significance had been in Odessa during Easter 1871, and that had been of a purely local character, an exceptionally ugly quarrel, so to speak, between local business competitors.[33]

Statements made by K. P. Pobedonostsev lend support to the assumption that anti-Semites did not expect rioting to occur as a result of the anti-Jewish newspaper campaign. Pobedonostsev was director general of the Holy Synod, that is, secular head of the Russian Orthodox Church, and an influential advisor to Alexander III, having earlier been his tutor. Pobedonostsev was himself openly anti-Semitic, but he definitely opposed popular violence of any kind.[34] In similar notes to the minister of the interior, N. P. Ignatiev (22 May 1881), and Alexander III (6 August 1881), the director general complained that the censors had permitted the publication of a certain newspaper article on 8 May (one example among many such instances) that incited the people against landowners, nobles (*pomeshchiki*), and Jews. What a "wicked irony" (*zlaia ironiia*), he thought. Officialdom was, quite inadmissibly, acting at cross-purposes. He himself had been asked to instruct the clergy to preach against the pogroms, and he had done so. Yet meanwhile the censors were allowing provocative appeals to be published over their imprimatur. This must be stopped. In the letter of 6 August to the tsar, Pobedonostsev further lamented that rather than enlightening the people, the press confused it and led it into mischief. Without newspaper agitation, he thought, the people would be calm.[35]

Now, after the spate of pogroms had already begun, Pobedonostsev called for strict censorship over anti-Semitic newspaper articles. Why had he not done so previously? He was by no means a friend of the press, his opposition to popular violence was not new; and he must surely have been aware of the press agitation against the Jews prior to 15 April. Evidently, before the actual outbreak of violence, Pobodenostsev did not expect the newspaper campaign to lead to rioting. Yet if so exceptionally sensitive— and hostile—an observer of the popular press failed to discern the danger, then it was only natural for other observers, official and nonofficial alike, to do likewise.

As soon as the anti-Semitic papers began linking Jews to the assassination of Alexander II and reporting anticipated anti-Jewish riots, the Russian-language Jewish press became concerned. But its appeals to the government to suppress the anti-Semitic articles remained unanswered.[36] Was the government intentionally inactive, expecting the anti-Semitic agitation to lead to street violence, as some conspiracy theorists suggest? Or is there another explanation?

Censorship in 1881 was governed by the "Regulations on the Press" of April 1865, which removed preliminary censorship from books of over a certain length and from periodicals published in St. Petersburg and Moscow. The provincial press could be exempted from preliminary censorship with special permission from the minister of the interior and upon the deposit of a sum of money defined by the regulations. Publishers of books exempt from preliminary censorship could be taken to court if the censors thought a book violated the law. Publishers and editors of periodicals exempt from preliminary censorship could either be taken to court or subjected to administrative penalties. The minister of the interior was empowered—after issuing three warnings—to suspend temporarily or prohibit altogether the publication of periodicals considered to be objectionable. Books and journals exempt from preliminary censorship were required to be inspected by censors during three-day and two-day precirculation waiting periods respectively; weeklies and daily newspapers were examined at the time of the final printing of each number.

This last measure allowed the government to discover blatantly objectionable works before or as they reached the public. If the authorities felt that a work was so harmful that the halting of its distribution could not await a court decision, they were empowered to stop its circulation immediately.

In some ways these 1865 regulations gave publishers much more freedom than they had enjoyed previously, but they also made publishers more responsible for themselves. Now, whenever a publisher issued a work, he had to weigh whether it would entail administrative or judicial action leading to fines, imprisonment, and the loss of his investment (that is, the confiscation of the edition he had published).[37]

Here we have another example of the Russian government attempting to deal with and allow for a new center of power, influence, and creative activity while exerting itself to retain the state's control—attempting to institute or make way for change without changing. There was a consensus in the government after 1865 that, on the one hand, preliminary censorship could not be reimposed where it had been removed but, on the other hand, administrative controls must continue and even be improved. The government did indeed adopt repressive administrative measures after 1865, and it used the courts as well. But it did so for the most part only against a small number of publications considered to be too radical in their criticism of the government, the established order, and accepted beliefs and ideas. The government's self-imposed restraint is evident from the fact that from 1865 and on through the so-called reactionary reigns of Alexander III and Nicholas II, the publishing industry in Russia continuously modernized itself and expanded, asserted its independence from the state on many important issues, and became recognizably European in character and organization.[38]

On the whole, during the 1870s, Russian censors very rarely interfered with publications dealing with the Jewish question, even though this issue became a frequent and lively topic of debate in a number of press organs. If anyone was subjected to restrictions, administrative warnings, and other measures, it was almost always the Russian Jewish press, for defending the Jews' interests and criticizing the existing situation too vigorously. At the same time, it would seem, the government took virtually no steps to tone down or prevent the extended press campaigns being conducted by certain newspapers against such things as the Jews' alleged exploitation of the peasantry, massive evasion of military service, and involvement in the revolutionary movement. One should note in this regard that Jacob Brafman's fiercely anti-Jewish books first appeared in the periodical press.[39]

Furthermore, it often seems to be forgotten that the pogroms of 1881 began while the relatively liberal Count Michael T. Loris-Melikov was minister of the interior. His tenure continued until 4 May 1881, when he was replaced by a Slavophile and anti-Semite, Count N. P. Ignatiev. During Loris-Melikov's "dictatorship of the heart," which began in February 1880, censorship regulations were relaxed to such an extent that during 1880 the entire Russian press experienced very few administrative measures (four warnings and two bannings of periodical publications); during January–March 1881 no administrative penalties were imposed on periodicals at all; and only after March 1881 were they begun again, and even then quite cautiously.[40]

Preliminary censorship, it will be remembered, was still the rule outside St. Petersburg and Moscow, and it was presumably stricter than the supervision over the press exercised in the capital cities. Yet in a special report to the tsar dated 30 September 1881, Minister of the Interior Ignatiev asserted that "the provincial censorship does not satisfy even the most unexacting demands."[41] If this statement was true in September 1881, when the more reactionary Ignatiev had already been in office several months, it was undoubtedly even truer during the previous spring, when Loris-Melikov was minister of the interior.

Consequently, in the circumstances prevailing in 1880–81, as long as anti-Semitic newspapers refrained from open calls to violence, there was no reason to expect that the government would take measures against them. Censorship measures were rarely being taken against any publications.

Other developments occurring within the Russian government also affected the Jewish question. By the spring of 1881, Loris-Melikov had yet to enact his full program. He was dissatisfied with the existing political situation and wanted to change it. Trying to maneuver between an extreme left and an extreme right, he inclined toward certain mildly liberal political reforms and some rather less liberal press laws than those then in effect. The minister's views on the press in general were expressed quite clearly in his report of 12 April 1881 to Alexander III. He found the existing situation "highly unsatisfactory." New laws were necessary to define precisely the rights and duties of the press. The "calm discussion of public questions" must be allowed. But "the stirring of passions and the slandering of personalities, practiced with impunity for selfish aims by certain organs of the press," must be stopped.[42]

Loris-Melikov was referring to attacks upon himself and his programs, not to inflammatory anti-Semitic articles. Nevertheless, or perhaps just because of this circumstance, his remarks throw light on the larger context within which the Jewish question was dealt with. His government's inaction with regard to the anti-Semitic press was no indication of support for the anti-Jewish view. Rather, it reflected the incomplete implementation of his political program. With his somewhat liberal tendencies, he probably would have suppressed the anti-Semitic agitation if, before his resignation, he had gotten into a position to carry out his plans fully.

As a matter of fact, some well-intended censorship measures *were* taken before the spate of pogroms began. According to Count Kutaisov, the provisional governor-general of the Odessa (*Novorossiisk*) region, Prince A. M. Dondukov-Korsakov, on 23 March 1881 instructed the president of the local censorship committee to prevent the appearance of articles that would arouse antagonism between Christians and Jews.[43] This was too little, too late, perhaps. But it was a totally unnecessary move if the government was intent upon allowing pogroms to be fomented. Recall also that in the town of Odessa itself, the home of *Novorossiiskii Telegraf*, energetic measures taken by the local administration reduced to insignificant proportions the riot that broke out there on 3 May 1881.[44] In sum, no rioting occurred in Odessa at Easter, the time the rumors had predicted; and when disorders finally did occur, they reached no dimensions of any consequence. These circumstances indicate that the rumors that began circulating in the town in March were the result of a spontaneous, popular movement rather than the work of some organizing hand supported by the government.

After the pogroms began, the press continued to play a role in developments. It did so, however, in such a way as to cast more doubt on the conspiracy theory. Cases are on record of individuals attempting, sometimes successfully, to spark anti-Jewish riots by reading anti-Semitic newspaper articles aloud to a crowd. In some instances these articles were reported as official pronouncements and linked with an alleged tsarist *ukaz* (decree) commanding the people to beat and rob the Jews. When asked why the *ukaz* had not been published and publicly displayed, the answer was that the Jews had bribed the officials.[45] The use of newspaper articles in this way indicates spontaneity, not planning.

The tsar, of course, could not have issued an *ukaz* publicly calling for pogroms without endangering Russia's moral and financial credit throughout the Western world. Furthermore, it is known for certain that Alexander III opposed the anti-Jewish violence.[46]

But why did the supposed organizers, whoever they were, fail to supply their agents with "decrees" more substantial than newspaper articles that merely hinted at the need for violence? According to one report, the leaders of the riot "read" the alleged *ukaz* from "theater announcements and restaurant menus." Surely this is an indication of the opposite of forethought or planning.[47] More than likely, what happened in fact was that some more or less educated, self-proclaimed mob leaders suddenly got what seemed a bright idea, to make public use of the material at hand, namely, the already familiar anti-Semitic press. So they simply stood up and read the appropriate articles before the ignorant crowd.

A close look at three such cases will prove to be instructive. On 7 May 1881, the governor of Poltava, P. A. Bil'basov, sent a report to the Ministry of the Interior in which he related the following incident: A policeman had informed the railroad shop workers of a certain small town that the governor had issued an order specifically forbidding attacks on Jews. The workers were surprised by this announcement and showed the policeman a copy of the newspaper *Gerol'd*. It contained a lead article describing anti-Semitic disturbances that had recently taken place in Argenau, near Poznan in Prussian Poland. In addition, the newspaper reprinted a proclamation that had appeared in that town during the disorders, calling on workers to beat the Jews. The Russian railroad workers told the policeman that they had understood this proclamation to be addressed to themselves and added that they thought the government must have approved of it since the newspaper was published in St. Petersburg. The policeman then explained the matter, and the workers, acknowledging their mistake, accepted Governor Bil'basov's order.[48]

This story illustrates the accidental, unplanned character of pogrom agitation. It demonstrates that there were local officials who made real efforts to prevent pogroms. And the fact that it was reported to the Ministry of the Interior indicates that Governor Bil'basov must have thought the central government would approve of his and his policeman's conduct.

A shortened form of the Argenau proclamation[49] appeared in an incident that Captain Rudov, a gendarme official in Kiev *guberniia*, reported to his superiors. Several days before riots broke out in the village of Iablonovka (May 1881), the peasant Andrei Zelenskii came to a Jewish neighbor and showed him a scrap of paper. On it were written the words "Wake up Christians, the time has come to be saved from the Jewish yoke, to expel them, otherwise you are done for." Zelenskii declared that this quotation was from a tsarist *ukaz* and that it had been given to him by the clerk Andrei Bondarevskii, who worked in the Iablonovka sugar factory. Bondarevskii, a nineteen-year-old youth, reported that at the end of April he had visited the district police station in Smela to present his passport. There the clerk of the police station, Usenko, showed him a newspaper (Rudov thought it was No. 91 of the newspaper *Syn Otechestvo*) in which news of the Argenau disorders was printed, as well as the provocative sentence quoted above. Usenko copied it out and gave it to Bondarevskii, who gave it to Zelenskii. When Zelenskii repeated it to the workers, Bondarevskii claimed that he tried to persuade him "not to talk nonsense" (*ne plesti pustiakov*).[50]

Pogroms did indeed occur soon after this incident, in Smela, Iablonovka, and other nearby villages. But while clearly revealing the anti-Semitic inclinations of certain Russian officials (in this case the police clerk Usenko, who may very well have been a riot leader in Smela) and of certain workers (Zelenskii, but perhaps not Bondarevskii), the story indicates no firm planning. Usenko, evidently having been impressed by the Argenau proclamation, simply threw a stone in the water. Its ripples might or might not have reached the desired destination.

On 9 June 1881, the governor of Ekaterinoslav *guberniia,* I. N. Durnovo, reported to the Ministry of the Interior the following: Sometimes individuals read newspapers to the peasants. It occasionally happened that these readers distorted what was written, probably unintentionally, through misunderstanding or even through the mispronunciation of certain words. In this way an article announcing the government's intention to improve the Jews' "material circumstances" (*imushchestvennyi byt*), spoken with a Little Russian (i.e., Ukrainian) accent came out as if it were written "strike out at the Jews' property" (*bit' imushchestvo*).[51] The governor may have been wrong in stating that these mistakes were unintentional. But they certainly have about them an air of spontaneity more than of solid organization.

The anti-Semitic press campaign was an important ingredient in preparing the way for the pogroms in 1881. But, as has been shown, the newspaper articles and the use made of them in the streets in no way indicate the existence of a preliminary master plan enjoying governmental approval.

*Chapter 5*

# RUMORS,
# HANDBILLS, AND POSTERS
◆ ◆ ◆

## *Rumors, Rumors*

IN THE PERIOD IMMEDIATELY FOLLOWING THE ASSASSINATION OF ALEX-
ander II, Russia became a rumor mill. Rumors of the wildest kind
circulated. One of the most fateful asserted that the tsar had issued an
*ukaz* instructing the people to beat the Jews. That no such *ukaz* was
officially published and displayed was attributed by the simple people to
Jewish chicanery and bribery, as were the steps taken by the authorities
to prevent or end anti-Jewish violence. As I showed in chapter 4, the anti-
Semitic press was particularly important in the spread of these rumors
prior to 15 April, the date of the outbreak of the first pogrom. After that,
the course of events itself was conducive to the generation of anti-Jewish
rumors: the people now had a living example, and not merely abstract
words, to influence their behavior. The forces working for law and order
found it almost impossible to lay the rumors to rest. Their extreme
persistence can be accounted for by both local conditions peculiar to the
year 1881 and factors characteristic of Russia in general. The behavior
of the Jews—whether haughty or frightened, the prevalent economic
antagonisms, and the widely held perception that the Jews stood outside
the law were among the local factors. The generally troubled atmosphere
prevailing as a result of the accession of a new and unfamiliar tsar led to
the manufacture and persistence of a wide range of politically dangerous
rumors, which spread along with those about attacks on the Jews. The
intrinsic naïveté and stubborness of the lower classes in the Russian
Empire, along with the historical tradition of spreading wild rumors in
the countryside, ensured that these rumors would persist. The endemic
ineptitude of local government officials, the strong anti-Semitic attitudes
of many of them, and the lack of formal instruments for dealing with
rumors contributed to the outpouring of fantastic claims and assertions.

The anti-Jewish rumors so important in preparing the way for the 1881
pogroms took various forms: the tsar had granted the people permission to

beat and plunder Jews. He had commanded the people to attack the Jews, under pain of royal displeasure and severe punishment for inaction. The Jews deserved a beating for exploiting the people economically. The Jews deserved a beating for participating in the revolutionary movement that had assassinated Alexander II. The Little Father wanted revenge to be taken on the Jews. He wanted them ruined economically, and even driven out of Russia. The property they had acquired unjustly must be taken from them.[1]

Some rumors asserted that the people were given three days to accomplish the purposes of the tsar's *ukaz*.[2] This number may have been picked following the first pogroms, in Elizavetgrad (15–17 April), and the major outbreak that soon followed, in Kiev (26–28 April), since rioting in both these places lasted three calendar days (from the afternoon or evening of the first day until the morning of the third).

The rumors sometimes got quite wild. According to the governor of Poltava *guberniia* (20 April), the story was told there that the tsar hated Jews because they showed disrespect for him. How? One day the tsar passed by a Jew in St. Petersburg who removed his top hat but not his skullcap. The ruler was so displeased that he ordered the skullcap to be nailed to the Jew's head.[3] Belief in such a story could easily pass over into belief in a tsarist *ukaz* to beat the Jews.

According to the *zemstvo* (local administrative assembly) board of Kherson *guberniia* (summer 1881), a rumor there had alleged that, after the destruction of their property, the Jews would be sold to the Turkish sultan for forty kopeks each.[4]

On 8 May 1881 a district police official in Ekaterinoslav *guberniia* reported rumors that were spread in his jurisdiction by people who had witnessed the Kiev pogrom. According to one such rumor, some men who stood out because of their distinctive clothing had demanded that the Jews of Kiev be beated and in turn threatened to beat anyone not heeding them. People expected these bullies to appear elsewhere as well.

On 21 May the superintendent of state domains in Ekaterinoslav *guberniia* reported that peasants there had attacked Jewish agricultural colonies after hearing that the tsar had issued an *ukaz* to plunder and drive out the Jews. The Little Father allegedly took this step because he had revealed governmental favoritism toward Jewish colonists in the allotment of land.[5]

According to another rumor, high-ranking officials were touring the countryside telling the peasants that the tsar had gone to visit some foreign country. Meanwhile, he had commanded that before his return all the

Jews and landlords should be beaten and their land and property taken. Another version asserted that Alexander III himself was going around the villages, disguised as a high-ranking official in order to hide from the persecution of the landlords, and that he was giving the peasants money so they would beat the Jews and landlords for murdering his father. One rumormonger alleged that some such person had indeed been arrested in the district of Ekaterinoslav.[6]

Stories about beating the Jews were often linked with talk of assaulting other non-Russian nationalities and the landlords for the purpose of taking over their land. The cry usually was, "Now we'll beat the Jews, later we'll beat the foreigners and the landlords; their land will be ours." Such slogans, linking the Jews with other groups, seem to have become popular after the pogroms began.[7]

Jews were in fact practically the only ones ever attacked.[8] But the threat of violence against other classes was taken seriously by the government. This is revealed in its ready compliance with requests from landlords to send troops to their districts in order to prevent rioting and, perhaps more significantly, in the frequently expressed fear that socialists might exploit the pogroms for their own ends.[9] All this supplemented the very pronounced anxiety regarding peasant uprisings in general that prevailed in government circles after Alexander II's assassination, and which I shall discuss below.

The mob had a ready explanation for the fact that the tsar's *ukaz* was not published and publicly displayed—the Jews had bribed the officials. The same explanation was given when police and troops acted energetically to prevent or end attacks on Jews. Sometimes rioters interpreted the opposition of the police as having been only for the sake of appearances. Some thought that even when troops were sent in specially to quell disorders, they were forbidden to take energetic measures.[10] This notion helps explain the mob's dispersing at the appearance of troops in a particular spot and then regrouping elsewhere, as happened frequently in Kiev. The rioters evidently thought that the soldiers were only ordering an end to a particular act of destruction, but not an end to the pogrom in general.

Kutaisov pointed out—and criticized—conduct by various officials that lent support to the assumption of Jewish bribery. For instance, in the villages surrounding Elizavetgrad, Kherson *guberniia,* certain military officers summarily flogged without trial peasants who were accused of having participated in the local disorders, in order to discourage further rioting. In many cases those flogged were persons pointed out by Jews. Later, soldiers accepted gifts of liquor from local Jews. The peasants,

Kutaisov concluded, thought the soldiers had punished them because of Jewish bribery, not because the tsar had prohibited popular violence against any citizens of the empire.[11]

In Berezovka, Kherson *guberniia,* local officials used money obtained from the Jewish community to hire one hundred peasants to come to the town and act as a deterrent to popular violence. The fact that these "guards" proved untrustworthy and joined the rioters when the pogrom broke out evidently did not weaken the belief in Jewish bribery.[12]

In Borispol', Poltava *guberniia,* Cossacks were brought in to suppress the pogrom. They were quartered in the homes of Jews and bought supplies in their stores, circumstances that, of course, strengthened the local population's assumption of a payoff as the only explanation for officials protecting the Jews.[13]

In the very important case of Elizavetgrad, the site of the first pogrom, Kutaisov accused the Jews themselves of giving impetus to the notion of Jewish bribery.

It should be borne in mind that Kutaisov himself was quite hostile to the Jews, believing that they were by nature and tradition economic exploiters, hated by the local Christian population. He opposed using any extralegal or overly forceful (violent) measures as means to prevent or end pogroms. Yet throughout his lengthy reports he made clear his opposition to popular violence against the Jews. His criticisms of official inefficiency and incompetence were candid, sharp, and telling. His dilemma was how to balance between these two potentially contradictory viewpoints. To be sure, Kutaisov's reports of the pogroms generally exaggerated the reprehensible character of the Jews' behavior and their responsibility for inciting the riots. Nevertheless, with some critical appraisal, these reports can still be taken as a fair indication of the realities of the time.

In April 1881, as part of the mourning ceremonies for Alexander II, the popular entertainments traditionally engaged in during the Easter holidays were prohibited throughout the empire by decree of the new tsar. According to Kutaisov, this circumstance was abused by the Jews in Elizavetgrad. As Easter approached, in the atmosphere of rumors about possible anti-Jewish riots, Christians made fun of Jews for being cowards. The Jews, in turn, because of the restrictions on popular entertainments and the increased vigilance of the local police in light of the spreading rumors, felt overconfident and became haughty. They figured that, in the absence of holiday merrymaking, the usual large crowds, drunkenness, and rowdiness would not occur. So the Jews replied to the Christians' taunts with insolent, mocking, antagonistic remarks. They portrayed the police measures as a Jewish victory and, according to some reports, told the Christians: "Your Russian holiday will be in our pocket. . . . We have bought your festivities." Such tactlessness further excited the Christians and led to the idea that Jewish bribery was responsible not only for the police measures but for the Easter restrictions as well. The latter rumor was so widespread that it prompted the police chief to issue a special declaration explaining the real reason for the prohibition of festivities. Kutaisov concluded that this declaration had little influence on the population, mainly because it was already so excited against the Jews, but also because some officials occasionally remarked that the antiriot measures were being undertaken at the request of the Jews.[14]

Kutaisov emphasized the incompetence of these officials. I, from my perspective, would be inclined to emphasize the blatancy of their anti-Semitism and their reluctance to protect the threatened minority. This, however, does not obligate us to assume that the officials involved were operating according to a planned program.

Dozens of contemporary statements recorded throughout the sources confirm that the rioters firmly believed in the lawfulness of their actions. They considered themselves to be loyal subjects of the tsar, even when confronted with the opposition of the authorities, who, they believed, had obviously been bribed by the Jews. Only at their trials, in most instances, did the accused acknowledge their mistake and admit that they had been misled by the false rumor of a tsarist *ukaz*. While officials were occasionally able to convince the people of their misapprehension before the outbreak of violence, most often they were not so successful.

There must be an explanation for the persistence with which people believed the rumors of an *ukaz*. Perhaps they were encouraged by paid agents. Or perhaps there were circumstances more general in character that enable one to explain this phenomenon without resorting to such a deus ex machina.

There is some evidence that the Jews themselves may have unwittingly encouraged the circulation of rumors, both before and after 15 April. I have already mentioned Kutaisov's report on the Elizavetgrad Jews' provocative remarks, made when the taverns were closed and troops brought in to maintain peace and public order. Officials elsewhere asserted that Jews behaved similarly when special protection was extended to them or when news arrived of rioters in other places being punished.[15]

Exactly the opposite type of behavior—displays of extreme apprehension and anxious turning to the authorities with entreaties for special precautionary measures—also tended to contribute to the belief by non-

Jews in a tsarist decree allowing attacks on Jews. Their panicky reactions were often quite visible. In a number of villages before Easter, they packed up their belongings and sent them into nearby towns or gave them to friendly Christian neighbors for safekeeping. According to several witnesses who spoke to both urban and peasant rioters, when they saw the Jews' panic, they thought it was an admission of guilt that they had exploited non-Jews and were responsible for the assassination of Alexander II, as well as a sign that the Jews knew about the tsar's *ukaz* and about the inevitability of the pogroms.[16] The panic was in reality none of these things, of course. But it is not unusual in human affairs for perceptions of reality to play a more important role in the unfolding of historical developments than reality itself, as many facets of this study demonstrate.

A number of other circumstances contributed to the tenacity of the rumor of an *ukaz*. A detailed discussion of economic factors will come later in this study. For the moment, however, the long-standing economic antagonism between Christians and Jews should be noted. This conflict may have been permanently more or less out in the open and constantly growing stronger, as some contemporaries contended; or it may have been generally subdued and emerged only as a result of the stresses of the pogrom period, as other contemporaries contended. In either case, by the spring of 1881 the Jews had come to be popularly viewed not merely as merciless exploiters who used only semilegal and illegal means to take advantage of the common people, but also as unscrupulous business competitors (see below, chap. 7). Hence the rumor of a tsarist *ukaz* to attack the Jews corresponded perfectly with the conviction of many people that it was necessary to throw off the Jewish yoke and relieve the Jews of their ill-gotten gains.

Another factor in the tenacity of the rumor of an *ukaz* was the widespread belief that Jews and their property were not under the regular protection of the law. People were aware of numerous legal restrictions on Jews and were often witnesses to maltreatment by government officials of alleged Jewish lawbreakers. Particularly impressive were the expulsions of Jews who had settled in various forbidden areas, such as most of the neighborhoods in the town Kiev and the fifty *verst* zone along the southern and southwestern borders of the empire. These expulsions were carried out regardless of the harm done to established economic interests.

Clearly, Russia's rulers regarded the Jews as a particularly wicked and dangerous group, with few interests in common with the indigenous population. Therefore they were placed in the position of partly ostracized half-citizens. Nevertheless, in spite of all legislative efforts, it seemed that these wily tricksters managed to go on defying the government, breaking the law, and getting rich at the expense of the non-Jewish population.[17] So some non-Jews must have felt that now the tsar was turning to the people for assistance in restraining and punishing the hated minority.

Jews, when arguing for legal equality and the abolition of the Pale, regularly stressed the prejudicial effects of the existing legal discrimination: it forced the Jews to be a burden on their neighbors, and it seemed to place them outside the protection of the law. Some non-Jews used the same arguments.[18] Count Kutaisov, on the other hand, favored retention of the Pale and certain legal restrictions. Nevertheless, he pointed out that the people did not view violence against Jews as a criminal act. They were convinced that this minority did not enjoy those personal rights that other citizens enjoyed because Jews were willing to bear any personal insult or violence if only it would give them the possibility of deriving some material benefit. Hence to beat a Jew was considered to be far less criminal than to assault any other peaceful citizen.[19] In spite of its anti-Semitic twist, Kutaisov's statement confirms the assertion that the Jews' inferior legal position contributed to popular animosity toward them and paved the way for belief in a tsarist *ukaz* to attack the Jews.

Another element in the tenacity of the rumor of an *ukaz* was the generally troubled atmosphere that followed the assassination of Alexander II. All students of the period agree that this was a time of "wavering of minds," of indignation, bewilderment, and anxiety.[20] If the tsar could be assassinated, then anything was possible. Moreover, a new tsar was always expected to grant the people special favors (*tsarskie milosti*).[21] Perhaps the anti-Jewish *ukaz* was such a gift. This assumption could only have been strengthened, even without intentional outside encouragement, by the news concerning Gessia Gelfman and the spread of the notion that the Jews were responsible for killing the tsar—so similar in concept, wording, and implication to the popular religious belief that the Jews were responsible for killing Christ.[22]

Plain, elemental stubbornness and naïveté were major ingredients in the tenacity of the rumor of an *ukaz*. Or perhaps the naïveté was in fact cleverly disguised cunning, serving the peasants' own interests as they perceived them. An officer of the gendarmes expressed the opinion in 1861 that "when they [the peasants] are up to something, it is cunning, not stupidity, that prevails." In either case, once the anti-Jewish violence began, it often took determined exhortations by officials at public meetings and clergymen in the churches to calm the people. And, of course, they were not always successful. In the summer of 1881 the rumor of an *ukaz* continued, and it appeared again in the spring of 1882, in spite of the forceful suppression of previous pogroms and the punishment of the rioters.[23]

In Borispol', Poltava *guberniia,* for example, the local police official was well known, trusted, and respected by the people. While he was busy with official duties in nearby Pereiaslav in June 1881, tensions grew in Borispol'. A policeman unfamiliar to the local population was sent to the townlet to calm things down, but the already excited population refused to listen to him and stubbornly concluded that the "real" policeman had not come because the authorities allowed beating the Jews.[24]

Cases were reported in Ekaterinoslav *guberniia* of peasants so strongly and naïvely believing in the existence of a tsarist command to attack the Jews that they destroyed their own huts because Jewish tenants lived in them.[25]

Not all rioters were so single-minded. In Elizavetgrad, Jewish-owned houses with Russians living in them were not touched. Neither were the homes of some Jews who had good reputations for always keeping accurate and honest accounts with Russian workers.[26] But naïveté and obstinacy were more often the rule with the rioters.

In the village of Cheriko in Chernigov *guberniia,* the *volost starshina* (a locally elected peasant official) tried to persuade the residents not to attack the Jews. The peasants demanded a written guarantee that they would not be punished for their failure to comply with the tsar's *ukaz.* The *volost starshina* gave this guarantee, but the mob remained unconvinced and undertook to destroy six Jewish homes as insurance.[27]

In some places the population respected and trusted the local Jews and so did only insignificant damage to their property. When asked why, these rioters explained that they did it simply so they should not be punished for disobeying the rumored imperial command. Occasionally peasants came to the local Jews and asked them to remove their valuables from their homes, since on the morrow everything belonging to Jews would *have to be destroyed.* Some peasants even supplied their own wagons to assist Jewish neighbors in removing their otherwise doomed possessions. In at least one instance the employees of a Jewish factory owner came to him to express their satisfaction with him as their boss. But they added that they could not disobey the *ukaz* unless he gave them a signed statement that he would be responsible before the authorities for his workers' inaction.[28]

Such elemental naïveté and stubbornness (or cleverly disguised cunning) as this should be seen in the context of Russian history as a whole.

Persistent wild rumors were always an integral part of life in the Russian countryside. The False Tsar Dmitri in the seventeenth century and the belief that Pugachev was Tsar Peter III in the eighteenth century immediately come to mind. Closer to the period under discussion were the persistent rumors of a second, genuine Emancipation to follow the first, unsatisfactory proclamation of 19 February 1861, which the peasants thought had been falsified by landowners and officials. The peasant uprising and massacre at Bezdna, Kazan *guberniia,* in April 1861 and the rumors that accompanied and followed these events—concerning the character of the "true" Emancipation and the "miraculous" powers and achievements of the revolt's leader, Anton Petrov—are another illustration of the tenacity with which the Russian simple people held on to wild stories promising them a better future. In 1875–77 revolutionary socialists tried to organize a popular insurrectionary conspiracy among the peasants of Chigirin *uezd,* Kiev *guberniia.* This incident is somewhat different in character from the others mentioned above because it involved planning and deliberate deception. The important point, however, is that the revolutionaries encouraged the peasants to believe that they had come as emissaries of the tsar.[29] In many other less spectacular and less consequential instances during the reign of Alexander II, wild rumors were spread and peasant riots against landlords (also called pogroms in Russian) were undertaken.

Belief in the tsar's genuine solicitude for the welfare of his people, which was blocked by wicked officials, served a certain psychological need. It gave hope for the future while making it possible to live in a sometimes almost intolerable present. And occasionally, when someone claimed to bring good tidings directly from the Little Father, it presented a way of protesting against existing circumstances without becoming disloyal to the tsar.

In addition, pleading that they were inspired to illegal acts by their wholehearted devotion to the tsar often enabled peasants to avoid punishment. Daniel Field has written a thorough and fascinating analysis of what he calls "popular" or "naive monarchism."

> The chances of practical success might be remote, but the myth of the tsar provided a ready-made excuse in the event of failure. Peasants could plead their delusion and foolishness, these pleas were accepted, and the peasants were sent home. The plea did require a sacrifice of pride, which peasants readily made: better to confess to folly and let the wise suffer penal exile.
>     . . . The myth of the tsar provided them with a pretext, which they

otherwise lacked, to probe the intentions and determination of the regime in behalf of their own material interests and with minimal risk. . . .

. . . The myth of the peasant made it possible for peasants to manipulate their reputation for naive monarchism. They maintained that they were naive, credulous, and deluded; officials, whether stern or indulgent, took these professions at face value, acknowledged the peasants' fulsome expressions of repentance, and let them go. Order was restored. The peasants avoided punishment, officials were spared the difficulties and dangers of judging and punishing large numbers of peasants.[30]

After the assassination of the "Tsar Liberator," the government *expected* a rash of rumors and disorders as a matter of course. The minister of the interior, Loris-Melikov, warned the governors on 27 March 1881 to take precautions to counter irresponsible gossip with the truth and to prevent or end disorders. The minister stressed the need for action, but also the need for officials to remain calm, circumspect, and cautious. The government feared popular unrest, but the emphasis was on caution rather than repression.[31]

The rumors were not slow in coming. Immediately after the tsar was killed, the story became pervasive that the landlords had murdered him to prevent a new land redistribution. Occasionally the new tsar, Alexander III, provoked hostility since he was considered to be a friend of the landowning classes and someone whom the noblemen had elevated with the intention of reinstituting serfdom. In some versions the Jews and the landlords together had killed Alexander II in order to reintroduce bonded servitude. The gossip about the reimposition of serfdom died down at the end of the spring, to be replaced by persistent stories of new land divisions. As I have noted above, the people expected special favors from the new ruler. They were, of course, especially interested in receiving more land. A police report of 28 April summarized the situation thus: the peasants did not know whether they were coming or going, whether they would get the noblemen's land or be returned to serfdom, and they seemed ready to riot in either case. Hence tension in the villages became acute throughout the empire during the spring and summer of 1881, without any connection to the discord that was causing Jewish-Christian friction in the Pale at that time. Officials everywhere feared that the extremely excited mood of the population might lead to peasant revolts against the landlords and the authorities, quite apart from the problem of the Jews. The government's attempts to suppress the rumors were, as usual, mostly unsuccessful. Some people thought that only a real tsarist manifesto reassuring the peasants of their actual rights could put an end to the rumors.[32]

On 23 May the new minister of the interior, Ignatiev, finally instructed the governors throughout the empire to tour their *guberniias* in order to calm the excited people and especially to counter the dangerous gossip about a new distribution of the land. Ignatiev emphasized that the repetition of disorders like the recent ones in the south against the Jews could not be tolerated and should be prevented by timely and appropriate measures.[33]

In sum, then, not only Jewish-Christian relations but also Russia's circumstances in general were conducive to the emergence of persistent wild rumors.

A circular of Ignatiev's dated 3 June was also issued in response to general circumstances, and not just to the Jewish question. Numerous governors had petitioned to have troops left in their jurisdictions throughout the summer in order to prevent the possible outbreak of antiestablishment disorders. The minister of the interior noted in his circular that he and the minister of war had obtained the tsar's approval for granting military commanders the right to cancel summer training exercises if governors so requested. But at the same time, Ignatiev asked the governors not to abuse this right, since the summer maneuvers were so important for the military preparedness of the army. The governors should request their cancellation only when all other deterrent measures proved to be insufficient to prevent rioting. In addition, the governors should enlist the aid of clergymen, public figures, and officials in countering false rumors among the village population.[34] I emphasize that this circular related to rural unrest in general, not only—perhaps not even primarily— to pogroms.

On 18 June, Count Kutaisov reported that even the wildest and most ridiculous stories were being circulated and believed. He thought that only constant exhortation by officials at public meetings and by clergymen in the churches might calm passions and reduce discontent and agitation.[35]

Prior to 15 April little or nothing was done to explain to the population the illegality of anti-Jewish rioting and the falsity of the *ukaz* rumor. Kutaisov stressed this point and was very critical of the local administration on account of it. In his view, many officials got so used to hearing the rumors that they did not consider it possible to prevent the "calamity" (*beda*), which in time came to be considered an "unavoidable evil" (*neizbezhnoe zlo*). The measures taken—usually the reinforcement of the local police by means of troops—were aimed essentially at combatting the misfortune when it occurred, not at preventing its outbreak altogether. Only a few officials, Kutaisov noted, expected that the measures taken by the police would be, by themselves, an effective total deterrent to any eruption of violence.[36]

To a certain extent the attitudes of officials, as perceived by Kutaisov, paralleled those of the press noted in chapter 4: disbelief in the possibility of any serious occurrence, then concern or resignation that something would happen—which the police and troops could undoubtedly control— then surprise at the force of the outbreak.

According to Kutaisov, not only did the administration not take steps to refute the rumor of an *ukaz* prior to 15 April, but after the Elizavetgrad pogrom the local administration made a blunder that served to strengthen belief in the existence of an anti-Jewish tsarist decree. This was the establishment of a public committee to assist the families of indigent persons arrested on suspicion of participating in the riots, discussed in chapter 3. According to Kutaisov, the committee's existence, even though short, had very unfortunate consequences. The rumor spread among the people that not only would those arrested not be punished, but rewards were being given to their families. "It seems to me," Kutaisov concluded, "that the establishment of such a committee sufficiently portrays the state of things and makes quite obvious with what attention and acumen the administration dealt with the problem of stopping ridiculous rumors which agitate the people."[37]

The problem of communicating with the population at large and giving it accurate information on the government's views and policies was by no means a new one. In 1859 a member of a commission on local government institutions observed:

> Virtually the only means for publishing laws and administrative directives to the people . . . is the reading of manifestoes and decrees in churches and public squares. . . . But public reading not only fails to accomplish its purpose, . . . it is positively harmful. Manifestoes and decrees are read unintelligibly by deacons or police officials; most of the people cannot hear; barely five percent are present; and, finally, even the most attentive and informed listeners are seldom able to get a true understanding of the substance of a decree or manifesto from a single reading. . . . Priests and police officials not only do not care about the correct meaning of the law but, unfortunately, are sometimes prepared to confuse the people intentionally in hopes of serving their own interest.[38]

In 1881, Count Kutaisov stated that his experiences everywhere he went led him to conclude that the peasants very much needed to have various questions of state and public life elucidated for them. But there were no established ways of giving the people these explanations. No one official had this task as his primary duty; and currently local officials were either of too poor quality or, because of the shortage of manpower, too overworked with other matters to engage in interpreting government policy. Consequently, because of the government's faulty communication with the people, rumors were able to circulate easily. Kutaisov was referring specifically to the anti-Jewish rumors.[39]

From this testimony one can derive an explanation of the administration's inaction with regard to refuting the rumor of an anti-Jewish *ukaz*. No regular procedures existed for explaining to the people the government's views on public issues. There were no officials specially trained or appointed for this task. Rumormongering not only was rife in 1881 but was historically a regular feature of Russian life. The best efforts of officials were usually unsuccessful in refuting and laying to rest the various outlandish stories circulating at any particular time. So there was no reason for officials then, or for us now, to think that their efforts would have enjoyed any particular success with regard to specifically anti-Jewish rumors.

Furthermore, perhaps officials kept Loris-Melikov's 27 March circular in mind and were more cautious than farsighted. Given the history of the preceding few decades, anti-Jewish violence probably seemed to be a much more remote possibility than anti-landlord violence. Hence, as long as the rumors were directed against Jews more than against landlords, and as long as the rumors remained loyalist by referring to a tsarist *ukaz,* then officials may have thought that the situation was not as bad as it could have been. This being the case, one can, without resorting to the notion of deliberate plotting, understand the failure of the Russian authorities to try to combat the unbridled anti-Jewish rumors.

In the past many writers on the 1881 pogroms assumed that the rumors of a tsarist *ukaz* were disseminated as part of a master plan for the pogroms. The rapid circulation of the rumors (occasionally portrayed, inaccurately, as having appeared simultaneously in different places) and the persistence with which they were believed impressed these writers. They assumed that whoever organized the pogroms sent agents, well supplied with funds, to ensure the successful spread of and belief in the rumors. Some asserted that the government took no measures either to counter the rumors or to protect the Jews in light of them.[40] The evidence just presented, however, indicates that none of these assertions and interpretations will stand up to close scrutiny.

## Date Fixing

Occasionally the anti-Jewish rumors that spread so stubbornly in 1881 were accompanied by mention of specific dates.[41] I have mentioned that, several weeks before the event, word spread that a pogrom would break out in Elizavetgrad during Easter.[42] The authorities in Kiev allegedly had advance knowledge of the date, 26 April, of the pogrom in that town.[43] People supposedly knew a week in advance that a pogrom was set to take place on 3 May in Odessa.[44]

At first glance some form of planning would seem to be indicated by this date fixing, but it does not necessarily signal the presence of an organized body behind the scenes. And a close look at the chronological pattern of the violence in 1881 reveals that, if there was indeed any planning, it was of a most elementary, loose, almost accidental kind, more aptly characterized as spontaneous than organized.

The Elizavetgrad pogrom broke out on a Wednesday afternoon, the fourth day of the Russian Orthodox Easter. I have shown in chapter 3 that the riot's beginning was related to a completely fortuitous event, the removal of troops from the town as the result of a mistake in judgment by a local official. The date of the Kiev pogrom, 26 April, was the second Sunday after Wednesday, 15 April; the date of the Odessa pogrom, 3 May, was the Sunday after 26 April. The pattern here was: religious holiday, Sunday, Sunday. On each of these days, as was well known to everyone at the time, religious feelings tended to run high, almost no one worked, heavy drinking was customary, and people spent their time strolling in the streets. It was therefore extremely easy to encourage an excited crowd to gather.[45]

Meanwhile, in the atmosphere of anti-Jewish rumors, it was natural for people to inquire about the date on which the violence was supposed to begin. It was equally natural for a Christian holiday or a Sunday to be picked, or in some cases an approaching market day or the day announced in advance on which the local troops were scheduled to leave for field exercises.[46] When Easter was mentioned as the date for attacking the Jews, as occurred in a number of places, this may simply have been an expression of the intensified popular anti-Semitism characteristic of that season.

A well-organized political body, a group of local troublemakers, or a spontaneously hatched rumor—in the circumstances each could equally well be cited as an explanation of the date fixing, and each would be an equally speculative interpretation. However, there are certain considerations that tend to rule out the assumption that a "well-organized political body" was responsible.

First of all, it may be asked why the Kiev pogrom was not set for 19 April, the first Sunday after the Elizavetgrad riots. Could it be that one Sunday was skipped over because of the spontaneous nature of the sequence of pogroms? The Elizavetgrad pogrom occurred on Wednesday afternoon and Thursday, too close to Sunday, 19 April, perhaps, to make an impression strong enough to lead to action. During the week following 19 April, however, there was time for the news and the impact of the Elizavetgrad violence to sink in and for rumors to fix the following Sunday as the date for rioting in Kiev. The news of the Kiev violence could then have led to rumors that Sunday, 3 May (the next convenient date), would be exploited for anti-Jewish violence in Odessa, which had remained quiet during Easter.

Second, if the pogroms were backed by some well-organized political body, then why in many cases were dates set for rioting that never took place, and why did riots occur later than the dates fixed in advance? For example: Odessa was supposed to have a pogrom on Easter Sunday (12 April), but anti-Jewish violence occurred only on 3 May. In Lubny, Poltava *guberniia,* rumors fixed dates for the riot several times, but the sources indicate that when it finally broke out (on 27 July), it was in an almost accidental fashion, unconnected with any date fixing. A group of drunken townsmen, encouraged by the generally excited atmosphere, started the trouble all of a sudden. In Berdiansk, Tavrida *guberniia,* Easter was set as the date. Rioting broke out in villages nearby, but only on 5 and 6 May; in the town itself, however, no violence occurred. Easter was also set as the date in Rostov-on-the-Don, but there too no pogrom occurred. Pogroms were announced by handwritten proclamations for the beginning of May in several places in Minsk *guberniia,* but they never took place.[47] In short, the connection between dates fixed in advance and actual outbreaks of violence was either nonexistent or quite tenuous.

## *Handbills and Posters*

Another means by which pogrom agitation spread was handwritten or printed handbills and wall posters calling on the people to attack the Jews. These were found attached to walls, fences, and trees or simply left lying around in the streets. The character of the written circulars that appeared in connection with the pogroms of 1881 indicates that they were an entirely peripheral phenomenon: they were few in number and of doubtful influence. In each case they seem to have been produced locally.

Almost all added calls for attacks on the propertied classes, and some advocated attacking the authorities. In the most important case of Elizavetgrad, there is no evidence that anti-Jewish circulars appeared prior to the events of 15 April. Many of the circulars that appeared were clearly a response to local violence rather than a cause of it. There is no evidence in this connection to support the contention that a conspiracy lay behind the 1881 pogroms.[48]

It seems that anti-Jewish proclamations were found in only a relatively small number of places and usually in very small quantities. The sources used for this study reveal their appearance in only nine *guberniias*—Chernigov, Ekaterinoslav, Kherson, Kiev, Minsk, Poltava, Tavrida, Vitebsk, and Voronezh (see table 5). The last was not within the Pale but bordered on it; no pogroms occurred against the Jews residing there. None occurred in Minsk or Vitebsk *guberniias* either. Among those where pogroms did occur, Ekaterinoslav was singled out by one source as having had no anti-Jewish proclamations appear within its boundaries.[49] Bessarabia, Khar'kov, Podolia, and Volynia *guberniias* may also have had none.

Of those who at the time reported the appearance of anti-Jewish notices, almost no one, Jew or non-Jew, indicated that their numbers were impressive. In the town of Kiev, prior to the pogrom there, the local press published reports about the widespread appearance of manifestos calling for the beating of Jews. The local Jews themselves tended to believe these reports. The reports, however, were evidently greatly exaggerated or altogether baseless, the result of rumors that the newspapers did not bother to examine carefully.[50]

It is clear that handwritten proclamations could have been prepared spontaneously by any anti-Semite or anyone who might expect to profit by anti-Jewish violence—for example, business competitors of the Jews or impoverished and unemployed day laborers.

In several cases, it seems, only Jewish residents found the offensive handbills in the streets and turned them over to the police. The manifestos found in this way generally called for an end to violence against the Jews and the beginning of attacks on the non-Jewish propertied classes, who were accused of being worse exploiters than the Jews since they owned all the land. Noting that, in conversations with peasants, Jews sometimes presented similar arguments, trying to turn the popular agitation and violence away from themselves onto others, Kutaisov and some local officials came to suspect that the handbills in question were actually prepared by persons within the Jewish community. These people presum-

## TABLE 5

### ANTI-JEWISH CIRCULARS, APRIL–AUGUST 1881

| Location | Guberniia | Date of Circular | Date of Pogrom | Format | Object of Attack | Provenance | Source |
|---|---|---|---|---|---|---|---|
| Mirgorod | Poltava | 21 April | None | ? | ? | Newspaper employee arrested before distribution | K.-A., 7 |
| Kiev | Kiev | 27–28 April | 26–27 April | Printed-typograph | All exploiters, land-lords, government | Socialist revolutionaries | K.-A., 80, 416 |
| Pereiaslav town | Poltava | after 27 April | 30 June | Rumored | Jews (boycott) | ? | K.-A., 155, 202–03 |
| *Pereiaslav uezd* | Poltava | None until 12 July | 12 July | None | None | None | K.-A., 203–04 |
| Berdichev | Kiev | 30 April | None | Ms. | Jews | ? | K.-A., 87 |
| Here and there | Chernigov | April–May | April, July, August | ? | ? | ? | Tsherikover (I), 355 Tsherikover (II), 456 |
| About 33 locations | Ekaterinoslav | None | 1–10 May | None | None | None | K.-A., 447 |
| Nikolaev | Kherson | 2 May | 1 May | Ms. | Jews, officials | 2 workers | K.-A., 272 |
| | | 5 May | 1 May (quickly ended by police measures) | Hand-written, hectographed in Odessa | Jews, privileged classes, authorities | Politically suspect persons | Kantor, 153; K.-A., 36, 83, 95–96, 270–73, 287 |
| Berdiansk *uezd* | Tavrida | ca. 5–6 May | 5–6 May | ? | Jews | ? | K.-A., 383–84 |
| Odessa | Kherson | None until 7 May | 3–7 May | None | ? | ? | K.-A., 393–94 |
| Gomel to Romny RR stations | Minsk | ca. 7 May | None | Ms. (illiterate, ungrammatical) | Jews | ? | K.-A., 56 |
| Pavlovsk | Voronezh | 18 May | None | Ms. | Jews | ? | K.-A., 97 |
| Lubny | Poltava | May, July | 27 July | ? | Jews | Jews' competitors? | K.-A., 158–60 |
| Dvinaburg | Vitebsk | 24–25 June | None | Ms. | Jews | Students | Kantor, 149 |
| (Dvinsk after 1893) | | July | None | Lithograph | ? | ? | Tsherikover (I), 355 Tsherikover (II), 457 |
| Pereiaslav town | Poltava | ca. 30 June | 30 June | ? | Jews and propertied classes | Jews? | K.-A., 203–04 |
| Nezhin | Chernigov | 7 August | 20 July | Lithograph | ? | ? | Tsherikover (I), 355 Tsherikover (II), 457 |

*Note:* No details were available about circulars that appeared in other places.

ably hoped both to deflect the mob and to influence local officials to maintain or increase measures for the prevention of popular violence, especially by calling in troops to reinforce the local police.[51] Whether or not Kutaisov's suspicions were correct, that he was able to find some basis for them indicates the paucity of anti-Jewish circulars in many places.

Meanwhile, what I have described in regard to whole *guberniias* was also true of individual towns and villages: some places had proclamations without pogroms, and some had pogroms without proclamations. Clearly the appearance of manifestos did not necessarily have any influence over the torrent of pogroms. Further evidence for such an assertion lies in the fact that the mobs never attacked non-Jews, in spite of some proclamations calling for this and some talk to this effect. Officials, of course, feared that with time rioters might begin to heed such calls.[52]

Some manifestos also called for attacks on the authorities, in addition to Jews and wealthy non-Jews.[53] These were obviously not connected with any conspiracy being hatched by circles within or close to the government. The authorities were fortunate in that, although mobs did indeed sometimes attack soldiers, they did so while remaining loyal to the regime. They simply believed that the local authorities had been bribed to hide the tsar's *ukaz* allowing assaults on Jews, a fact that offered little consolation to jittery and beleaguered Russian officials.[54]

The proclamations calling for attacks on wealthy non-Jews and officials in addition to Jews were undoubtedly written by revolutionary socialists or their sympathizers. In some cases the authorities managed to expose the local troublemakers who were the source of anti-Jewish circulars.[55]

The historian Eliahu Tsherikover's statement that all the printed proclamations were monarchist in character is simply not true. Perhaps the lithographed circulars that he mentioned as having appeared in Dvinsk, Vitebsk *guberniia* (July 1881) and Nezhin, Chernigov *guberniia* (7 August 1881), were purely monarchist, but there is no way of knowing, since the author does not cite their specific content. However, I find it significant that no pogrom occurred at all in Dvinsk and that the one in Nezhin took place on 20 July, almost three weeks before the appearance of the circular there.[56] The handprinted, hectographed circulars found in Nikolaev, Kherson *guberniia*, were not monarchist. They called for attacks on Jews, wealthy non-Jews, and even the authorities.[57]

The only other explicit case of a printed circular that I have been able to uncover in the sources used for this study relates to the town of Kiev. On the night of 27–28 April, police there arrested a group of revolutionary socialists in the act of printing a proclamation on a typograph. The document had obviously been written in response to the previous two days of rioting in the town. It claimed that the riots were one-sided; that the people should not attack just the Jews; that they should not attack poor Jews at all; rather, they should destroy the exploitative capitalists, the kulaks (wealthy peasant moneylenders), the landlords, and the government agents who protected the oppressors of the people.[58]

Manifestos such as this one were among the factors that led local officials to blame the pogroms on revolutionary socialist agitation. Later, when this explanation was rejected, the authorities feared such proclamations as a danger sign that the revolutionaries might try to divert to their own ends the anti-Jewish violence that had already begun.[59]

The most important point to be made about the circulars is that *no* anti-Jewish handbills or wall posters, printed or handwritten, monarchist or revolutionary, appeared before 15 April insofar as official investigations and unofficial witnesses could discover.[60] Furthermore, in many instances manifestos appeared in a particular place only after a pogrom had begun there or even after it had ended.[61] Some of the notices, by their references to recent violent events, revealed clearly that they were merely a response, an afterthought, to the pogroms, and not a cause of them.[62]

The evidence set forth in this chapter demonstrates that the circulation of anti-Jewish rumors, their persistence, and the responses to them of government officials can all be explained without assuming the existence of an organized conspiracy. The available evidence also makes it clear that, to a certain extent, the actual occurrence of pogroms on the dates fixed in advance was an accident, a coincidence. On those occasions when this happened it was a matter of the aroused populace having seized upon the rumors of a set date, and when the day arrived, if local officials were not competent and adroit, the pent-up anger and expectancy of the mob just broke all bounds. There is no need to refer to an outside organization in order to explain the matter. As for popular manifestos and leaflets, these were a common instrument of the revolutionary movement. If some group in the government or some organization close to the government—or any organization at all, for that matter—had decided to use the means of the revolutionaries—inciting popular violence—for antirevolutionary ends, would it not have adopted this device as well? Yet before the first pogrom there were no manifestos. And the most likely explanation of those that appeared later, both the purely anti-Jewish and the clearly revolutionary, is that they were a reflexive attempt to promote and exploit a situation that had already developed spontaneously and unexpectedly.

*Chapter 6*

# MYSTERIOUS MESSENGERS
# AND GREAT RUSSIAN RAIDERS

◆ ◆ ◆

LARGE NUMBERS OF PEOPLE WERE ON THE MOVE IN THE UKRAINE
during the spring and summer of 1881: businessmen, government
officials, students, pilgrims, tourists, and itinerant laborers. According
to those authors who see a "hidden hand" behind the anti-Jewish violence,
some of these travelers were really messengers sent from Moscow or St.
Petersburg. Their job was to prepare the ground for the approaching riots,
warn local officials, and instruct them about how to deal with the rioters.
Officials were allegedly told to cooperate with the troublemakers, or at
least to treat them leniently, and certainly not to use firearms against
them. The proponents of the conspiracy theory go on to assert that the
mysterious messengers were followed by bands of Great Russians (people
belonging to the dominant ethnic group in the empire who came from
the core provinces of the center and northeast), financed and sent from the
interior *guberniias* specifically for the purpose of setting the pogroms in
motion. Once this aim had been achieved, the Great Russian raiders
moved on to other places in order to continue their sinister work.[1]

In the pages that follow I will examine several contemporary accounts
of strangers who appeared in various places where pogroms took place and
stirred up the muddy waters then in flux. A close-up picture of one aspect
of the events of 1881 will emerge. This picture will suggest who the
mysterious messengers and some individual riot leaders were and will
leave the impression that there was in fact no conspiracy behind the events
of that year, but rather that individuals acted on their own, taking
advantage of local conditions to promote their own narrow interests.

Explicit statements about mysterious messengers have been preserved
in testimony given by an eyewitness, P. Sonin. In mid March 1881,
Sonin recalled, he was in Elizavetgrad and visited his good friend I. P.
Bogdanovich, the chief of police. Bogdanovich was known as an honest
and benevolent man, who treated non-Russians and non-Orthodox Christians very humanely. On the day Sonin visited Bogdanovich, the police

chief was quite perplexed. He explained that he had been visited earlier in the day by a retired state councillor from the capital who had spoken about his recent visits to Ekaterinoslav, Kherson, Nikolaev, Odessa, and Balta. He expressed a liking for Elizavetgrad, but he lamented that there were so many Jews there and wished they could be induced to leave Russia.

We may note that if the state councillor did indeed express such a desire, he did so as part of a rather small minority. Though this view became more widespread during the 1890s and thereafter, it was very rare in government circles during the early 1880s and in no way reflected governmental policy.[2] Prior to the pogrom in Kiev, some wealthy businessmen and also some workers openly expressed the view that it was necessary to expel the Jews from the region, "because they arrest the general course of life and are an obstacle to the blessings of the government's undertakings."[3] Perhaps the retired councillor was expressing the viewpoint of these businessmen and others like them.

In any case, he had gone on to note that during the coming Easter season, because of the public mourning for Alexander II, all spectacles, stage plays, amusements, games, and so on were strictly prohibited. He was curious to know if the police chief had any fears about the possible occurrence of disorders. When Bogdanovich asked in wonder why he should fear such an eventuality, the state councillor replied that the people might want to compensate themselves for the loss of their merrymaking. There was some evidence of this among the lower-class riffraff. If, "God forbid," violence against the Jews were to begin, the gentleman had continued, no one would hold the police chief responsible. He could not be expected to foresee such a thing, for it would be an unanticipated outburst of popular indignation. But if the mob began to attack wealthy non-Jewish citizens and businessmen or German merchants, that would be a different matter. That would be "a completely false step." The police would be held responsible. Bogdanovich, according to Sonin, did not know what to make of these words.

A few days later the police chief told Sonin that the retired councillor had left town, after excusing himself for being unnecessarily bothersome, since it turned out that he did not need Bogdanovich's help with his business after all. What that business was he had never explained.

Later two other strangers came to Elizavetgrad and stayed in the same hotel as the state councillor, one dressed like a merchant, the other like a dandy coachman. They evidently had a lot of money, and they visited tearooms, taverns, inns, and the suburbs where the poor lived. What they did and said the police chief did not know. From Elizavetgrad they went in different directions to other places in the vicinity. Sonin also reported that about twenty strangers came to Elizavetgrad by railroad the day the pogrom broke out or the day before. They were dressed like shop salesmen or coachmen and were "clearly" the leaders of several gangs that began to attack Jewish shops and homes without any evident cause.[4]

According to Sonin, strangers dressed like shop salesmen and coachmen were active in Kiev and Odessa too. After their arrival in Kiev, the rumors of the approaching pogrom became noticeably more definite. Later, during the rioting itself, individuals dressed like ultrafashionable dandies were among the leaders who urged the mob on. They disappeared before the end of the pogrom and so were not arrested. In Odessa these types were vociferous in announcing the existence of a tsarist *ukaz* to attack the Jews. In concluding his account, Sonin remembered how contemporary stories about the pogroms had left "the definite impression" that the riots had all taken place according to a fixed pattern prepared beforehand by unknown persons, "just like the 1905 pogroms."[5]

Sonin's testimony may be trustworthy. Let us assume for the moment that it is. If there was a conspiracy by some organized body, it must have been one working outside the regular governmental channels. Otherwise, why not give the local police chief more direct and more explicit orders, even if only orally? I am reminded of Gogol's *Inspector General*. Perhaps some unknown party was trying to mislead Bogdanovich into believing that his superiors wanted anti-Jewish violence. If so, the attempt was not successful, for, as is shown in chapter 3, the police chief tried his best to prevent any disorders.

But Sonin's testimony does not necessarily lead to the conclusion that there was a conspiracy by some organized body. The retired state councillor could have been acting on his own initiative. From the account available, one cannot learn whether he was actively promoting anti-Jewish violence or not. Perhaps he was simply a tourist or traveling businessman with anti-Semitic inclinations. It would have been natural for such a person to want to expound his views to the chief of police, the official most closely in contact with the hated minority nationality.

My remarks thus far have been based on the assumption that Sonin's testimony is trustworthy. It is highly likely, however, that this is not the case. Sonin wrote quite vividly, sometimes even quoting, as it were, conversations between himself and the Elizavetgrad police chief, or between the latter and the mysterious retired state councillor. Yet Sonin was writing twenty-eight years after the event (in 1909), and from memory, as he himself admitted. His recollections could not possibly have been completely accurate, which is clear from the fact that on two significant points his account differs from those of other witnesses. First of all, only toward the end of his article, and only in regard to Odessa, does he mention rumors about a tsarist *ukaz* to beat the Jews. But the sources leave no doubt that such stories were also widespread prior to and during the Elizavetgrad and Kiev outbreaks. Second, unlike Sonin, none of the other sources mentions dandies as having appeared in Elizavetgrad.

Apart from inevitable lapses in memory, Sonin was writing under the striking impression created by the 1905 pogroms, as is clearly revealed by the remark I have quoted from the conclusion of his article. In 1905 conditions were entirely different from those of 1881. But since he was convinced that the 1905 anti-Jewish riots were organized, it must have been quite simple for him to project this assumption backward to 1881. Remembering the encounter between his friend the police chief and the state councillor, our author could easily have given it, in his mind and therefore in his article, a much more concrete and sinister form than it had in reality.

Let us return to the question of the rather well-dressed pogrom leaders. While Sonin seems to have been mistaken about the appearance of such persons in Elizavetgrad, other contemporary sources confirm his claim that they appeared in the town of Kiev. Count Kutaisov, for example, in his report devoted to the pogrom in Kiev, stated that some witnesses there had spotted persons directing the crowds in various places who were, if not dressed quite like gentlemen, yet cleaner than the masses, sometimes even wearing fancy jackets (*pidzhakakh*). These characters went into shops, clarified if they were Jewish- or Christian-owned, then told the mob whether or not to attack.[6]

The Austrian consul in Kiev depicted similar scenes. Unidentified strangers entered the shops of German and other non-Orthodox Christian merchants, told them to remain calm, because only the exploitative Jews would be attacked, and instructed them to put pictures of Christian saints in their shop windows. Some mob leaders reportedly came to houses in the center of town and asked the watchmen on duty to tell them the names of Jewish residents. Other reports reaching the Austrian consul mentioned persons who went around with written lists of the Jewish homes to be destroyed.[7]

It is highly unlikely that these dandified strangers who acted as mob leaders were government emissaries. If they were supposed to be secret agents, then it is difficult to see why they made themselves so obvious. Perhaps they wanted to be noticed and recognized as agents of the government without claiming to be acting in an official capacity, thereby making known the capital's approval of the pogroms without implicating the government too openly. If so, then why did they not reveal their mission to the local authorities? Most importantly, why did they have to flee to avoid arrest if they had official approval to act?

They could have been agents of the Holy Brotherhood. This possibility will be discussed in chapter 11.

Another possibility is that the strangers themselves (Sonin spoke of twenty or so) made up the whole organization, which was acting totally on its own. If so, then they were largely dependent on many other causal factors beyond their control, that is, accidental, spontaneous factors, insofar as their "organization" was concerned. If twenty unknown men could induce the populations of several major towns, and perhaps other, smaller settlements as well, to rise against the Jews, then surely organic developments within the populations affected were much more important than the influence of a few "organizers."

These dandified strangers could perhaps have been business competitors of the Jews (more or less well-to-do themselves and therefore better dressed than the common run of the population) or anti-Semitic students and intellectuals who resented the Jews' entering into Russia's intellectual and cultural life and thereby presenting them with stiff competition in the free professions. Anti-Jewish feelings were not limited to peasants and workers; Christian tradesmen and businessmen were often fiercely anti-Jewish as well, and a number of contemporary sources note that significant sections of the intellectual classes in Kiev and elsewhere were very hostile to the Jews.[8]

For the period after the beginning of the wave of pogroms, another explanation of the appearance of dandified mob leaders may be offered. Many Jewish ready-made clothing stores were plundered in the course of the rioting in different places. There are eyewitness reports of the Kiev pogroms that state explicitly that rioters took clothes from Jewish shops and dressed up in them.[9] Perhaps, then, chance participants in the plundering of clothing stores, feeling a new self-confidence on account of their new finery, moved on to as yet unaffected localities where, as a result of their "superior knowledge and experience," they were naturally bolder than the local people and tended to become leaders of the mob.

Some Jews in Kiev, looking for evidence of revolutionary socialist influences, noted persons in the crowd who had "evidently, changed their clothes in order to hide their belonging to the more cultured [*intelligentnaia*] class."[10] This reference is vague; it seems to imply that these characters were better dressed than the rabble, but not dressed in the fashion one might have expected of *intelligenty*. If so, then again it might be an example of rioters dressed in stolen clothing—a case of climbing partway up the social ladder rather than, as the Jews at the time thought, partway down.

In sum, the rather well-dressed mob leaders, rather than being agents of some organization, were probably business competitors of the Jews, or anti-Semitic students and intellectuals, or even run-of-the-mill rioters— just somewhat bolder than the mass—wearing plundered clothes. It is likely that no dandies appeared in Elizavetgrad. They did appear in Kiev a week and a half latter. At least some of them could have been participants in the Elizavetgrad pogrom who were not displaying the fruits of their earlier activities. The same could have been true of dandies noticed elsewhere.

In the countryside the situation was somewhat different. A rather clear-cut case occurred in Kherson *guberniia,* where a certain peasant went around to several villages claiming before the local village elders that he was a tsarist envoy and secret police agent who had been commissioned to oversee the destruction of Jewish property. Without having succeeded in causing any pogroms, he was finally arrested. His only successes had been in forcing some Jewish tavern keepers to sell liquor cheaply. The several local officials whom he had succeeded in duping lost their jobs and were brought to trial for criminal activity as well.[11]

"Suspicious persons" were also reported wandering about elsewhere in Kherson *guberniia* and through villages in Kiev *guberniia,* making all kinds of "outrageous [anti-Jewish] proposals." In Kiev *guberniia* they were known to be illiterates with strongly anti-Jewish feelings. The peasants arrested there were not always the only ones involved in inciting to violence, but the reports of these incidents in no way indicate the existence of an organized movement.[12]

The assertion that mysterious messengers were sent from Moscow and St. Petersburg in order to give instructions to the local officials in the Ukraine seems to be refuted by the behavior of many of these officials. First of all, some officials took measures, even energetic and successful ones, to prevent rioting. In some instances the troops went so far as to fire on the mob with the result that there were non-Jewish casualties (see chaps. 3 and 8). Second, in many instances rioters were arrested, tried, convicted, and punished. Great Russians from the interior provinces were among those who suffered this fate; they got no special consideration.[13] Did the officials who took these steps not get the message from Moscow and St. Petersburg, or did they refuse to heed it? Third, if local officials knew in advance about the pogroms, then why did they initially tend to blame this violence on the socialists (see chaps. 10 and 12)?

These questions lead to a whole series of others. If there was a plot, clearly not everyone was in on it. Why not? Perhaps there were strong factions within the government opposed to such a policy. Or perhaps the central government, remaining unified within itself, double-crossed its local representatives in order to cover up the tracks of those really responsible for the pogroms. But why should it do this, if its aim was to exploit the rioting, to channel discontent away from itself, and to increase its support among the people? Why encourage the people to riot, then punish them for doing so? That was surely counterproductive. In addition, the central government, including Ignatiev, initially accepted publicly the explanation that the pogroms were inspired by revolutionary socialists. Did the authorities not realize that such publicity was liable to win sympathy for the revolutionaries from anti-Semites among the people? If some group within the ruling circles planned the pogroms, with some set purpose in mind, it must have been exceptionally dull-witted not to realize from the beginning that there was an explanation much better calculated to serve reactionary and anti-Semitic purposes, namely, the one adopted later, which stressed the antagonism allegedly aroused by Jewish exploitation. This was not a new charge. The delay in picking it up is another indication of the government's initial surprise at the turn of events.

Apart from the "leaders" discussed above, there were bands of ruffians who moved from place to place spreading violence as they went. Everyone agrees that these gangs were composed mainly, though not exclusively, of Great Russians. That they represented some association or organization is highly doubtful. Their presence and their behavior can be explained very well without resorting to that: one merely has to investigate the social and economic conditions in southwestern Russia in 1881.

## Chapter 7

# THE GEOGRAPHICAL PATTERN
# AND SOCIOECONOMIC FACTORS

◆ ◆ ◆

MANY STREAMS FLOWED TOGETHER TO CREATE THE TURBULENCE OF the 1881 pogrom torrent. A careful analysis of the dates and locations of the various pogroms reveals an interesting and rather unexpected pattern. Upon examination of the economic background against which the pogroms took place, this pattern becomes more understandable, and a picture of the people responsible for it emerges.

Russia was undergoing significant economic changes. In the spring of 1881, as in previous years, the Ukraine acted like a magnet, attracting unemployed laborers from all over the empire, and especially from the central region. But economic conditions that year were especially difficult. Great Russians from the interior provinces and local residents found themselves competing for scarce jobs. Both groups of unemployed, as well as those who did have work, inevitably came into contact with Jews, who found themselves concentrated in the western and southwestern regions of the Russian Empire on account of the laws establishing the Pale of Jewish Settlement. The manner in which these groups interacted was important in the spread of the 1881 pogroms.

Also of great importance were the relations between the Jews and their business and professional rivals in the towns, since the rioting almost always moved from towns to villages. In the especially tense atmosphere of the time, eyewitnesses of pogroms, moving from the place to place, spread the news and sparked new rioting, sometimes intentionally, sometimes unwittingly. Railroad workers were especially important in this process. Government officials, when trying to understand the waves of pogroms, tended to ignore the important role played by urban and industrial factors and focused on alleged Jewish harmfulness in the countryside. Why they did this, and the real nature of Jewish-peasant relations, are other important elements in understanding the movement of the 1881 violence. Finally, in order to complete the picture, the resemblance of pogroms occurring in different places must be accounted for.

+ first wave of pogroms, 15–20 April
△ second wave, 21 April–10 May
○ third wave, 30 June–16 August
MINSK
CHERNIGOV
Borzna
Konotop
Nezhin
Ichnia
Romny
VOLYNIA
Brovary
Kiev
Berezan'
Vasil'kov
Pereiaslav
Lubny
Borispol'
Volochisk
Kanev
POLTAVA
Smela
Dnieper R.
KIEV
Cherkasy
Zhmerinka
Lozovaia
Novomoskovsk
PODOLIA
Znamenka
Aleksandriia
Pavlograd
Elisavetgrad
EKATERINOSLAV
Golta
Aleksandrovsk
Anan'ev
KHERSON
Orekhov
Mariupol
Berezovka
Kishinev
Tiraspol
Nikolaev
Berdiansk
Melitopol'
Kherson
Maiaki
TAVRIDA
Odessa
BESSARABIA
Azov Sea
BLACK
SEA


MAP 2. *Sites of Pogroms, 1881*

The pogroms may be envisioned as having occurred in several waves. The individual incidents ranged from relatively insignificant disturbances, lasting only a couple of hours, to major violence, lasting whole days. The former involved the smashing of windows in Jewish homes and stealing liquor from Jewish taverns; the latter included assault and battery, rape, and massive plundering and destruction of private and business property.

As a rule, the pogroms moved from large towns and townlets to nearby villages, and along railroad lines, major highways, and rivers to towns and villages farther away. The table below illustrates this point. (The dates when pogroms began in each place are given in parentheses.)

Railroad Connections
Elizavetgrad (15 April)—Aleksandriia (19 April)
Anan'ev (26 April)—Tiraspol' (27 April)
Kiev (26 April)—Brovary (27 April)—Konotop (27 April)
Kiev (26 April)—Zhmerinka (27 April)
Aleksandrovsk (1 May)—Orekhov (4 May)—Berdiansk (5 May)
Aleksandrovsk (1 May)—Mariupol' (7 May)

Road Connections
Kiev (26 April)—Vasil'kov (27 April)
Kiev (26 April)—Zhitomir (29 April)

River Connection
Kiev (26 April)—Kanev (27 April)—Smela (3 May)—Cherkasy (29 April)

The movement was continuous in time and space. It was sporadic as well. That is, rioting would occur in a large town and for some days thereafter spread to adjacent areas. Then it would stop for several days or even weeks, only to break out again in another large town, generally quite a distance from the previous area of action, and spread from there. For example, between *15 and 21 April* pogroms occurred in and around Elizavetgrad, Aleksandriia, Anan'ev, and Kishinev. Between *26 April and 10 May* pogroms occurred in and around Kiev, Brovary, Konotop, Romny, Vasil'-kov, Zhmerinka, Volochisk, Kanev, Smela, Cherkasy, Novomoskovsk, Pavlograd, Anan'ev, Tiraspol', Nikolaev, Melitopol', Orekhov, Aleksandrovsk, Mariupol', Berdiansk, Kherson, Maiaki, and Odessa. The Pereiaslav area was struck on *30 June* and, along with Berezan', again on *12– 14 July*. The Nezhin and Borzna areas were hit off and on between *15 July and 16 August*. Warsaw, Poland, suffered a pogrom on *Christmas Day 1881*. All of these places were either large towns or *uezds*—that is, district administrative centers—or large *mestechki*—that is, settlements having markets and fairs that gave them an urban character. None of the places named had a population of less than three thousand; the vast majority had more than twelve thousand.[1] From this list we can see that it is more accurate to speak of several waves of pogroms rather than a single wave.

Knowledge of the identity of those who spread the rioting would help explain this pattern. The pattern in which the disorders moved from place to place does not reveal with any certainty whether the persons involved were ideologues and paid agents acting according to some master plan or individuals acting spontaneously on their own initiative. Nevertheless, it does strongly suggest the latter possibility rather than the former. If the pogroms had been planned, one might have expected either simultaneous outbreaks in many farflung places[2] or a greater element of continuity, with the wave moving from one place to another close by, encompassing an ever larger contiguous area, with no breaks in the timing. Neither of these patterns was followed. The mixture of continuity and disjunction in the actual occurrence of the pogroms would seem, then, to indicate an overall spontaneous character rather than a calculated plan.

Persons from several groups in Russian society were among those who spread and incited pogroms. None of them need have had any connection with a conspiratorial center.

As I noted in chapter 1, after the abolition of serfdom in 1861, the southern and southwestern regions of the Russian Empire entered a period of steady economic growth. Both industrial and agricultural capitalism developed rapidly. Between the 1860s and the 1890s, the number of industrial enterprises more than doubled, and the value of their output increased more than six times. New towns and industrial townlets appeared, and the urban population more than doubled. An industrial proletariat emerged: the number of workers more than quadrupled.[3]

The reader will recall that coal and iron ore mining, relying heavily on Western European capital and technology, accounted for much of the industrial growth in the southern and southwestern regions. Agricultural machinery too was supplied from these regions to all of Russia. However, even on the eve of World War I, the area remained predominantly a farming region, with the manufacture of foodstuffs the leading branch of industry.[4]

It is important to remember that from the 1860s the construction of new railroads connected this territory with both the Black Sea and the interior of the empire, making possible the movement of grain in both directions. At the same time, industrialization and urbanization in Western Europe as well as within Russia were increasing the demand for marketable foodstuffs. Local farmers responded to these capitalist incentives. They spread the cultivation of grain in particular across the steppes and began to use agricultural machinery and hired laborers extensively. For a while the Ukraine, New Russia, and the southwest region became the granary of Europe, the leading exporter of wheat and barley.[5]

Also after 1861, as I pointed out earlier, peasants all over Russia found their land allotments too small and their living expenses, taxes, and financial obligations too high. Therefore, if they could not rent or buy more land, they often left home and sought work as day laborers in the fields of others or in towns, construction sites, river ports, sea ports, and factories. Most worked at unskilled, occasional jobs, often simply as porters, lackeys, coachmen, and so on; few found permanent positions. Still, tens of thousands of Great Russians from the central and northeast provinces were continually attracted to the relatively richer southern and southwestern regions. During the spring it was natural and normal for even greater numbers than during the rest of the year to arrive, since agricultural, construction, and transportation work—as a rule—then became readily available.

New arrivals were especially numerous in the spring of 1881, since an industrial depression, which had begun during the preceding winter, threw many factory hands in St. Petersburg and Moscow out of work. These outsiders supplemented local peasants who were also seeking employment away from home. The situation was especially difficult in 1880–81 because of local crop failures that led to near-famine conditions. No one had much hope of finding gainful employment. Outsiders came nevertheless, tending, of course, to wander from place to place as they looked for work. Some of them must have been organized into *artels,* the traditional Russian associations of independent laborers and artisans who banded together for collective work and shared earnings. These men naturally traveled in groups, which can explain any appearance of organization in their activities without their necessarily having been involved in a larger conspiracy.[6]

Conspiracy theorists sometimes admit these facts, but they interpret them merely as evidence of the fuel available to make pogroms. The spark to light this fuel, they believe, had to come from some organized body.[7] Such an explanation, however, is superfluous.

Let us review the situation in March—April 1881. The tsar had just been assassinated, and the people were perplexed, uncertain about the future. Rumors about anticipated anti-Jewish rioting were rife. Large numbers of unemployed were to be found in the big towns. Many of these were moving from place to place to seek work; many were strangers far from home.

The Great Russian workers in particular, being far from home, undoubtedly felt a strong sense of rootlessness, alienation, and anonymity. Many must have lost all hope in their search for employment. They were hungry, homeless, embittered, and given to occasional acts of thievery and assault. Cases are on record of unemployed laborers in this region during this period committing crimes simply in order to be thrown into jail, where they were at least guaranteed something to eat. A pogrom had the advantage that it promised, as a bare minimum, a bellyful of vodka. All of this must be viewed alongside the rowdiness and inclination to rough living characteristic of these men. Any adventure, any outlet, was likely to be eagerly seized upon.[8]

The Great Russian unemployed were not alone. Some of the local unemployed were likewise rowdy, rough, and away from home. They too, of course, were affected by the generally confused, uncertain, and tense atmosphere of the time. They may not have felt as rootless, alienated, and anonymous as the Great Russians, but their hopes of finding employment were just as dim. Furthermore, the Ukrainians had a long tradition of violent antagonism to the Jews to spur them on. In the past it had manifested itself in the Khmelnitski massacres of 1648–49 and in the murderous activities of the *Haydamaky* in the eighteenth century, especially from 1734 to the large-scale massacres in 1768. In both instances the Jews had been singled out for particularly cruel treatment. The perpetrators of this anti-Jewish violence were admired as national heroes in the popular oral tradition (for example, folksongs were dedicated to them) and in literature (for example, T. Shevchenko's *Haydamaky* of 1841).

Many urban natives of the southwestern region were also quite embittered. Some resented their dependence on Jews as employers, moneylenders, and suppliers of articles of basic necessity (including liquor).[9] Others felt intensely the pressure of Jewish business and professional competition, which had grown as more and more Jews took advantage of the opportunities offered by the expanding Russian economy during the reign of Alexander II.

The great mass of Jews remained extremely impoverished. Indeed, Russia's economic development, especially the rapid expansion of the railroads, affected some large groups in the Jewish population quite negatively (for example, small craftsmen lost business to factory-produced goods, and wagoners, porters, and innkeepers were made superfluous as more and more people and goods traveled by train), thereby intensifying the overall pauperization of the Jewish masses. The number of Jews who had lately become well-to-do businessmen, industrialists, and professionals was a very small fraction of the whole Jewish population. The degree of Jewish success also varied from place to place. Still, in recent years the Jews, especially in the towns, had become more economically visible than ever, since some of them were establishing new stores, shops, offices, warehouses, banks, mills, and factories, wearing fine clothes and jewelry, and buying and building fancy new homes.

Economic and professional rivalry perhaps accounts for the relatively large number of artisans who participated in the urban riots[10] and for the passivity or approval with which the better-off classes looked on. The Jews' more well-to-do business competitors, merchants, industrialists, and professional people, while not participating actively in the riots themselves, may have contributed by spreading rumors, reading anti-Semitic newspaper articles aloud, and even assisting in the impromptu organizing of rioters on the spot (for example, dividing them up into groups and sending them to different parts of town). One did not have to belong to any secret organization in order to undertake such activity.[11]

The officially appointed municipal rabbi of Elizavetgrad charged that the Jews' competitors from the trading and professional classes were the main inciters to rioting in the locality for which he had responsibility. The governor of Poltava *guberniia* strongly implied that the pogrom in Lubny (27 July 1881) was caused by the Jews' business competitors. He noted that the Jews there were too few to subjugate the local population economically or to be widely resented as exploiters; their presence was inconvenient only to the local artisans and small traders. These evidently incited the rather well-to-do workers who were the main participants in the rioting.[12] Prince P. P. Demidov San Donato, a liberally inclined contemporary student of the Jewish question who moved in high government circles, was convinced that "if the enmity of the trading and industrial classes toward the Jews be not the chief cause of the anti-Jewish movement in towns, in any case it affords the movement considerable moral support."[13]

The business competitors of the Jews were not active in spreading the pogroms from place to place, but other groups were. Many contemporary reports confirm that outsiders, mainly Great Russians, came from places where pogroms had recently occurred or, in some instances, were still in progress. They spread news of the rioting, in which they themselves may have participated, and in some cases actively encouraged the local people to imitate their tempestuous fellow countrymen.[14]

Other contemporary reports mention natives of different places returning home after business trips, quests for outside employment, visits to relatives, pilgrimages (especially to Kiev), and so on, and spreading the word about pogroms. The diffusion of rioting from large towns to nearby villages usually followed this pattern. Local peasants who had been in town rushed home with the exciting news. The local population had already been agitated by the widespread rumors about a tsarist *ukaz* ordering attacks on the Jews, but the rumors alone were seldom enough to provoke violence. Eyewitness reports of rioting elsewhere, especially if they included allegations that officials had failed on purpose to suppress the violence immediately, so that the rumor of an *ukaz* seemed to be true, and especially if the news was brought home by returning natives, often gave just the fillip the village population needed in order to push it over into violence.[15]

Apart from these factors, in the psychological atmosphere existing in the spring and summer of 1881, any small tavern brawl could lead to widespread violence. Disputes over unpaid bills, or the amount of liquor served or consumed, or broken glasses and dishes, were common at all times. Similar clashes in the marketplace were equally common and equally dangerous. There is no need to assume, as conspiracy theorists do, that organizers paid agents to start the brawls that led to pogroms.[16] The person whose shouts about a Jewish tavernkeeper beating him led to the outbreak of the Elizavetgrad pogrom was reportedly an half-idiot townsman, well-known locally as a fool.[17] In many cases officials trying to prevent the outbreak of rioting warned the Jews, or asked them, to avoid even the most insignificant quarrel.[18]

Among the most active pogrom makers were railroad workmen.[19] They, of course, had ready access to travel by rail, so they could easily spread the word about pogroms in different places and thereby encourage others to join in the excesses. In some cases, not only the men actually working on the trains could move about, but even machine-shop workers had free passes to travel on the lines for which they worked.[20] Thus railroad workers were in a better position than most other groups to travel about expressing their dissatisfaction with existing conditions. In addition, they were sometimes well organized and felt a sense of solidarity among themselves. They were under no serious supervision by the authorities. Most had left their villages and begun working for the railroads only in the previous fifteen years, with the great expansion of the railroad network.

They generally lived in miserable conditions, in shacks and camps near the tracks and stations. Little or nothing was being done to improve their situation.[21]

Government officials at the time noted many of these factors and added that the railroad workers tended to be particularly turbulent and troublesome because the revolutionary socialists had influenced them to some extent. (Other factory workers, especially those in arsenals, were also mentioned in this regard.) Even officials such as Kutaisov, who discounted altogether the direct significance in the pogroms of the revolutionaries, admitted the fact of their influence on the railroad men.[22]

The report of Governor Shostak[23] of Chernigov *guberniia*, dated 16 May 1881 illustrates quite vividly the role of the railroad men in the pogroms. Shostak stated that on the eve of the pogroms in Nezhin *uezd* at the end of April, the local railroad authorities were given a petition signed by a group of railroad machine shop workers who demanded free tickets to travel on the line. Meanwhile a large meeting of the workers was held to discuss this petition. The governor admitted that he had no solid facts but speculated that the question of attacking the Jews may also have been discussed at this meeting. He left open the possibility of outside, socialist, influences. Shostak went on to note that the Kiev and Konotop railroad workers had already received free tickets on the Kursk-Kiev line, which passed through Kiev, Nezhin, and Konotop. Allegedly there was some socialist influence among these workers. More certain was that the Konotop pogrom was begun by railroad machine shop workers, near the railroad station, while the Kiev pogrom was still in progress (27 April). Governor Shostak thought the leaders were probably Konotop workers who had taken part in the Kiev riots and then used their free tickets to hurry home and spread the news. A witness reported that a person in a white cap (*v beloi shapke*) got off the train from Kiev, went to the nearby workshops, and shouted, "Now we'll work in the Kiev fashion." When the riot began, he disappeared in the crowd.[24]

Recall that under the initial impact of the pogroms, coming so soon after the assassination of Alexander II, the new tsar, Alexander III, and his government adopted the view that revolutionaries had caused the disorders. Soon, however, this theory was rejected, and no historians have attempted to revive it. All the evidence indicates that only after the rioting began did the revolutionaries make some hesitant and generally ineffective efforts to encourage and exploit them.[25] So the man in the white hat was almost certainly not a revolutionary. To assume that he was a railroad worker acting more or less spontaneously is at least as plausible as to assume that he was an agent for the government or the Holy Brotherhood.

As for the unemployed who moved from place to place by railroad, they did not necessarily need some secret benefactor to finance their travels, as conspiracy theorists assert. They may have moved along on freight trains as hobos, paying no fares and riding as long as they remained undetected.

Then again, many of those moving along the railroad lines were probably contract laborers, their transportation arranged by the contractors who hired them. It was common in the early spring for the railroads to bring such workers to southwestern Russia packed into freight cars. In the fall the men traveled home the same way.[26]

As elsewhere, the industrial workers in Russia who appeared on the scene during the early stages of their country's modernization process were essentially dislocated and disoriented peasants, struggling to get accustomed to a new lifestyle, that is, struggling to become proletarians, under very severe working and living conditions.[27]

In some places workers made all their purchases at establishments (inns, taverns, food stores, clothing shops) belonging to Jews who lived nearby. Often Jews were suspected of engaging in all kinds of criminal and exploitative activities (theft of passengers' baggage at railroad stations, dealing in stolen goods, carrying on trade, especially in liquor, without a license, paying exceptionally low wages to their factory hands, making them work on religious holidays, and so on). Hence it seemed to many that all their belongings and the fruits of their labor fell unfairly into the hands of these urban swindlers.[28] In the circumstances, many members of Russia's nascent proletariat undoubtedly identified the commercialized and relatively urbanized Jews with urban life in general and urban life with their own miseries. The Jews, then, quite naturally became a major focus for their resentment and hostility. Persons from the ruling circles conspiring to make pogroms were not needed in order to incite the workmen to anti-Jewish violence.

The 1881 pogroms were initially, and perhaps essentially, an urban phenomenon, the result of Russia's accelerating modernization and industrialization process.

There is no basis whatsoever for accusing the rural peasants of having initiated the waves of pogroms: only after the rioting began were the villagers drawn in. Dozens of small settlements experienced anti-Jewish disorders, but invariably as echoes of pogroms that had occurred recently or were still occurring in nearby large towns. Statistics compiled and analyzed by T. S. Fedor indicate that the eight *guberniias* where pogroms occurred (Chernigov, Ekaterinoslav, Kherson, Kiev, Podolia, Poltava, Tavrida, and Volynia) were among the most rapidly urbanizing and industrializing areas in European Russia during the last quarter of the nineteenth century. Relatively high percentages (43–76 percent) of the "persons occupied in manufacturing" were located in cities in five of these *guberniias* (Ekaterinoslav, Kherson, Kiev, Poltava, and Tavrida). In general, Fedor's contentions that much of the industrial growth in Russia took place outside towns and that much of the new urban population engaged in commerce and transportation, do not present any problems for my contention that the pogroms were essentially urban in character and related to the modernization process. The main point is that persons with an agricultural background and peasant value system had become dislocated. The resulting discomfort was felt most intensely in the towns, where the pogroms began. Fedor's findings may be interpreted as indicating that the spread of rioting to villages was connected, at least to some extent, with the large number of persons engaged, more or less as newcomers, in rural manufacturing and cottage industry (*kustar*). However, the influence that the peasants' traditional psychology had on the outbreak of violence must not be ignored. I shall return to this topic below.[29]

A few high government officials at the time noted that pogroms were very rare in villages far away from the urban centers, where, because the authorities were so distant, it would have been easiest to start riots and they would have had the least chance of being suppressed quickly.[30] In other words, the pogroms did not burst forth simply as a spontaneous expression of *peasant* hostility toward the Jews.

Yet for decades prior to 1881 (and for decades thereafter as well) the Jews were regarded by most government officials as much more harmful, and therefore much more likely to arouse hostility, in the villages than in the towns. As soon as the minister of the interior, N. P. Ignatiev, rejected the theory that incitement by revolutionary socialists had caused the pogroms, he immediately adopted the view that the riots were a spontaneous protest against Jewish exploitation, especially in the villages. So pervasive was this view that one of the main means favored by Ignatiev for ending the rioting was the removal of Jews from villages, a measure that completely ignored the urban origins of the waves of pogroms.[31]

How can such blindness on the part of officials be explained? First of all, their orientation was overwhelmingly rural-agricultural rather than urban-commercial-industrial. Officials paid much less attention to the urban classes and the incipient proletariat that was becoming urbanized than to the rural population, the so-called native population (*korennoe naselenie*). They directed almost all their solicitude and concern (not unmixed with paternalistic condescension, and even contempt) toward the peasants, for whom they professed a strong affection.[32] This mind-set naturally blinded all but the most astute and unbiased to the urban character of the pogroms.

An exchange of opinions that took place in the High Commission for the Review of Existing Laws Concerning the Jews in the Empire (1883–88) vividly illustrates this point. The commission's majority, including its chairman, Count K. I. Pahlen, favored the gradual emancipation of the Jews and on some questions took positions uncharacteristic of Russian officialdom.[33] For example, Pahlen and his colleagues pointed out that the 1882 May Laws were a response to the pogroms of 1881–82 and supposedly aimed at removing the conditions for rioting in the future. One provision prohibited Jews from henceforth moving into villages. But since the pogroms had almost all begun in the towns, the commission majority noted, this regulation in no way corresponded to its announced aim; therefore it should be abolished.[34]

The high commission's minority, however, remaining true to tradition, totally ignored the urban origins of the pogroms. To these men, the fact that, of 259 recorded pogroms, 219 had occurred in villages, 4 in Jewish agricultural colonies, and only 36 in towns and townlets was sufficient proof that the riots were essentially a rural phenomenon. The May Law prohibiting more Jews from moving into the villages was justified in the view of the commission's minority, since fewer Jews in rural areas meant less exploitation of peasants, which would presumably reduce tensions and the possibility of more rioting.[35]

Populist revolutionaries had discovered in the previous two decades that the peasants in the villages were, as a rule, peculiarly passive and unlikely to rise up in revolutionary action. This does not mean that the peasants invariably refrained from violence, as government officials were nervously aware. The potential for violence was always present, especially after the assassination of Alexander II. But peasant insurrection in Russia was almost always sporadic, spontaneous, disorderly, and lacking in direction—in a word, anarchistic. If rebellious peasants saw a purpose for themselves, it was usually directed at immediate, narrowly conceived ends, not the establishment of a new regime. Most important of all in the present context, peasant violence was generally unsustained and likely to die down as quickly as it flared up. Patience and submission were readily at hand, able to return quickly and replace sudden outbursts of anger and audacity.[36]

The Marxist analysis and critique of the populists, which only later gained popularity in Russia, was in some ways more sensitive to this reality. The Marxists argued that the urban proletariat, not the village-based peasants, would make the revolution to establish a new order, since the proletariat would be more class-conscious, unified, better organized, and more aware of long-term comprehensive goals. The Marxists, of course, had in mind a mature working class, not the peasants recently become wage laborers who started the pogroms. Nevertheless, the fact that in 1881 rural peasants acted—or reacted—in the wake of urban unrest might not have surprised Marxist thinkers, had there been any, as much as it did others. The populists, however, were as startled as anyone by the outbreak of the pogroms.

The minister of the interior, Ignatiev, and other government officials also expressed surprise at the peasants' sudden aggressiveness, in light of their habitual passivity. In his appeals for anti-Jewish legislation to protect the peasants, Ignatiev labeled the sudden waves of massive peasant violence as uncharacteristic (*stol' nesvoistvennoe russkomu narodu dvizhenie*), and therefore all the more indicative of the peasants' exasperation over Jewish exploitation.[37] It was particularly comforting for Ignatiev, as a monarchist and Slavophile, to stress the passivity of the peasants; it was especially useful for him, as an anti-Semite, to stress their exasperation at the Jews. Still, apart from the hypocricy and hyperbole involved in Ignatiev's formulation, and in spite of the paradox evident to the distant observer aware of the government's constant fear of peasant uprisings, the factors of customary peasant passivity and initial government surprise are data that the historian must take into account when explaining the anti-Jewish violence of 1881.

Whenever contemporary Jews argued for equal rights, they claimed that everyday relations between Jews and peasants were amicable, even quite friendly. It would seem that this claim had some justification, given the numerous cases of local peasants who protected individual Jews and their possessions and who tried, often successfully, to restrain their neighbors from carrying out pogroms,[38] or who, after the rioting ceased, of their own free will returned property they had plundered, expressed their regret over what they had done, and in some cases even offered to compensate the Jews for their losses. Count Kutaisov found that in the Kiev area occasionally "there was revealed among the peasants a remarkable good-naturedness [*dobrodushie*], diametrically opposed to the rage with which they had acted during the disorders." The report added that "it was as if they had given vent to all their accumulated bile, all their anger toward the Jews, and considering their aim reached, did not try to extract any material benefits."[39]

I note that studies of peasant justice (*samosud,* mob or lynch law) in contexts having nothing to do with the Jews contain similar descriptions of peasant frenzy being whipped up by the very act of perpetrating violence against presumed criminals and then being followed by complete calm or remorse.[40]

Though we must now recognize the importance of the urban element in the 1881 pogroms, we must not fail to explain the role of the rural peasantry, which did, after all, participate in the violence in large numbers. My observations about their psychology will also apply to a certain extent to their fellows who had gone looking for work in the towns and factories.[41]

The rural population in the Ukraine was clearly quite ambivalent toward the Jews. To some degree relations were good and mutually beneficial, but at the same time they were marked by mutual suspicion and resentment, and occasionally even outright hatred.

Village Jews were often on quite friendly terms with their neighbors. They bought their produce, transported it to market, made them loans on the security of standing crops or other items, gave them jobs, and supplied them with liquor and manufactured products from the towns. After all, as one historian has noted, "the income of the small trader depended upon the size of his 'permanent' clientele, which in turn depended upon his *interpersonal relations* with his clients," that is, his "ability to meet their regular and extraordinary consumption needs," to purchase their produce, and to extend them credit from one season to the next.[42]

Still, the peasants viewed the Jews as aliens. Their religion, language, food, clothing, and manners were all different, strange, mysterious. The laws of the empire marked the Jews as distinctly inferior by discriminating against them even more than against the peasants themselves. Yet the peasants found that they were often dependent on Jews in many ways, and they naturally resented this. Some felt a vague sense of guilt and resentment about wasting their money on the Jews' liquor. These feelings actually led to action for some peasants, as illustrated by cases reported in the Pale at this time of individuals and even whole villages deciding on their own to abstain from liquor altogether.[43] Furthermore, apart from the normal hostility to tradesmen and merchants (as unproductive,

nonphysical workers) found in every agrarian society, the peasants suspected that the prices the Jews paid for agricultural produce were exceptionally low and that the interest they took on loans, if not the prices they
charged for manufactured products, were exceptionally high. The laws of
economics that dictated the behavior of the Jews did not interest the
peasants. Once aroused to violent action, they may have felt that by
destroying and plundering the Jews' possessions they were merely appro-
priating property that did not rightly belong to the Jews.[44]

As a result of this ambivalence, on the surface relations were generally
calm while underneath there flowed a current of turbulence. The intrusion
of exceptional circumstances could at any time bring this turbulence to
the surface in a wave of violence. Such exceptional circumstances existed
in 1881. A new, unknown tsar had ascended the throne in the wake of
the violent assassination of the "Tsar Liberator," and the peasants were
uncertain whether the new regime would improve or erode their position.
Meanwhile an economic depression and crop failures had worsened the
ordinarily miserable circumstances of the poorer classes. Before Easter a
rash of rumors had broken out; it spread persistently: the tsar had given
orders to beat the Jews because they had participated in the assassination
of Alexander II. Finally, news arrived of pogroms in the towns. The
weather was unseasonably hot; everyone was irritable. Tsarist officials were
overly placid and often incompetent.

The Jews at the time believed the peasants rose up against them only
because of outside agitators. However, one does not have to embrace a
conspiracy theory in order to accept this view. As I have shown, sometimes
the agitation from outside was the work of individuals or small groups;
sometimes it was simply the result of stress and strain created by the
political, social, and economic atmosphere in the spring of 1881.

For decades calm had prevailed. Then it suddenly ended as reverbera-
tions from the surge of violence in the towns reached the countryside. The
pogroms of 1881 spread spontaneously from towns to villages as a rule.
They were carried by migrant workers, railroad men, and homecoming
peasants who were acting under the influence of very difficult economic
circumstances and who were joined, especially in the towns, by business
and professional competitors of the Jews. After billowing up in one or
more places, the rioting moved along, and then died down, only to rise
again at a later date in another area. A relatively small number of towns
and townlets was affected; a relatively large number of villages became
involved. Nevertheless, the pogroms were more the result of Russia's

modernization and industrialization process than of age-old religious and national antagonisms.

Some writers have argued that the pogroms all followed the same pattern, a feature that indicated that they were planned and centrally directed. Commenting on the Warsaw pogrom of 25 December 1881 (New Style), the last one to occur within the empire during that year, the historian S. M. Dubnow had this to say: "It would seem as if the official pogrom ritual did not allow of the slightest modification. The disorders had to proceed in accordance with the established routine."[45]

To a certain extent the various pogroms do bear a resemblance to one another. The same rumors were spread everywhere; the violence generally started in a Jewish tavern; attacks were usually confined to property rather than including persons; strangers often participated; police and officials were often irresolute. Such uniformity may, of course, be explained by the simple sociological principle that similar conditions tend to produce similar behavior patterns. If credible parallels can be drawn, for example, between riots so distant in time and place as those in the United States in 1943 and 1968 (racial riots involving whites and blacks), on the one hand, and those in Russia in 1881 and 1903 (involving Christians and Jews), on the other hand, then surely similarities between the different disorders within Russia would be expected, apart from any centralized planning.[46]

The case of the pogrom that took place on 10 May 1883 in Rostov-on-the-Don supports this assumption. Everyone agrees that the government at that time firmly and unambiguously opposed anti-Jewish rioting. Nevertheless, the Rostov incident occurred, and it followed a pattern very similar to the riots of 1881. A quarrel in a Jewish tavern started the affair; disgruntled outsiders, psychologically ready for pogroms, took part; the authorities and troops, forbidden to use firearms against the mob, were irresolute; Jewish property was plundered and destroyed; military reinforcements, riding horses and wielding whips, finally ended the rioting and arrested the rioters. The 1883 pattern followed that of 1881. If the government changed its policy during these years, as is asserted by those writers who see the hand of the government in the 1881 violence, then this similarity of pattern presents a difficulty. But if there was no shift in policy, if the government always opposed pogroms, then the parallels are less surprising.[47] Meanwhile, recall that the 1881 pogroms spread as participants and news of earlier riots moved from place to place. Such linkage surely contributed to the uniformity of pattern that year.

This uniformity, however, must not be exaggerated, for striking differences in the pogroms can also be noted. Strangers were not present in every instance, and their absence from the villages is particularly notable. The vigor and competence of the authorities on the spot varied from place to place. The amount of damage caused varied as well. Some riots lasted only a few hours, some several days. It should be noted that those that lasted three days began in most cases on the afternoon of the first day; military reinforcements arrived on the second; the last vestiges of the rioting were mopped up on the third. In other cases rioters who thought they were doing something of which the government approved ended the disorders after three days of their own accord, thinking that this was the amount of time fixed in the tsar's *ukaz* for beating the Jews.[48] The seemingly preordained pattern is thus explicable as a result of local circumstances. Central planning need not have played any role.

Uniformity of pattern, then, turns out to be a weak reed indeed when made to support the conspiracy theory of the 1881 pogroms.

*Chapter 8*

# ACTION AND INACTION
# IN DEFENSE OF THE JEWS
◆ ◆ ◆

*Preventive Measures Before the Start of Trouble*

LOCAL OFFICIALS TOOK VIRTUALLY NO MEASURES TO COMBAT THE RU-
mors that announced the existence of a tsarist *ukaz* calling for anti-Jewish
violence. Some conspiracy theorists maintain that the authorities did
nothing to prevent the actual outbreak of rioting or to end it once it had
started. Of these authors, some could not have seen the correspondence
between officials on the subject of the anti-Jewish disorders.[1] Others
ignored it, evidently feeling that it did not reflect what was really happening on the spot.[2] A few historians allege that confidential instructions
were given, orally and in writing, that, if anti-Jewish disorders occurred,
local officials should deal leniently with the rioters.[3] No written instructions of this sort have ever been revealed. And the evidence for oral
instructions is very flimsy. Apart from contemporary popular rumors,[4] it
is based, as far as I can tell, on the testimony of only one witness, P.
Sonin, who, as I have pointed out, was writing from memory, twenty-
eight years after the event, and under the impression made by the more
recent Kishinev and Gomel pogroms of 1903 and the various pogroms of
1904-6.[5]

The documents available concerning the events of 1881 give an entirely different picture of the government's behavior in defense of the
Jews. That picture is kaleidoscopic, revealing officials caught in all kinds
of dilemmas and complications. In contrast to the rumors about officials
receiving instructions to aid and abet anti-Jewish rioting, the sources
demonstrate incontrovertibly that instructions were given to prevent such
violence. A review of the Elizavetgrad pogrom shows how an error in
judgment created the conditions that enabled the first pogrom to take
place, after effective measures had been taken initially. The major pogrom
in Kiev offers a good case history of how decidedly anti-Semitic officials
confronted large-scale violence in a large and important town. Actual

circumstances, and not only anti-Semitic attitudes, operated to determine the behavior of officials and the course of events.

The Russian autocracy of the nineteenth century was famous for its efforts to impose an authoritarian regime on the people of the empire. Yet it is an amazing fact that the police forces available to fight pogroms in 1881 were grossly inadequate in both numbers and training. As a result, it was quite common for civilian officials to call on the military for reinforcements. But this was not such a simple solution as it appears to be at first glance. All kinds of logistic and administrative problems arose when troops were called in to maintain or restore law and order.

The character of Russian officials must, of course, also be taken into consideration. Their anti-Semitism, their degree of competence and skill, the dilemma of having to confront their fellow-Christians in order to protect the alien Jews, the fear that severe repressive measures could evoke antigovernment passions—all these played a role in the behavior of those responsible for keeping the peace.

The central government authorities had to deal with the question of how to handle officials who were guilty of participating in the anti-Jewish violence, whether or not to reward those who successfully prevented such violence, and how to organize aid to the victims of the pogroms.

Besides calling in troops, all kinds of other measures were taken to combat rioting. In this regard the sources reveal that many clergymen and church officials played a much different role in the events of 1881 from that generally attributed to them. Because of the benevolent intervention of Christian churchmen, many Jews remained untouched by the violence. More broadly, a splendid case study is offered by Rostov-on-the-Don, a town where comprehensive measures were taken that effectively defused a very explosive situation.

On the whole, a review of the efforts to maintain law and order in 1881 shows a complex situation over which no one had complete control, not even the government.

As for measures taken before the outbreak of violence, in Kherson *guberniia* the police chiefs of both Elizavetgrad *uezd* (31 March) and Aleksandriia *uezd* (5 April) told the policemen under their supervision to be especially attentive in fulfilling the duties assigned them by law and to take all measures necessary to prevent possible disorders. On 10 April, in view of the heightened possibility of Christian-Jewish clashes during Easter, the governor of Kherson *guberniia,* following instructions issued by the governor-general of the Odessa region, gave similar orders to all the police chiefs in the *guberniia.*[6]

As the first anti-Jewish riot of 1881 was being suppressed, on 17 and 18 April, Minister of the Interior Loris-Melikov gave orders to the governors-general of the Odessa, Kiev, Khar'kov, and Vilna regions to see that strict measures were taken to prevent further disturbances in the Pale area.[7] Ignatiev, on 6 and 23 May, also gave such instructions (see chap. 5, sec. 1, and chaps. 10 and 12).

These directives about taking "all measures necessary to prevent further disorders" were, admittedly, vague. They prescribed no specific actions. In some cases they may have led to no special steps whatsoever. But this was not the case in the town of Elizavetgrad, site of the first pogrom of 1881.

The police force of the town numbered 87, while the population numbered 43,300.[8] As I have noted in earlier chapters, during the first three days of the Easter holiday (celebrated in Russia for a full week), troops were brought in to reinforce the police, and all taverns were closed. Complete calm reigned. On the morning of the fourth day, 15 April, the chief of police, I. P. Bogdanovich, dismissed the troops and allowed taverns to reopen. The pogrom began at 4:00 P.M. in the marketplace when a Jewish tavern keeper was accused of hitting a Christian customer (a fellow known in the town as a simpleton) who had smashed a drinking glass.[9]

The Elizavetgrad police chief made an error in judgment that anyone in his position might have made: The population seemed to be calm. Troops could not be kept in the town indefinitely. Anyway, how would it look on his record if he relied on military reinforcements for too long a period? Were not he and his subordinates competent to control matters? So the police chief let the troops go. Perhaps he was not very eager to protect the Jews, but that possibility does not coincide with what we know about his character as a decent official who treated non-Orthodox Christians and non-Russians very humanely (see above, chap. 3). Thus to see his behavior as part of a plot demands a good deal of imaginative thinking.

Also, it is difficult to see why the police chief would bother to restrain the population, and perhaps risk deterring it altogether, by calling in troops if his intention was to allow (or promote) violence. If he was trying to conceal his connivance in the pogrom, then from whom? European public opinion?—this seems very far-fetched. His superiors?—this answer eliminates the possibility of a governmentally sponsored program of pogroms. The Russian people?—if officials wanted to use pogroms to direct the enmity of the people away from the regime and to stimulate patriotic feelings, then it is puzzling why the government's role was hidden. Even more puzzling is why the government would initially take measures that might sharpen the people's antagonism toward it. Kutaisov stated that the population was indeed irritated that troops were brought in to reinforce the police; some townsmen were insulted that the government did not trust them to maintain law and order.[10]

The major pogrom in Kiev presents similar problems for anyone trying to interpret it as the result of a government-supported intrigue. On 15 March 1881 the governor-general, A. R. Drentel'n, received information from local police officials that some act of public violence was being prepared in Kiev by revolutionary socialists. The governor-general took this information seriously. On 16 March he gave instructions about how troops were to be called, distributed, and used in case of disorders that the police alone were unable to handle. At this date no one seems to have given any thought to the possibility of anti-Jewish riots.[11]

After the Elizavetgrad pogrom special orders were passed down from Minister of the Interior Loris-Melikov to Governor-General Drentel'n to the governor of Kiev, N. P. von Gesse, to the police chiefs of the town of Kiev and of the other districts in the *guberniia*. If riots broke out, the most energetic measures were to be taken to suppress them at the very beginning. Meanwhile the police were to remain alert; any signs indicating the possibility of Christian-Jewish clashes were to be reported immediately up the bureaucratic ladder. Governor von Gesse instructed the police chiefs to give him reports on the mood of the population at least every three days.[12]

An attempt to begin rioting on 23 April was suppressed. Only on 26 April did the full-scale pogrom begin. Rumors had set this date, a Sunday, beforehand. So, when it arrived, officials told the Jews to remain in their homes and not to open their stores and shops. The Jews reportedly responded to this cautious advice with anger, especially since the Russian officials would not promise to end immediately any violence that might erupt.[13] The authorities' noncommittal attitude may have been a spiteful kind of harassment of the Jews, or the officials may simply have wanted to impress upon them the importance of refraining from any provocative behavior.

Though Governor-General Drentel'n in private expressed very hostile feelings toward the Jews, he nevertheless drove his carriage through the streets of Kiev during the riots and urged the population to restore calm and public order. His admonitions were, according to Kutaisov, generally ignored, being drowned out by the mob's "senseless shouts of 'hurrah.' " At best, Drentel'n's exhortations had only a temporary effect: as soon as his carriage pulled away, the rioters resumed their pillaging.[14] According to one report there were instances when the mob threw stones at Drentel'n's carriage,[15] and according to another he was at one point knocked over and trampled upon when, in order to chase away rioters, he entered a store being looted.[16]

The evening after the Kiev pogrom broke out, Drentel'n issued a public declaration to the people of the town. He asked that everyone try to contribute to the restoration of calm, that spectators stay away from riot areas, and that the people refrain from gathering in the streets in crowds. Persons who disobeyed would be dealt with severely. The governor-general also threatened the use of firearms if the rioting resumed, and in fact, one person was killed and two wounded when troops fired on a Kiev mob on Monday, 27 April. According to the town's chief of police, V. D. Novitskii, three or four people were killed or wounded by troops on 28 April, and, when news of these shootings spread through the town, the rioting ceased, not to be renewed. On 3 May, Drentel'n issued a proclamation calling on the people to return property "picked up in the street" during the Kiev pogrom.[17]

Drentel'n's report to Ignatiev, dated 16 May, provides another indication that the governor-general was not plotting pogroms and that he did not think the minister of the interior was doing so either. Otherwise we must assume that the two were communicating in an elaborate code wherein everything meant the opposite of what it said.[18] Drentel'n noted that work in the fields was due to begin in early June and would absorb the simple people's attention. Still, riots could start anew before then: the Christian population was still agitated; and the Jews, getting over their initial panic and seeing themselves under military protection, might once again do things to incite the population against themselves. Consequently, Drentel'n thought it wise to remain on guard by keeping in force all the preventive measures taken previously.[19] As usual, the governor-general did not hide his antipathy to the Jews, but he also made clear his opposition to violent attacks upon their persons and property.

In spite of all his efforts, Drentel'n failed to prevent pogroms in Kiev *guberniia;* and in the town of Kiev the rioting even reached major proportions. If the governor-general was not involved in a plot to allow this development, was he, then, simply incompetent?

Contemporaries as well as later historians were highly critical of the behavior of the troops in the town of Kiev. At worst they were indulgent toward the rioters; at best they were indecisive. By their relative inaction they allowed the disorders to develop to practically unmanageable dimensions.[20]

Kutaisov, after his thorough investigation, gave a highly plausible answer to the critics of Drentel'n and the army: There were not enough troops free in Kiev to appear at the scenes of anti-Jewish rioting, which occurred not because the local authorities were incompetent but because initially it was difficult to foresee the nature of the disorders. No one could foretell that they would be confined to attacks on Jews. The authorities feared something much more serious from the point of view of the government, a fear clearly indicated in the police reports of 15 March. There were numerous military arsenals in Kiev, full of arms. Clearly, it was impossible to leave these without the necessary protection. Furthermore, the town was large and spread out over broken terrain, and it was impossible to cover the whole area with the number of troops available. Another factor was the totally unexpected speed with which the riot spread once it had started. Finally, there was the problem of the large crowds that tended to gather at the riot sites. Many people in these were simply curious spectators who happened to be out for their normal Sunday stroll. In their presence the officers and their troops naturally tended to refrain from acting too severely, especially by using weapons. Otherwise, innocent persons would undoubtedly have been injured, the crowd would have become exasperated, and the disorders, which until then had not seemed so terrible, might have turned into a serious and complete insurrection. Kutaisov concluded that in spite of the military's relative restraint, it still succeeded in preventing the wealthier, central sections of the town from being attacked. Drentel'n's public threat of force if the anti-Jewish rioting continued, issued on the evening after the rioting began, when the character of the disorders had become clear, and the actual use of force the next day were adequate indications to Kutaisov that the governor-general and other local authorities were not disposed to indulgence toward the mob.[21]

Prior to the 1881 pogroms, and even afterward until the 1890s, the disorders Russian troops were called upon to prevent or repress were almost always in the rural areas. There the encounters "appear to have been rituals in which government and peasants abided by mutually understood rules, rather than unpredictable confrontations." "As a general rule, at least until the mid-nineties, the arrival of the army in a recalcitrant village was immediately followed by peasant capitulation."[22] Rarely were the 1881 pogroms in the villages an exception to this rule.

Urban disorders were an entirely different matter, and here the army had very little or no experience. Disturbances in towns tended to be more violent than in the countryside. Perhaps—along with the factors discussed in chapter 7—the relative anonymity of people in the towns and the relative ease with which persons involved in disturbances could lose themselves and find hiding places contributed to the propensity for greater violence. This was in sharp contrast to the villages, where everyone, including officials, knew and could identify everyone else and there was almost nowhere for offenders to conceal themselves. The 1877 regulations on the use of the military domestically, to be discussed below, did not help matters; the only role they envisioned "for the army in popular disturbances was that of crowd control and forcible crowd dispersion—a role which suited the condition of rural, not urban Russia. The framers of the [1877] rules, never dreaming of the ferment which would breed in the Empire's cities and towns, . . . failed to take into account the most elementary features of urban geography. . . . The rules contained no prescription for dealing with snipers or with instances of looting and vandalism spread over scores of city blocks, as the army was shortly to discover."[23]

Not only in Elizavetgrad and Kiev were preventive measures taken before the trouble started. The cases of local officials reporting to their superiors, and on up to the minister of the interior, on measures taken to prevent or suppress pogroms are too numerous to mention individually. Literally dozens of instances are on record. Many urban and village officials, though not all, of course, were able to report upon the success of their actions in preventing pogroms or in keeping the violence down to clashes between individuals. The contemporary Jewish press contained many expressions of thanks to local officials who had stood firmly against pogroms.[24]

## The Police Force and the Army

Of the measures taken the most common was the calling in of troops to reinforce the local police, who almost everywhere were very short of manpower and of low professional quality. Minister of the Interior Loris-Melikov was well aware of the problem. As early as 12 April 1881, he had reported to the tsar the need to unify the functions of the police, which were divided among several different police commands, and to reorganize completely the rural police forces.[25]

Two contemporary accounts dramatically illustrate the situation.[26]

The governor of Poltava *guberniia* reported that in Poltava town 76 police-men served a population of 40,000; and in Kremenchug 50 policemen served a population of 35,000. *Uezd* towns (that is, district administrative centers) in the various *guberniias* averaged 9–16 policemen. Wages were very low, seven to twelve rubles a month, with the result that only very poorly educated persons would join the force to work for such low wages and the turnover rate was very high. Most had no knowledge at all or else very confused conceptions of the obligations of officers of the law. Such a police force was unsatisfactory in times of quiet; it was all the more so in disturbed times. As far as military personnel was concerned, in the *uezd* towns the local garrisons regularly numbered about 70 soldiers, but only about 20 might be available for crowd control, barely enough to guard arsenals, treasury offices, and banks.[27]

The governor of Kherson *guberniia* reported that the local police force did what it could to keep order, but since it was poorly armed, poorly disciplined, and too few in number (see table 6), it did not have the means to be entirely successful. Of the seventeen towns in Kherson *guberniia,* only Kherson and Elizavetgrad had relatively large police forces. Three towns had 12–16 policemen, seven towns had 6–10 policemen, and five towns had 5 policemen each.[28]

Local officials frequently explained their inaction or their failure to prevent or end rioting by the inadequate manpower available to them. Some remained inert because they feared for their own or their subordi-nates' safety in the face of an angry and numerically superior mob.[29]

Not only were there insufficient policemen in Russia. Occasionally concern was expressed that there might not even be enough military forces to go around in order to protect all the places of Jewish habitation that seemed to be threatened. Governor-General Drentel'n stated that the whole Russian army would not suffice if troops were sent to every village and townlet requesting them. Given the army's need to engage in summer

TABLE 6
POLICE AND POPULATION IN KHERSON *Guberniia*, 1881

| Town | Total Population | Jews | Christians | Police |
|------|------------------|------|------------|--------|
| Aleksandriia | 15,980 | 4,794 | 11,186 | 13 |
| Anan'ev | 15,210 | 7,650 | 7,560 | 16 |
| Berislav | 6,847 | 4,525 | 2,322 | 7 |
| Elizavetgrad | 43,299 | 13,000 | 30,299 | 87 |
| Kherson | 49,807 | 23,000 | 26,807 | 138 |

training exercises and its other duties in regard to defending the state from foreign attack, peasant uprisings, and revolutionary socialist assaults, this expression of concern may be taken as genuine and not exclusively a reflection of anti-Semitic prejudice and unwillingness to protect the Jews. Again to cite Drentel'n, he felt that such large numbers of troops were being pulled back from the borders in order to prevent anti-Jewish riots that the position there was really significantly weakened. This fact, he thought, should be kept quiet in order not to make a "disadvantageous impression" within Russia or abroad.[30] I shall return to this issue below.

Meanwhile, the decision to call in troops did not necessarily mean the prevention of, or a quick end to, rioting. Logistical and administrative problems had to be solved, decisions had to be made about when, where, and how to use the troops available to best advantage, how many to use, and how long to keep them in a particular crisis area (so that their continued presence contributed to calming rather than antagonizing the local population)—all these were real problems confronting officials. Apart from inexperience, incompetence, inefficiency, and the personal animosity to Jews that many local officials undoubtedly nourished, even in the best of circumstances, mistaken decisions were likely, and Jews would consequently suffer. There is no need to assume the existence of an anti-Jewish conspiracy in order to explain such occurrences.

Logistic and administrative difficulties were formidable for officials who needed to employ troops to combat pogroms. On 3 October 1877, Tsar Alexander II approved the "Rules Determining the Method for the Call of Troops to Aid the Civil Power." These regulations remained in force until 1906 and have been summarized by William C. Fuller, Jr.

If the civil authorities were short of police they could summon troops [for various duties, including]

. . . to prevent or stop popular disorders. . . .

. . . Governors-general, governors, *gradonachal'niki* (city officials with the rank of governor), *ispravniki* (rural colonels of police), and *politseimeistery* (urban colonels of police) possessed this right [to call for military aid], as did senators conducting a full-scale investigation (*reviziia*) in a particular province. *Ispravniki* and *politseimeistery* could summon troops on their own authority only if help in the execution of a judicial sentence was required.

Although [the framers of this law] attempted to include careful controls over civilian power to call out the troops, the decree of 1877, as was characteristic of much tsarist legislation in this period, contained many ambiguities and allowances for "exceptional circumstances." All civilian officers were, for example, to appeal for troops to the commander of the appropriate military district, or if he was unavailable, to the provincial military chief. But if neither could be reached, the civilians were permitted to contact the closest military commander. Again, requests for aid were supposed to be made in writing, but in "extreme emergency" could be made orally. At any rate, requests were to contain a precise description of the reason for calling out the troops, accompanied by a statement detailing the number of troops required. Civil officials were not themselves to command the troops, but were to transmit their instructions concerning the placement of guard posts and pickets through the military officers present. If, all else having failed, the civil official decided that weapons had to be used, he was to inform the military commander, who was to order armed action entirely in his own manner, but only after the riotous or disobedient crowd had been warned three times by drumbeat or trumpet. The army could, however, resort to force without civilian instruction in self-defense or to protect human life. When the senior army officer on the spot terminated armed action, all authority for the preservation of public order was to revert exclusively to the civilian power. The civilian power was, further, to decide itself when the troops summoned could be released to return to their quarters.

. . . [The] plan had been to satisfy the reasonable security needs of the civilians while shielding the army from unwarranted and burdensome civilian requisitions.[31]

It is clear that many difficulties could arise in the application of the 1877 law—and they did. If soldiers were not on hand before the outbreak of violence, or if plans to bring them in had not been made in advance, precious time passed before their arrival—if they were not already busy elsewhere. The civilian authorities first had to make formal requests for military reinforcements. Then the military commanders had to issue orders. The troops had to be made ready to move. Only then could they be transported to the trouble spot. A further obstacle arose if the troops' destination was far from a railroad line and they had to march there. Meanwhile, local officials sometimes did not know the rules governing the summoning and disposal of troops, or which military district to call them from. Thus more time was lost.[32]

Snags also developed when there was no understanding of the lines of command and the distribution of authority between civilian (police) officials and military commanders. This sometimes accounts for the "suspicious" inactivity of troops on the spot during rioting: they simply received no definite instructions about how to act or what to try to achieve. In some such cases, the police authorities thought their responsibility ended once the troops appeared since these would suppress the riots alone. The military authorities, meanwhile, thought they must await orders from the police officials. As a result, both remained inactive, unless some officer on the spot decided to act in a specific instance.[33]

That this type of problem was not confined to the pogroms of 1881 is indicated by a complaint registered in January 1882 by a general of the Warsaw Military District. According to the general, only civilians were supposed to order the troops into action in cases of civil disorders. However, it happened all too often that civilian officials failed to accompany the soldiers into the streets, so the soldiers became "helpless witnesses to urban criminality." In order to avoid such situations, the general would have liked "military officers to be less dependent on the instructions of the civilians." During the nineteenth century this problem of lines of authority was never solved to everyone's satisfaction.[34] It had surely not been solved in 1881.

Occasionally inexperience and incompetence led to the troops' being divided into units so small that they proved powerless to disperse the mobs. Instead of concentrating the forces available at a few chosen points, the authorities attempted to cover as much ground as possible. In these cases, the undersized companies of soldiers often became mere spectators of the destruction going on, or else they succeeded in chasing the rioters away from one spot only to have them regroup elsewhere.[35] In later years the mistake, as one military source expressed it, of "[fragmenting] half companies into tiny commands of a few men each," or, as another source stated, "[splintering] such military entities as companies and platoons into nondescript, officerless groups of two or three men," continued to be made in dealing with disturbances having nothing whatsoever to do with the Jews.[36]

There is no way of knowing whether any particular Russian official was inefficient and incompetent, or whether his behavior resulted from his reluctance to defend Jews, that is, a more or less conscious decision to act upon anti-Semitic sentiments. In either case, such behavior need not be taken as an indication that the particular official was involved in an anti-Jewish plot. Psychologically and in practice every Russian official found himself in a dilemma. At best, he felt a closer tie of kinship to his fellow Christians than to the Jews; at worst, he despised and hated the latter and viewed them as parasitical aliens. Yet now he was placed in the position of being obligated to defend these outsiders against the native population. A certain reluctance to act was only natural.

Meanwhile, failure to suppress the rioting at its very beginning, or any visible official passivity, especially on the part of troops called in to reinforce the police, served to encourage the notion that the government approved of the pogroms. Contemporaries were fully aware of this. They emphasized in particular the very harmful effect on neighboring communities of news of official inaction in Elizavetgrad and Kiev.[37] Yet many officials feared that too severe repression of a mob could lead it to turn against the government, in the official mind the worst thing that could happen.[38] Again, a certain reluctance to act was only natural.

These problems help account for the fact that sometimes troops were forbidden to use their arms against anti-Jewish mobs, while at other times they did fire, even wounding and killing some persons.[39]

Greater perspective on the problems described above is gained if one notes the attitude of the military authorities toward using the army to repress popular uprisings in the years after 1881, as troops were called upon to act against the civilian population more and more often. The minister of war generally resisted civilian calls for military intervention domestically. For example, he rejected a plan that was proposed by the minister of the interior, Tolstoi, in 1882 to redeploy troops in various places, particularly in the Pale, to prevent workers from rioting and to forestall pogroms. In the view of the military, the garrisoning of the army must be based upon strategic principles, that is, the danger of war, rather than internal security needs. There were no units to spare for the control of civilians; if necessary, the industrial interests should hire their own police forces. Most important of all, it was felt that the adoption of Tolstoi's plan would in practice entail the severe disruption or termination of the troops' training exercises. As the Kiev district military commander argued on this occasion, "to abstain from training troops in peacetime, on the mere supposition that disorders might occur [cannot be agreed to] by any state which is concerned with the military readiness of its forces in the event of a clash with an enemy."[40]

While conceding that the army had a role to play in helping contain and repress civilian discontent, military men complained more and more as the century wore on that civilians were summoning troops without reason—thereby disrupting training and military preparedness—and that they did not appreciate the true function of the army. There were other complaints as well. Police duties were considered to be "somehow 'dishonorable' or unworthy of the army." Too often soldiers were not allowed to resort to force, so the mobs eventually lost their fear of them. Also, troops used for crowd control were especially susceptible to demoralization, especially in cases when they were forced to use their arms or when, in order to avoid bloodshed, they were forced to retreat.[41]

The civilian authorities, meanwhile, had very real security needs in situations where their finances, powers, and resources were indeed limited. Still, they were the ones who had ultimate responsibility for maintaining law and order in Russia. The army, for its part, tried to persuade "the other ministries, especially those of the Interior and Justice, to hire more policemen, or to create their own special police forces." In sum, as William C. Fuller, Jr. has noted:

> it was in the traditional interest of civilians to use as many troops as necessary, even more than necessary, to stabilize the Empire, just as it was in the professional interest of the army to extricate the troops, insofar as possible, from this very kind of service. The conflicts which resulted from this tug of war were not unimportant episodes in a history of civil-military cooperation and mutual respect, for the conflicts subtly changed the way in which civilians and soldiers related to each other in tsarist Russia.[42]

Those instances in 1881 when local officials actively participated in rioting,[43] and the responses of the higher authorities to these incidents, can also be understood without resorting to a conspiracy theory. Some officials, like Ignatiev, were inclined to give official offenders light punishments. Others favored very strict penalties. Still others called for awards to be given to those officers on the spot who were particularly successful in preventing or ending pogroms.[44] Tsar Alexander III's reaction to petitions for such awards reveals quite vividly the problem that officials faced. The tsar answered, "If we allow these rewards, then immediately, from all sides, we will receive similar requests. Yet I find the occasion too deplorable (*a povod ia nakhozhu slishkom priskorbnym*)." In the end, though, Alexander agreed that a number of awards should be made.[45]

## Financial Assistance and Other Measures Taken by the Authorities

The ambivalence of officials about caring for Russia's Jewish population is similarly manifest in their implementation of another measure that could have served to stem the tide of anti-Jewish rumors and passions. This was the matter of financial assistance to pogrom victims. Such aid, whether given directly by the government or raised by private donations, with adequate publicity could have had the moral effect of demonstrating official sympathy for those who had suffered and official condemnation of anti-Jewish violence. Some conspiracy theorists mistakenly claim that no public assistance was given or even allowed to be given to pogrom victims and took this as a sign of governmental complicity in the anti-Jewish movement.[46] The documents, however, reveal a rather more complex situation.

The governor-general of the Odessa region, Dondukov-Korsakov, shared the customary prejudices against the Jews and their economic activities and railed against them at length in his reports. He viewed them as supremely crafty businessmen, capable of extracting profit from any situation, even one apparently disastrous to themselves. On 29 April 1881 the governor-general claimed to have information about a number of big Jewish tradesmen in Elizavetgrad who intended to declare themselves bankrupt. They would then submit a petition for a large loan from the State Bank, ostensibly in order to keep the local bank from folding. The loan, however, would in fact greatly exceed the losses suffered by all the wealthy Jews of the town. Indeed, the bulk of the damage done in Elizavetgrad was done to the poor Jews. The governor-general therefore concluded that claims about the amount of Jewish losses were greatly exaggerated. They could be made good by the municipal administration and the local wealthy Jews, and there was no need for widely publicized outside assistance. Governor-General Dondukov-Korsakov was only one of many Russian officials who thought the Jews exaggerated the amount of their losses. Others were Count Kutaisov, Governor-General Drentel'n, Governor Durnovo of Ekaterinoslav, a town *duma* (council) commission in Elizavetgrad, the mayor of the town of Kiev, and a special commission there.[47]

The Jews' calls for help in all directions, meanwhile, led Baron Horace Guenzburg, president of the Jewish community in St. Petersburg, to ask the government for permission to send five thousand rubles by way of the *guberniia* administration in order to meet the primary needs of indigent Jews ruined in Elizavetgrad. And the Odessa Jewish Society of Shop Assistants (*prikashchiki*) proposed to call a meeting in order to raise more money for aid to the Elizavetgrad pogrom victims. However, Dondukov-Korsakov reported that he would allow neither proposal. He told Guenzburg to deal directly with the town board or with representatives of the Jewish community in Elizavetgrad. And he told the shop assistants' society not to get involved, since this matter was not among the subjects that, according to its charter, it was allowed to discuss.[48]

As a matter of fact, action had already been taken to assist Elizavetgrad Jews. And it had been initiated by the governor of Kherson *guberniia*, Erdeli, who was under the jurisdiction of the governor-general of the Odessa region, Dondukov-Korsakov. On 17 April, as soon as he arrived in the stricken town, the governor met with the town *duma* in order to discuss charity measures for indigent Jewish victims. The governor instructed the *duma* to determine the amount of the Jews' losses and to organize charitable activities immediately. The town, working through a specially established Jewish committee, assigned 1,000 rubles for a start, mainly to supply food. In the end over 160,000 rubles, obtained from donations, were distributed.[49]

Meanwhile, the same Governor Erdeli allowed a public committee to be established in Elizavetgrad to help the families of needy non-Jews arrested on suspicion of participating in the rioting. The people, of course, got the impression that the government would not only not punish those arrested but would even reward their families.[50]

In May, Governor-General Dondukov-Korsakov saw to it that Jewish agricultural colonists in Ekaterinoslav *guberniia* received governmental assistance after a peasant attack ruined their properties. Other places as well reported the establishment of special committees to collect donations for the pogrom victims.[51]

This motley record can be explained by the conflicting feelings and obligations that Russian officials experienced when they found themselves having to protect Jews.

In addition to calling in troops and seeing to financial assistance for pogrom victims, other measures were instituted to combat anti-Jewish violence. In numerous places night patrols were initiated before rioting began; taverns were closed; Jews were warned to refrain from even the least provocative behavior. After the spate of pogroms got under way, officials took other measures. They sometimes tried to reason with the mobs: some told the people that the pogrom agitation was of a seditious character; others explained the ridiculousness of the anti-Jewish rumors, the criminality and punishability of attacking the Jews, and the bad economic consequences that would result. Clergymen, noblemen, *zemstvo* members, and other local notables, responding to requests by officials, also admonished the people to remain calm. Rumormongers and inciters were arrested. Posters calling on the people to beat the Jews were removed by order of the authorities. The passports of persons residing in hotels, inns, and boarding houses were checked, and anyone who lacked a passport, or who was considered suspicious or a threat to public tranquility, Jew or non-Jew, was expelled. Large gatherings on the streets were forbidden, and people were warned not to stand about as spectators if rioting began, because it hindered the police and was dangerous if physical force had to be used against the rioters. In a few instances troops immediately flogged arrested rioters, both as a punishment and as a deterrent, and then released them.

That the sources mention the clergy a number of times as having assisted in combatting pogroms is particularly interesting in light of the prevailing assumption that churchmen were the worst enemies of the Jews among the Christian population and eager to provoke violence against them.[52]

Among officials who, after 15 April, requested churchmen to preach against the pogroms were Governor-General Drentel'n and the governors of Chernigov, Ekaterinoslav, Kiev, and Tavrida *guberniias*.[53] The governor of Chernigov *guberniia* thought the clergy should explain to the people that any violence was against the Christian religion and, in addition to being a serious crime before the law, was a grave sin before God. The governor of Tavrida *guberniia,* in a letter to the local clergy, stated that the "Christian-Orthodox people are persecuting people guilty of nothing [*khristiane-pravoslavnye liudi presleduiut ni chem ne vinovatykh liudei*]." On 3 June 1881, Ignatiev instructed the governors to enlist the aid of churchmen in combatting false rumors in the villages that might lead to violence, whether against Jews or otherwise.[54] That same month, the director general of the Holy Synod, K. P. Pobedonostsev, who was particularly fearful that the pogroms might turn against the government, had a sermon drafted that warned against further disorders. The sermon was to be read in all churches.[55]

The clergy did not always respond positively to appeals for assistance from the authorities, and many churchmen looked upon the anti-Jewish violence with indifference, if not emphatic approval. Nevertheless, in April 1882, by decree of the Holy Synod, with Pobedonostsev at its head, thirty-two churchmen were awarded decorations for outstanding service in the suppression of anti-Jewish rioting.[56]

After 15 April some officials posted public proclamations explaining the falsity of the rumor of an anti-Jewish *ukaz,* the illegality and punishability of the pogroms, and their harmfulness to the state and the economy. Typical was the proclamation, posted on 28–30 April, of Governor Bil'basov of Poltava, who himself was not favorably disposed toward the Jews. Nevertheless, he felt a grave responsibility, he said, to prevent any violence in the streets. He thought that a clear declaration on his part would be believed over the pogrom rumors and that it would be very conducive to restoring calm. So he proclaimed that: Any arbitrariness, disorderly conduct, or violence would be strictly prosecuted. The Jews, just like

Orthodox Russians, were subjects of the tsar and enjoyed equally the protection of the laws of the empire. Attacks on Jews would be prosecuted just as if they were attacks on Orthodox Christians. The government's measures were intended to promote harmony among the population, to protect the safety and calm of each and all, and to allow everyone to be peacefully occupied in his honest labor, without fear for his property. Therefore, decisive measures would be taken to suppress any disorders.[57]

On 27 April 1881 someone in Kiev sent a message to the director of the Department of State Police. The document as printed gives no indication about who wrote it; the author may have been Governor-General Drentel'n. The writer claimed that, given the present mood of the population, newspaper articles dealing with the anti-Jewish riots occurring in various places were dangerous. By stimulating religious hostility and the thirst for plunder they served to increase the excitement and irritation of the people, who were already aroused by rumors of anticipated, legally approved assaults on the Jews. Consequently, the author of this document suggested, private newspapers should be restricted to reprinting official government announcements about the riots.[58]

It seems that a general measure to this effect was undertaken only in late March or April 1882, soon after the exceptionally bloody pogrom that took place in Balta. At that time the official publication of the Ministry of the Interior, *Pravitel'stvennyi Vestnik,* lectured the Russian press on its responsibilities, asserting that the task of the press was to calm the public, rather than to inflame it by the circulation of unfounded rumors and unreliable information. The paper also announced a regulation banning any account of a pogrom that had not appeared first on its pages. It pledged that "from now on it [the newspaper] would accurately report all cases of 'Jewish disorders' in accordance with the official information received from the governors."[59]

Referring to this last statement, one conspiracy theory historian claimed that it "clearly implied that the government knew beforehand of the imminence of new pogroms."[60] A different interpretation is, however, quite possible. To be sure, the newspaper's statements constituted an indirect admission of the government's inability to promise an end to the rioting. But they do not necessarily reveal any anti-Jewish designs on the part of the regime. Most likely, the government's announcement was intended to be what it purported to be, namely, a preventive measure, along the lines of the suggestion made by the individual from Kiev mentioned above. Meanwhile, at least one responsible official had enacted such a program as early as March 1881. The provisional governor-general

of the Odessa region ordered the chairman of the local censorship committee to take measures to prevent the appearance of articles in the local press
that aroused antagonism between Christians and Jews.[61]

A most vivid insight into antipogrom measures taken prior to 15 April
is given by the police chief of Rostov-on-the-Don, Nordberg, in two
reports (dated 4 and 10 April 1881) to his superior, Governor I. N.
Durnovo of Ekaterinoslav. On 31 March, when Nordberg returned to
Rostov from a vacation, he was informed about dangerous rumors spreading in the town. Unskilled workers were allegedly preparing to assault
students at the local real school (high school), as well as local Jews, during
Easter, as punishment for the participation of a student and a Jewish
woman in the assassination of Alexander II.

Nordberg immediately took measures to verify these reports and reveal
the cause of their appearance. He sent plainclothes policemen into hotels,
boardinghouses, and taverns to gather information. During three days of
investigations it was found that rumors were indeed spreading among the
workers. But most people tended to view them as just talk, though they
did not rule out altogether the possibility of something happening. The
original source of the gossip was not uncovered by the investigation.
Nordberg speculated that if some specific group was responsible, it was
probably the unemployed unskilled workers then present in large numbers
in Rostov. These laborers suffered greatly from the current exceptionally
high cost of living and were not particularly averse to violence in the
streets. Shaken by the recent murder of the tsar, they were easy prey to
agitators, who might have been the generally undisciplined factory and
railroad workers of the area. The police chief stated in both his reports
that he did not think a riot would really occur. He thought the local
Christian citizens of the well-to-do classes were more worried than the
situation warranted.

These views of Police Chief Nordberg probably reflected the attitude
of most Russian officials of the time. But this man did not rest content with
such conclusions. Assuming that energetic preventive measures would not
be superfluous—they might encourage the whole population to calm
down—Nordberg acted, purposefully and with skill. In this he differed
from many of his contemporaries.

The poorest unemployed were given jobs cleaning and paving the
streets and clearing an area to make a public square. The capital to finance
the project was obtained from donations and the municipal treasury. The
aim was to allow the workers to earn enough money so that they would
not be threatened by starvation, at least until work in the fields and on

the river became available. In addition, free dining rooms were established during Easter week. Because of the prevailing mood, Jews donated much money to this project. Both uniformed and plainclothes police were instructed to keep an eye on hotels, taverns, and all gathering places of workers, to identify nonlocal people, and to notice if they acted suspiciously. Extra troops were brought in during the holidays to reinforce the local garrison and the local police and were instructed to make extra patrols through the town and to be on standby in case of need. On the first three days of Easter, all taverns were closed until the afternoon.[62]

Early in May, after the wave of pogroms had already begun elsewhere, more measures were taken in Rostov at the suggestion of local Christian citizens and with the approval of Durnovo, the governor of Ekaterinoslav. With the help of the citizens, a census of all workers in the town was conducted. A citizen supervisor was appointed over each factory, shop, mill, or other establishment having numerous employees. Announcements were made that if violence broke out, the workers were obligated to appear at their place of work immediately; their absence would be considered proof of their participation in the rioting. Preparations were also made so that, if necessary, workers who opposed the violence could be used against the mob. Meanwhile, in order to assure the availability of such antipogrom workers, officials and citizens went around to the factories to explain that ruining the Jews would disrupt all trade and industrial relations. This would probably lead to the ruin of many Christian employers, which would in turn leave their workers without jobs.[63]

All the elements that would seem to promote public disorder were present in Rostov. It was a large port city and a trading and industrial center.[64] Many strangers were present, looking for work, impoverished, embittered, restless, and ready for a measure of wild fun and plunder. Rumors about anticipated pogroms were spread, and, later, news of pogroms in other places added to the agitated mood. Yet thanks to the measures taken by the authorities, no rioting occurred in Rostov in 1881 or 1882.

In spite of the proclamation condemning pogroms issued by Governor Bil'basov of Poltava, the *guberniia* was struck by pogroms. In May, Governor-General Totleben of the Vilna region and Governor I. N. Durnovo of Ekaterinoslav, both of whom may have held views quite hostile to the Jews, issued proclamations similar to Bil'basov's.[65] Yet no pogroms took place in the whole Vilna region; but they did occur in Ekaterinoslav *guberniia*.

These cases demonstrate not only official opposition to the pogroms, but also the fact that taking measures to prevent riots was not always a guarantee against violence. Contrary examples abound throughout the sources—the measures taken were sometimes successful in preventing riots, and at other times they failed.

The government was not free to turn the tap of violence on and off at will, as some conspiracy theorists claim.[66] It simply was not powerful enough or competent enough to exercise such control over the population at large or even over its own officials. Some of these were more anti-Semitic than others, and some were more competent, imaginative, and energetic, than others. There is no evidence that the occurrence or absence of pogroms depended upon participation or nonparticipation of government officials in an organized plot. Rather, the officials' behavior and their success or failure in preventing pogroms were determined by the degree to which each one, especially on the local level, fell under the influence of his own anti-Semitic feelings and by the degree of his administrative-executive competence.

*Chapter 9*

# PUNISHING THE RIOTERS

◆ ◆ ◆

THE PUNISHMENTS METED OUT TO RIOTERS DURING AND AFTER THE
1881 pogroms are another possible index of the government's intentions.
At first sight, given the circumstances, the penalties appear to have been
exceptionally light in most cases. Relatively few persons were arrested,
and many were released before being brought to trial. According to one
report, a total of 3,675 persons were arrested, but only 2,359 were
brought to trial. Precise figures for the different towns and villages are
unavailable. In Elizavetgrad, 600 were reportedly arrested, in Kiev, about
1,400, in Odessa, 1,000.[1] In most cases, only if the behavior of the
accused was extreme (especially if they disobeyed too blatantly or physically attacked the authorities or the troops), and only if the evidence
against them was thorough and unequivocal, were they actually subjected
to some punishment. With rare exceptions this ranged from several
months to one year in prison. Occasionally offenders were flogged. Jews
who tried to organize themselves for self-defense were also arrested and
penalized. Persons who returned stolen and plundered goods voluntarily
were granted immunity from prosecution. Furthermore, Jews were warned
against, and non-Jews discouraged from, concluding private agreements
whereby the latter would recompense the former for destroyed property
in return for a promise that no legal proceedings would be begun in the
matter. Officials told the Christians, generally peasants, that they would
have to pay only if they were convicted in court on the basis of clear
evidence regarding the amount of the damage done.[2]

The mass of people at the time must have interpreted the authorities'
noticeable leniency in regard to the judicial aspect of the pogroms as a
sign of approval. To be sure, some rioters were prosecuted. But that was
probably just for show, just to let people know who was still the boss.
No one would suffer too much. People must have felt that, after all, the
mob was only doing the job set out for it by the government. Writers
who see a plot behind the pogroms generally agree with this view: The
leniency of the courts was intentional. There would have been no sense in

145

punishing the people severely when they were only doing the dirty work expected of them. Also, if the judicial inquiries were too thorough, then many officials and persons close to the ruling circles might be implicated.

In the summer of 1882, when cases arising out of the pogroms of that year were tried, the courts finally began to impose severe penalties. By then, though, according to conspiracy theorists, the government's policy had changed: anti-Jewish riots were no longer necessary. And the new minister of the interior, D. A. Tolstoi, who replaced the more viciously anti-Semitic and less sophisticated Ignatiev, would by no means tolerate violence in the streets.[3]

The government's behavior in regard to the judicial aspect of the pogroms can, however, be explained without assuming the existence of a conspiracy. In fact, the actions of the authorities in these stormy events become fully explicable only when one assumes that there was *no* plot.

The approach taken by conspiracy theorists greatly oversimplifies the reality, ignores the character of Russian legal institutions and the Russian judiciary, obscures the difficult position in which the authorities found themselves, and fails to explain certain instances when severe, and even extra judicial, punishments were in fact administered as early as 1881. In order to appreciate these factors one must examine the status of the rule of law in late nineteenth-century Russia, the considerations that guided the administration in its judicial thinking, and the situation of the judiciary after the reforms of 1864.

The Russian masses had no clear conception of their legal rights and obligations. Nor were the legal possibilities for punishing the rioters always clear-cut. There were arguments both for and against using a firm hand and administering strict and immediate punishment. Russian law, as it stood in 1881, turned out to be unprepared to deal with the situation that developed in the southwestern region. This crisis, and the several pogroms in 1882, eventually led to the promulgation in 1891 of a law dealing with "attacks by one part of the population upon another." Meanwhile, the complexity of the situation in 1881 rendered it certain that the courts would have no easy job in administering justice. On the side of severity, summary punishments outside regular channels were sometimes administered. But on the side of clemency, persons returning stolen goods voluntarily were usually promised that they would suffer no punishment. One must look at what lay behind the authorities' behavior in these particular cases. The most worrying, though not the only, concern of officials was to avoid a boomerang effect, whereby too severe punishments would result in exacerbating hostility to the government. Jews engaged in self-defense were also among those arrested. This must be explained, as must the role of the officials' anti-Semitism in determining how they punished rioters. An example of hostility to the Jews being combined with legal formalism is presented by the manner in which officials handled the private deals that Jews sometimes made with peasants about compensation for property destroyed during rioting. Another look at the pogrom in Kiev will also be instructive, since events there brought together the various factors influencing Russian officials and demonstrate the constraints within which they worked when the time came to punish rioters.

Nineteenth-century Russia was not a state governed by the rule of law. Wide latitude was given for administrative fiat. Consequently there is some basis for the assumption that if the regime had wanted to ignore the established legal codes and court system in order to take a strong stand against the rioters and punish them swiftly and severely, it could have done so. However, the unambiguous adoption of such a mode of action was in fact precluded by the framework within which Russian officials acted, quite apart from any sympathy or support they may have given to the pogroms.

The considerations that guided the administration were: at least a minimal inclination to legal formalism; the underdeveloped character of Russian law, that is, its unpreparedness to deal with attacks by one part of the population upon another (as distinct from insurrection); the complexity of the crime committed, in regard both to the large number of people and to the different types of criminal activities involved; the fear that the fury of the mob might turn against the regime; and a greater or lesser degree of antipathy toward the Jews as exploiters of the simple people. These concerns alone are enough to enable one to understand why official behavior was marked by an indecisiveness that left the overall impression of leniency.

Russia was moving—even though slowly, painfully, and spasmodically—in the direction of the rule of law. The Great Reforms of the 1860s had been a significant leap forward toward that goal. This is how one historian summarized the 1864 statutes on the judiciary:

> [They] embodied, with a varying degree of thoroughness, the accepted principles of western European jurisprudence: equality of all before the law; access to an impartial tribunal and the right to be heard; acceptance of the maxim *nullum crimen nulla poena sine lege*, that is, no action is punishable

unless adjudicated, after a fair trial, as a violation of the law; uniformity and relative simplicity of judicial procedures; separation of the judicial from the legislative and the executive power; irremovability of the judges, except for misconduct in office; publicity of proceedings; representation of the parties in civil cases and of defendants in criminal cases by qualified members of the bar; trial by jury; election of judges of the lower courts; preliminary investigation of criminal offenses by examining magistrates (*sudebnyi sledovatel . . .*) instead of by the police.

The new system of law courts was one of great simplicity. Minor civil and criminal cases were tried by justices of the peace. . . . Appeals from the decisions of these courts were taken to the county session (*mirovoi sezd*) of the justices of the peace. . . . The more important cases were tried, with or without jury, by district courts (*okruzhnoi sud*), and might be appealed to the local higher courts (*sudebnaia palata*). . . . The reorganized Senate was retained as the supreme court.

The principles proclaimed by the statutes of 1864 were not consistently applied in practice. Military courts, ecclesiastical courts, and township courts dealing with petty cases involving only peasants were retained.

. . . Within the sphere of their jurisdiction the courts proved reasonably efficient, businesslike, and honest.[4]

The exceptions to the 1864 statues, by which extra legal judicial authority was vested in administrative officers, in almost every case involved political crimes against the state or against the officially sanctioned, landlord-dominated, social and economic regime.[5]

To a certain extent, then, Russian officials saw themselves as acting within a fairly well-defined legal framework. Incompetence, bribery, corruption, and influence peddling were rife, but perhaps they were becoming less so than ever before.

The people, meanwhile, did not always have a clear conception of their legal rights and obligations. As some officials at the time realized, one major root of the mob violence against the Jews in 1881 was an absence of respect for the law and legal processes. Arbitrary and severe punishments meted out swiftly by administrative fiat, in this view, might have had the desirable immediate effect of cooling the passions of the mob. But in the long run the danger of popular violence would return, since the people's veneration for the law would in no way have been deepened.[6]

The governor of Poltava *guberniia*, P. A. Bil'basov, addressed himself to this problem. He wanted the rioters to be brought to trial and punished as quickly as possible, even if the penalties inflicted were light. Bil'basov reasoned that the population, after all, respected the judicial authorities much more than it respected the police, whose actions it habitually interpreted as being arbitrary and tyrannical. Therefore, the least bit of judicial condemnation would suffice to convince the masses that anti-Jewish violence was indeed illegal and that the rumors about rioting being permitted were false. Tensions would be reduced and the disorders would end.[7]

Calls by officials for strict and immediate accountability before the law were numerous in 1881.[8] They were supplemented by the proposal of several officials to administer summary justice outside the regular legal channels.[9] That responsible persons made such a suggestion serves to indicate the initial panic into which some officials were thrown by the rioting. As a rule, officials stated that if the rioters were not handled with a firm hand, then either the people's belief in an imperial *ukaz* allowing them to attack the Jews would be strengthened, or their faith in the power of the government would be seriously weakened. And in either case they would be encouraged to continue rioting. But the firm hand, most officials felt, must remain within the boundaries set by existing legal institutions as far as possible.

At this point, however, the authorities encountered a grave problem—Russian law was underdeveloped and unprepared to deal with the unusual situation created by the anti-Jewish riots. I leave aside for the moment the question of whether this was not simply an excuse used by anti-Semites to justify their inaction.

Count Kutaisov reported that in the days before the beginning of the pogrom in Pereiaslav, Poltava *guberniia* (30 June), three cases of disorderly conduct occurred. They were stopped in time, before developing into real riots, and the guilty parties were quickly tried and convicted. The sentences, however, did not, and could not, influence the population to be calm; they were too light. The justice of the peace had done everything demanded of him by law, given the specific circumstances of each case. The general problem of taking steps to calm the whole population was not within his sphere of duty; it was the direct obligation of the administration alone.[10] This was the legal situation in a case when no rioting had yet occurred. What about afterward?

In 1881, Russian legal codes contained detailed provisions for dealing severely with cases of insurrection. But they failed to define any special penalties for cases in which one group in the population attacked the persons or property of another group. While resembling insurrection, this offense was not really the same. The only laws in the Russian Codes applicable here dealt with "disorderly conduct in public places" and "simple theft." These laws were, in fact, the ones applied.[11] However, persons guilty of these crimes were merely subject to imprisonment (usually for three months) or relatively light fines.

It was clear to all that the leniency of the punishments did not fit the enormity of the crime, since the disorderly conduct was very often accompanied by beatings, rapes, serious plundering, and destruction of property. Consequently, in June 1882 the minister of justice, D. N. Nabokov, issued a circular instructing the courts in such cases to apply both the rules regarding "disorderly conduct in public places" and "damage to movable and immovable property." The fear that the fury of the mob might turn on the government, as well as the hope that the rioting might be ended with less harsh measures, may account for the delay until 1882 in applying the relatively severe rules about "damage to movable and immovable property."[12]

Nabokov's circular of 1882 served as the basis for a law of 1891 dealing with "attacks by one part of the population upon another." That law provided for exile, long terms of imprisonment, and hard labor for persons participating in a crowd, regardless of whether it was organized beforehand or not, that did violence to persons or property on the basis of religious, racial (tribal), class, or economic hostility, or on the basis of rumors that disturbed public tranquility.[13] The Russian legal codes were finally prepared to deal with the likes of the 1881 pogroms.

Not only were there no laws providing for circumstances such as the 1881 pogroms, but the crime itself turned out to be quite a complex phenomenon. The authorities were confronted with the problem of how to imprison, prosecute, and punish hundreds, or even thousands—sometimes whole villages—of offenders against public peace and order. For purposes of fixing appropriate punishments, they had to distinguish between inciters, leaders, mere followers, persons who attacked Jews physically and perhaps were involved in rape or murder, those who destroyed property or stole it from homes and shops, persons who simply picked up goods that had been strewn about the streets, mere spectators arrested in the tumult, those who disobeyed or attacked officials and troops, and persons who resisted arrest. Trustworthy witnesses and evidence had to be gathered about events that took place in a context of tremendous confusion, excitement, and emotional strain. Decisions had to be made about which courts were competent to try the various offenders.

In some cases, as even conspiracy theorists admit, summary justice outside the regular legal channels was in fact applied by officials who ignored the Gordian knot of legal complexities and aimed at ending the rioting as quickly as possible. In the villages near Elizavetgrad and Kiev, certain military officers resorted to flogging rioters in order to stop the spread of the excitement and to convince the population of the illegality of attacks of Jews. Some rioters were given corporal punishment in Odessa as well. These were mainly youths whose parents requested that they be chastised in order to discourage them from such misbehavior in the future.[14]

A certain Captain Rudov pursued this course in the townlet of Smela, Kiev *guberniia*. On the day the riot there ended (5 May) he had the rioters flogged publicly. He made no distinctions as to age, sex, or degree of guilt and even included some Jews who had tried to defend their property by physical violence. This proves that the captain's actions were not the result of Jewish bribery. Alexander III called Rudov "energetic and wise" when told of his conduct. Even later, in 1883, when pogroms broke out yet another time, the tsar advised officials to flog the chief instigators thoroughly.[15]

Kutaisov, always a stickler for adherence to the law, was more critical of Captain Rudov: His actions were against the law. They were made pardonable only by the exceptional circumstances in which he found himself as military commander. These included the lack of assistance from the frightened local authorities, the fact that there was no place to keep several hundred prisoners, the spreading rumors about an *ukaz* to beat the Jews, and the real threat of more pogroms. However, Kutaisov admitted, the beatings were actually quite successful in helping to restore calm and to convince the people that there was no anti-Jewish tsarist *ukaz*. Many peasants returned to their villages, told what they had seen or experienced, and thereby persuaded people primed to riot to change their minds.[16]

Another extralegal form of justice occasionally used involved the billeting of troops. Villages whose residents had participated in pogroms were required to quarter soldiers for a certain amount of time at their own expense. This step was taken not only in order to have forces immediately available in case of renewed rioting but also because of the large number of rioters, not all of whom could be identified, imprisoned, or tried, and the need officials felt to penalize them in some way in order to discourage further disorders.[17] Billeting troops as a rule imposed quite a heavy burden on the peasants. As one recent historian of the Russian army has noted, the "mere presence [of military units] could entail severe economic disruption, if not ruin for a village" especially if "civil [or] military officials [decided] to extract punitive damages from a village occupied by the army, damages which went to defray the cost of the occupation." It was most usual in such cases for the army to take animals from the villagers to provide the troops' meat rations. However, "for many peasants the ownership of a domestic animal could be the margin between relative prosperity and destitution."[18]

Persons who returned stolen and plundered goods voluntarily were usually granted immunity from prosecution. A close look at this policy indicates that it was probably not motivated by anti-Semitic sentiments. Rather, it seems to have been adopted after considering the interests of Jewish riot victims and making a quite realistic appraisal of local conditions. The police and officials often manifested a genuine concern that as much property as possible be returned to the Jews. Stern threats of prosecution with no mitigation of punishment could be expected only to lead to the destruction of the plundered goods or their disposal in the nearby steppes and rivers. It was with the aim of preventing this misfortune that the authorities in a number of instances gave rioters a grace period within which they might return stolen goods with no fear of punishment. It was announced, however, that after this interval searches would be made, and anyone found with stolen goods would be prosecuted. Reportedly, as a result of such declarations, many people did indeed return goods they had taken.[19]

A. R. Drentel'n, the governor-general of the southwestern (Kiev) region, in consultation with the procurator of the Kiev district higher court, revealed another legal aspect of the possession of stolen goods. Some persons simply picked up Jewish property that had been flung about the streets, without otherwise participating in the disorders. According to Drentel'n, this happened often during the Kiev pogrom. Most of those apprehended with stolen goods were arrested on streets that had not undergone any rioting and only because policemen noticed that they were carrying, with no effort at concealment, goods unlikely to be their own. When questioned, they explained that they had taken the things because they were lying around unattended, and they generally gave up their newly found acquisitions as soon as they were stopped by the police. Drentel'n, with transparent disingenuousness, said he thought that this behavior was the result of the simple people's not realizing that taking the items was illegal. Rather than theft, this was more like a violation of the rules governing "the appropriation of lost and found articles," a misdemeanor subject to prosecution only after three weeks of not declaring that a lost article had been found. Consequently there was no legal basis for bringing to trial persons arrested during the rioting whose only crime was the appropriation of goods found in the streets.[20] Apart from the deceit and hypocrisy that probably lay behind the anti-Semitic Drenteln's analysis of the situation, the legal authorities faced a genuine problem here.

There was also another concern, in addition to determining who was guilty of what. The legal authorities had to avoid the boomerang effect that too severe judicial measures might have. (This same concern had made officials reluctant to use firearms during the rioting.) They realized that swift and stern justice was necessary in order to persuade the people to end the rioting, but severity in defense of the Jews might only anger the already highly agitated population even more and ultimately lead to attacks on the regime itself. The prevention of just this eventuality was, after all, the most important goal of officials; this was the main motive in general for wanting to end the riots. Alexander III had just come to the throne in circumstances seemingly fraught with revolutionary potential. Hence his new regime was sure to be most cautious. As a solution to the problem, on 15 May 1881, Minister of the Interior Ignatiev instructed local officials to see that very severe penalties were imposed on all recognized riot instigators and leaders and on any intellectuals who were arrested (Ignatiev then suspected that the revolutionary socialists were involved in organizing the pogroms), while lenient treatment was to be accorded to the mass of uneducated followers.

The rule of more severe penalties for leaders than for followers was logical and was subsequently incorporated into the antiriot law of 1891. But Ignatiev and others made it clear that they favored the distinction not necessarily for legal reasons (determining varying degrees of guilt in the pursuit of justice) but mainly for reasons of state (political considerations about reducing social discontent and guaranteeing internal security).[21]

Later, in 1882, the regime was much more self-confident. The minister of the interior, Tolstoi, was much more experienced as a high government administrator than Ignatiev had been. Unlike his predecessor, he had no Slavophile dreams and no overriding anti-Semitic prejudices. His primary political value was social order imposed from above. So he could, and did, relatively fearlessly adopt a policy of severe penalties for everyone taking part in pogroms.[22]

Considerations about how to avoid angering further the already agitated population probably lay behind the arrest of Jews who tried to organize themselves for self-defense. There is no need to assume that the authorities involved were manifesting support for a pogrom movement. It is more likely that they were trying to prevent the exacerbation of the situation, such as occurred in Elizavetgrad. There, when it was thought that shots were being fired at the rioters from inside the synagogue, the raging mob became even more furious. And this pattern was repeated elsewhere.[23]

Any official who opposed the pogroms to any degree would, of course, want to prevent such incidents. In Odessa efficient police action did in fact succeed in keeping the riot short and mild. Still, about 150 Jewish students and workers were arrested, their homes searched, and their primitive weapons (sticks and iron bars) confiscated. Jewish student activists at the time saw something "sinister and systematic" in the arrests. It would never have occurred to these valorous Jewish youths that the authorities wanted to prevent further incitement of the rioters, so one can easily understand how they sometimes concluded that an anti-Jewish conspiracy was afoot.[24]

In Berdichev the police chief was allegedly bribed into allowing the Jews to organize and defend themselves against potential rioters who were expected to arrive by railroad. Twice itinerant laborers were turned back and forced to move on without leaving their train when they were met by Jews armed with clubs.[25] Clearly, the police chief here had received no orders from his superiors to allow a pogrom. And if some nongovernment organization was behind the riots, we might ask why *it* did not bribe the officer to arrest the Jews.

My discussion thus far has left aside the role played by official anti-Semitism in determining the uses made of Russian law by the authorities. Perhaps most Russian officials hated the Jews as exploiters of the simple people. Some expressed their antipathy in actions, aiding and abetting or remaining passive before the mob. Many, though, limited themselves to statements of sympathy for the rioters, which, however, did not necessarily indicate that they fully approved of the riots. As anti-Semites who felt a certain degree of paternalistic responsibility for the non-Jewish masses, many officials surely felt they "understood" the anger of the people against the Jews, and even sympathized with it. But as authorities responsible for law and order and aware of the danger of revolutionary outbreaks, they could not agree with the method chosen to express this anger or allow it to be put into operation without interference. They could, however, deal with rioters relatively leniently when the time came to initiate judicial proceedings.

A vivid example occurred in the *guberniias* of Tavrida and Ekaterinoslav. After the pogroms ended, the authorities received reports that some Jews were trying to conclude private agreements with peasants who allegedly had participated in the disorders. These transactions concerned compensation for property damaged and destroyed during the rioting. The Jews attempted to convince the peasants that it would be more to their advantage to repay the losses voluntarily than to be forced into repaying by the courts. In some cases the Jews declared that they would be satisfied if they were compensated for half or even less of the amount that they claimed to have lost. The simple peasants, frightened at the prospect of being brought before the authorities, found such offers tempting. In order to guarantee such bargains, it was stipulated that neither party could raise any questions about them in court.

As far as the authorities were concerned, this was simply a new way for the Jews to exploit the peasants. In order to prevent such alleged swindles, local officials were ordered to explain to peasants and Jews the legal procedure for satisfying claims for losses incurred during the rioting. Only the administrative authorities and the courts were competent to determine who the guilty parties were and what punishments they deserved. The Jews' losses should be compensated only in cases when the guilty were convicted in court as a result of the Jews proving the amount of their losses and the identity of those who caused them. The private agreements that were being concluded should be considered "transactions based upon false assertions" and therefore void and subject to punishment as swindles.[26]

Here hostility to Jews as exploiters of the simple people combined with legal formalism to harm the interests of the victims of the pogroms. Perhaps a desire to prevent further exacerbation of the peasants' frustrations, with its attendant danger of more outbreaks, also played a role. There is no need to assume that the government officials involved necessarily supported the tendency toward pogroms. Even those who opposed the rioting most strenuously could have approved of these measures.

The treatment of rioters in Kiev is almost always cited by conspiracy theorists in support of their view. A careful analysis of the facts, however, reveals that the case was quite complicated and that it brought together all the factors influencing Russian officials that I have outlined: legal formalism, the underdeveloped character of Russian law, the complexity of the crime, fear of a boomerang effect, and outright hostility to Jews.

During the 1881 pogrom in Kiev, Governor-General Drentel'n was the man directly in charge of policy in the town. As I have demonstrated, conspiracy theorists see him as one of the main characters involved in the pogrom plot and accuse him of being directly responsible for the failure of the authorities to suppress the Kiev riot quickly and efficiently. Drentel'n, in a report dated 3 May 1881 to his superior, the minister of the interior, explained his treatment of those arrested.

An investigation had revealed that the main motive of the attacks on the Jews was hatred for enslaving the Christian population. The mass of local people, both the lower and upper classes, was convinced that the Jews were responsible for many of the difficulties and deplorable occurrences of the preceding year and that they had even made possible the assassination of Alexander II. Hence, Drentel'n concluded, trying those accused of rioting at the place of the crime, according to the regular legal order, and with the participation of a jury would be no guarantee of proper, unprejudiced verdicts. Acquittals could surely be expected in most cases. Meanwhile, only certain categories of the accused could legally be tried in the local higher court, without a jury. And there the regular legal procedure was accompanied by many formalities, which slowed the decision-making process. Speed, however, was very necessary.

Over one thousand people had been arrested in Kiev and filled the only place of detention available. A typhoid epidemic had ended only recently, and there was the danger that it might break out again. In addition, there was the danger of more rioting and more arrests. All these considerations made Drentel'n want to get the prisoners out as quickly as possible.

Furthermore, the governor-general thought that only verdicts delivered rapidly could "reestablish in the minds of the population the justice which was violated and satisfy those who had suffered," that is, the victims. Quick and strict verdicts, especially in regard to instigators and leaders, were also in the interest of the regime, to demonstrate to the population that wild excesses were intolerable and entailed serious penalties. Therefore Drentel'n decided that several pogrom cases—those involving ring leaders, persons arrested in the act of pillaging, and persons who resisted arrest—should be handed over to the Kiev district military court and dealt with as they would have been in time of war.

We have seen Drentel'n's lenient treatment of persons arrested while leaving the scene of rioting with stolen goods, and his justification of such a policy.

Persons accused simply of disturbing the peace should have been tried before justices of the peace. Two problems, however, arose here. First, the law defined quite insignificant penalties for the usual cases of this misdemeanor. Second, since all the police charge sheets referred to robberies committed by the mob during the rioting, the justices of the peace might argue that they had no jurisdiction. Hence, because of the serious character of the crime, Drentel'n decided to impose administrative penalties on all those arrested for disturbing the peace. This meant that anyone having a permanent home, family, or regular business in Kiev would be released from jail under bail of persons known for their trustworthiness. All others would be deported to their home towns and villages and prohibited from returning to Kiev, which was quite a significant punishment for laborers seeking employment in the Ukrainian capital. Reportedly, at least 274 persons were actually expelled.[27]

Minister of the Interior Ignatiev, in a report to the tsar dated 14 May 1881, wrote that he approved of Drentel'n's decisions concerning the treatment of those arrested. The minister added that he had taken steps to ensure, insofar as possible, that the authorities elsewhere acted similarly when dealing with rioters. In notes to Drentel'n and the Odessa and Khar'kov governors-general, Ignatiev explained that from the government's point of view it was important to end the pogrom cases (that is, to punish the rioters) as quickly as possible, because long, drawn out trials would only continue to incite the discontent in society.[28]

Count Kutaisov visited Kiev while the district military court was still trying the accused rioters. Some of those handed over to it initially had been dismissed without a trial. The rest were gradually being examined. Kutaisov thought that the court was by no means satisfying the expectations of Governor-General Drentel'n, who had assumed that it would deliver severe verdicts, necessary because of both the gravity of the accusations and the need to discourage future riots. What happened in fact was that some of the accused were declared not guilty altogether because of the difficulty in identifying rioters and separating them from the mass of mere spectators. In many other cases, those of people being tried for robbery and disorderly conduct, it could be proven only that they had been involved in destroying property and were therefore guilty of disorderly conduct alone. From this the judges concluded that the rioters were not out for material gain but just wanted to express their hatred of the Jews. So the court acquitted them of the charge of robbery, and on the charge of disturbing the peace it gave them merely light sentences.[29]

In several other places as well, relatively light punishments were justified by the courts on the ground that the riots were against exploiters and so, with few exceptions, did not involve the normal motives found in criminal cases of robbery.[30]

The public prosecutor in the Kiev district military court was a man named Strelnikov, whose main interest seemed to be in indicting the Jews for exploiting Christians and thereby causing the riots. Consequently he was not very motivated to have severe penalties meted out to the rioters. Strelnikov observed that some of the accused, who had pulled a military captain from his horse, had committed an act that deserved the death penalty, but the exceptional circumstances of the riot made this impossible. When a Jewish witness complained about the overcrowded conditions and aggravated economic competition caused by the existence of the Pale of Jewish Settlement, Strelnikov replied, "If the Eastern frontier is closed to the Jews, the Western frontier is open to them; why don't they take advantage of it?"[31]

Strelnikov's behavior did not please persons higher up in the administration. On 14 June 1881 the director of the department of police, V. K. von Plehve, reported to the tsar that the Kiev military court had not justified the hopes placed in it. It had treated the accused rioters very leniently and the whole matter in a very perfunctory manner. Therefore its verdicts had little influence in stemming the tendency toward pogroms. Von Plehve's superior, Ignatiev, undoubtedly shared his view. The tsar wrote on the report, "This is reprehensible."[32]

Such central government dissatisfaction was not confined to the Kiev instance or even to cases related to the 1881 pogroms. Describing Russian military courts of this period in general, a recent historian drew the following enlightening picture:

[Late nineteenth-century tsarist] military courts were not merely kangaroo tribunals from which the government could always squeeze any sentence it desired. The structure of Russian military justice, the legal education of military judicial personnel, and the attitudes and practices of that personnel all buttressed due process of law.

After the military judicial reform of 1867 the majority of military trials were public, and the adversary system obtained in military as well as civilian courtrooms. In fact, save for the absence of jurors, military and civilian criminal procedure were identical; the procedural articles of the military judicial code were transcribed word for word from the corresponding articles of the civilian legal statutes.

Of course, in specific cases governmental pressure could and did influence military court decisions. But in bending to the wishes of civilian authorities, subverting the law in the interests of repression, military judges were acting against their training and instincts.

Generally, military courts strove to respect due process in the trials of civilians. Thus, improperly prepared indictments were frequently dismissed. Further, on occasion military courts handed down sentences in strict accord with the law regardless of whether this was vexatious to the civil government or to the Emperor himself.[33]

This author was not referring to the 1881 pogroms, but he could very well have been, as we have seen above.

Count Kutaisov commented that whatever the motives of the military court, the sentences it handed down did not satisfy the needs of the time. The court was empowered to apply the laws of wartime to the case, and the people expected severe penalties. When they heard that the accused were given only light punishments or acquitted altogether, they became convinced that the use of the military court was only a temporary measure taken to frighten them. But it was not so frightening after all. It appeared to the people that in order to get a conviction when a whole group was involved, the court must have much more precise proof against each of the accused than in cases involving only isolated individuals. Such were Kutaisov's impressions of the impact made by the military court's verdicts.[34]

We should note, however, that the Kiev district military court was not entirely passive. While most of the punishments were quite lenient, from one to eighteen months in prison, at least one of the convicted got four years at hard labor, and at least four were sent to Siberia.[35]

In contrast to the view of Count Kutaisov, one may cite the opinion of the Austrian consul in Kiev, Tsingaria, which has been used by some conspiracy theorists to support their case. In messages to Freiherr von Heimerle, the Austrian minister of foreign affairs, Tsingaria claimed that Drentel'n had the rioters tried in a military court knowing in advance that they would receive light sentences. His aim was to give the appearance of severity without really harming Christians on account of the Jews. This was in order to cover up the inadequacy of antiriot measures taken initially and to remove any suspicion that the government was implicated in or passive to the disorders. According to Tsingaria, it was no secret that the governor-general and his subordinates were acting according to instructions from St. Petersburg to be indulgent to the mob.[36]

The falsity of Tsingaria's view is clear from what has been said above on the basis of official Russian government interdepartmental communications unknown to the Austrian. From these it appears that Drentel'n was sincere when he expressed the expectation that the military court would pass severe sentences. He certainly got no instructions from above to grant clemency to the guilty. On another point, however, Tsingaria was undoubtedly correct—that the governor-general wanted to cover up his incompetence in suppressing the rioting or preventing it altogether. But this concern was in relation to his superiors, not to the outside world.

The case of Kiev exemplifies the ways anti-Jewish rioters were punished in 1881. The punishments were generally light, but this had nothing to do with an anti-Jewish plot. As with other facets of the pogroms, Russian officials, especially the anti-Semitic ones, faced a number of dilemmas, the most severe being, on the one hand, the desire to be indulgent toward the rioters, their fellow-Christians, and on the other hand, the need to defend the Jews in the interests of broader considerations of state security and public order. Drentel'n, Kutaisov, and Strelnikov all held anti-Semitic attitudes, but each responded differently to the problems presented by popular anti-Semitism, and in ways not to the liking of the others. Being anti-Semitic was not the only factor dictating how people behaved in this crisis. The troubled waters of 1881 were marked by many swirling eddies. Conflicting interests, considerations, and circumstances wrenched matters out of the hands of the authorities, even in an area over which they had enormous control, the area of social discipline and justice in the courts.

*Chapter 10*

# THE AIMS OF THE "CONSPIRATORS"
◆ ◆ ◆

CONSPIRACY THEORISTS HAVE ADVANCED A NUMBER OF THESES TO explain what the presumed reactionary conspirators expected to achieve by the pogroms. Some of these explanations are more persuasive than others. But when each is analyzed together with the public and private responses of conservative and reactionary figures, then the case for a conspiracy once again falls apart.

The most obvious aim might have been to weaken the Jews' economic power. Another might have been to generate support for an anti-Jewish legislative program, such as the minister of the interior, Nicholas P. Ignatiev, actually produced toward the end of 1881. But Ignatiev was no master schemer, as is shown conclusively by extensive evidence. First of all, he issued various memoranda and instructions clearly indicating his opposition to the pogroms. Second, the fact stands out that he changed his explanation of the violence, initially seeing it as socialist inspired, and only later, after impressive evidence came in, blaming Jewish exploitation of the popular masses. This change in explanation must be examined in detail in order to appreciate fully the thinking and concerns of the Russian authorities in 1881. Finally, it can be demonstrated that Ignatiev had no plans for anti-Jewish legislation prior to the fall of 1881. Another goal of the alleged pogrom planners could have been to use the Jews as a lightning rod: the violence would presumably direct the people's justified anger at the regime away from the government while generating loyalist and nationalist passions. Some writers thought the riots were planned as a means of discrediting Michael T. Loris-Melikov, who was minister of the interior when they began, and who had the reputation of being a liberal. Other writers thought the pogroms were Ignatiev's work, launched in order to promote his idea that the country needed a conservative consultative assembly. Another aim attributed to those who supposedly sponsored the pogroms was to encourage Jewish emigration. Here again the case for a conspiracy does not hold up.

161

The pogroms were intended to weaken the Jews' economic power, asserted one thesis.[1] They certainly achieved that—in individual cases. And it is well known that many officials considered this to be a major objective of the Russian government. But would officials have pursued a policy of *violence* in the streets at a time when, for fear of disrupting and damaging economic life in the Pale, they even recoiled from adopting a policy of decisive *legal* measures against the Jews' economic activities?[2] Furthermore, what could pogroms of the type undertaken in 1881 really accomplish in this regard? Apart from the ruin of some individuals, they could hardly achieve more than temporary disruptions of the Jews' trading activities. In addition, as events proved, they would be costly to non-Jews as well, both those who were customers and those who had other business ties with the Jews.

Officials on the spot emphasized this last point from the first days of the rioting. If trade fairs were disrupted, they noted, not only Jews would suffer, but so would Russian manufacturers and financiers who had sold goods on credit or loaned money to Jewish businessmen. Goods would not be sold and debts would not be paid. The depression in trade and industry already being experienced would be intensified, and more people would be thrown out of work. Agricultural producers would lose too. Without customers for their products they would have to sell cheaply or, when possible, await better times, thereby being left without money to pay for labor during the coming busy summer season. Some authorities on the spot were accused by contemporaries of acting to protect the homes of wealthy Jewish businessmen more diligently than the dwellings of the impoverished Jews. If these accusations were true, then the officials involved may have been reflecting such general commercial concerns as those just mentioned—they may even have been among those who expressed them in writing. At the same time, some officials noted that the rioters who were arrested left their families without breadwinners so long as they were in prison.[3]

Some conspiracy theorists attributed a more subtle purpose to the men who allegedly arranged the pogroms: they wanted to generate support for a harshly anti-Semitic legislative program, after twenty years of relative liberalism in regard to the Jewish question. True, innumerable officials expressed the view that it was necessary to protect the Jews, but this was usually tacked onto assertions about the need to combat their supposedly pernicious economic influence. As officials often stated their message: such relations must be established between Christians and Jews as would remove the hostility that led to pogroms. In the view of those historians who see a plot here, these expressions were simply an excuse for promoting the implementation of anti-Jewish laws. They noted the following sequence:

| | |
|---|---|
| Spring 1881 | Pogroms break out. |
| Fall 1881 | Special *guberniia* commissions are established and given instructions that encourage them to make anti-Jewish recommendations. |
| Early 1882 | The special Committee on the Jews in St. Petersburg produces a legislative project for severely restricting or abolishing the few civil rights Jews enjoy. |
| | Minister of the Interior Ignatiev takes part of this program to the Council of Ministers. |
| 3 May 1882 | The May Laws are adopted: Jews are not to be permitted in the future to move from towns to villages, to acquire land in rural areas, or to conduct trade on Sundays and Christian holidays. |

To show that Ignatiev and other anti-Semites exploited the pogroms is no proof that they planned them. Furthermore, the table above is very schematic and only a pale reflection of the rich texture of events in this period.

The conspiracy theory assumes that Ignatiev was insincere all along: he did not really oppose the pogroms but intentionally allowed or encouraged them; he did not really believe his own statement that Jewish exploitation evoked the violence and therefore required drastic anti-Jewish preventive measures; he was simply a hypocritical anti-Semite manipulating events to serve his own ends.[4]

Ignatiev was viewed by many of his contemporaries as an outstanding liar and hypocrite.[5] And there is no dispute about his being an anti-Semite. But at least three important pieces of evidence indicate that the picture drawn of him as a master schemer is inaccurate. First, when the violence began, Ignatiev was serving in the relatively uninfluential post of minister of state domains, from which he could not have swayed the course of events, certainly not in an official capacity. Nor could he have known that he would soon be appointed to the powerful position of minister of the interior.[6] Furthermore, none of the available sources indicates in any way that Ignatiev ever took steps to encourage the pogroms. What they do reveal, however, and quite vividly, is that as minister of the interior he strongly promoted the application of measures calculated to end the rioting, a point to which I shall return below.

Second, Ignatiev changed his explanation of the pogroms. Third, he had no plans for anti-Jewish legislation prior to the fall of 1881. This is another point to which I shall return below.

Ignatiev's initial response, like that of Loris-Melikov before him, was to blame the revolutionary socialists. During the first few days of rioting, Loris-Melikov thought the disorders were simply a manifestation of the usual anti-Jewish feelings that were displayed to one degree or another yearly at Easter. By 18 April, however, he was talking about "evil-intentioned instigators."[7]

On 6 May, the day after Ignatiev became minister of the interior, he sent a circular to the governors that declared the aims and program of the new government and was published in all the newspapers. In it Ignatiev asked officials and society to join actively in the fight against sedition. He added:

> The movement against the Jews, which manifested itself recently in the south, represents a sad example of how people otherwise loyal to the Throne and the Fatherland can fall under the influence of evil-intentioned persons, who stir up the worst passions of the popular mass. The later then falls into willfulness and arbitrariness and acts, without being aware of it, according to the plans of the revolutionaries. Such violations of the public order not only should be strictly prosecuted, but carefully prevented. For the first duty of the government is to safeguard the population from all violence and wild arbitrariness.[8]

That same day Ignatiev submitted a report to the tsar. He noted the arrest of a number of persons for trying to renew the anti-Jewish violence in Odessa. Among them were students already known to the government for their political unreliability. This circumstance, Ignatiev declared, supported his supposition that, though the immediate cause of the disorders was dislike for the Jews, the real instigators were the revolutionaries. They provoked the population to become unruly, hoping that, as it became accustomed to open violence in the streets, it would eventually be prepared for genuinely revolutionary action.[9]

On 12 May, when requesting permission from Alexander III to send Count Kutaisov on his fact-finding mission, Ignatiev repeated his assertions of 6 May. He notified local officials that the count was coming in order to clarify the connection between the pogroms and the activities of the revolutionary socialist party. In his formal instructions to the tsarist emissary, the minister called upon him to clarify the general social causes of the hostile relations between Christians and Jews and to elucidate the immediate causes of the disorders, the timing of which led to the conviction that they had occurred under the direct influence of elements hostile to the government. These hostile elements perhaps wanted to ascertain the capacity of the population for creating disturbances and the means available to the government to suppress them. [10]

In several memoranda the minister made a point of mentioning the element of Jewish exploitation. However, it should be noted that he did this only in private communications, not in those published in the press—perhaps in order to avoid further inflaming popular passions. Furthermore, Ignatiev's emphasis throughout this whole period was on the role of the revolutionaries.

The sincerity with which Ignatiev held this view may be gauged by his quarrel with Governor-General Drentel'n of the Kiev region, another strongly anti-Semitic official. On 30 April, Drentel'n too assumed that the socialists played a leading role in the rioting. [11] Then, on 14 May, Ignatiev reported to the tsar that Governor-General Drentel'n now claimed that the riots had no political character and were not planned but were, rather, an explosion of accumulated grievances against Jewish exploitation. If enemies of the government took part, then they were just trying to take advantage of what seemed to be a good opportunity. But they did not lead the masses. Ignatiev disagreed, saying that he himself could not accept Drentel'n's view, especially in light of the revolutionary proclamations printed and distributed during the pogrom in the town of Kiev. There was no doubt, Ignatiev thought, that the party that issued the proclamations played a leading role in the riots. [12]

On 23 May, Ignatiev sent another circular to the governors ordering them to tour their *guberniias* with the aim of calming the excited people by explaining the falsity of the dangerous rumors about a new division or distribution of land. Repetition of disorders like the recent ones in the south against the Jews could not be tolerated, the circular emphasized, and should be prevented by timely and appropriate measures at the local level. [13] This linking of the land problem with the pogroms indicates that the central government continued to take quite seriously the notion of socialist influence in the pogroms.

Ignatiev's explanation of the pogroms was echoed by the tsar, who received his information from the minister. On 11 May 1881, Alexander III received a delegation of prominent Jews. He told them that all his subjects were equal before him, that the Jews were merely a pretext for the riots, and that the violence was really the work of "anarchists." He concluded by noting the role of Jewish economic dominance and exploitation in engendering hatred of the Jews. This final part of the tsar's statement did not appear in the press—once again indicating the government's caution when popular passions were likely to be inflamed.[14] Many local officials, independently of the minister of the interior and the tsar, came to the same conclusion, that the revolutionaries were to blame for the widespread eruptions of pogroms. So did an agent of the Holy Brotherhood who was specially sent by his organization to investigate the disorders, and so did some Jews.[15] This was a natural response in the circumstances of the spring of 1881.

Only under the impact of detailed reports from government agents on the scene, such as Kutaisov, Drentel'n, and others, and only after the passage of some weeks (in August 1881, it would seem[16]), did Ignatiev actually blame Jewish exploitation alone for having provoked the people's spontaneous violent protest.

This about face, performed quite quickly by Drentel'n, but rather slowly by Ignatiev, is indeed striking, and it is one of the best pieces of evidence available in general indicating a lack of planning on the part of the government.

Conspiracy theorists claim that the central authorities blamed the socialists while knowing all along that they were not responsible for the pogroms. If this is true, what did the government expect to gain from such a tactic? To answer this question let us assume for a moment the role of the reactionaries who supposedly planned the whole affair and try to see the world as they presumably saw it.

First of all, we want to instigate and exploit anti-Jewish violence. We assume that the non-Jewish population in the Pale is basically anti-Semitic, and viciously so. We also assume that the people are in general strongly loyalist. For this reason we decide to take steps to have rumors spread about a tsarist *ukaz* ordering or permitting attacks on Jews. Then, when attacks actually occur, we allow them to be suppressed, sometimes more vigorously, sometimes less so, all in order to keep matters under our control. Unfortunately, some part of the rioting mob suffers punishment. To calm the people, we tell them that they have been fooled by the socialists into breaking the law. At this point a few liberal-minded persons, an altogether tiny minority in Russia, should turn against the revolutionaries and support our regime more fervently. So should some socialist-inclined Jewish youths.

Now, if this were the whole of the plotters' purpose, then it turns out that they planned pogroms so the government could suppress them—in order to gain support from a handful of people.

The popular masses could respond to the "socialist" explanation in either of two ways. On the one hand, they could be expected to conclude that the socialists had led them astray and betrayed them. Hostility to the revolutionaries and support for the government would thereby be generated. On the other hand, the presumably anti-Semitic masses could easily have become embittered toward the government, which protected the hated Jews, and more favorably inclined toward the socialists, who were evidently anti-Jewish. The presumed planners, with any foresight, would have perceived the danger of such a response developing. Some socialists did in fact become aware immediately that it might be to their advantage to have the masses believe they were anti-Semites.[17] It is doubtful that conservatives and reactionaries would have taken the risk of encouraging such a belief, especially in the spring of 1881, when their main fear was precisely an upsurge in the strength of the revolutionaries.

If, by contrast, one assumes that the pogroms were spontaneous and a surprise to the government, its initial response becomes easily understandable. The revolutionary socialists had just succeeded in assassinating Alexander II, and the government was as yet unaware of their actual impotence. It was only natural for officials to attribute the new troubles to the most prominent adversary on the horizon. Later, as evidence accumulated that the revolutionary socialists were not responsible for the anti-Jewish violence, the government began to emphasize its long-held assumption that the Jews exploited the Christian population mercilessly and concluded that this alone must have finally provoked the outburst of violent hostility.

The all-pervasiveness of the notion of Jewish exploitation long before April 1881; the likelihood that this explanation of the rioting would readily generate popular support for the government among the masses; the fact that "Jewish exploitation" was so much more useful than any other slogan if one intended to promote an anti-Semitic legislative program; the additional circumstance that a certain risk was implicit in the "socialist" explanation—all these factors make it highly unlikely that anyone planning pogroms, whether clear-sighted or not, would have first explained them as socialist inspired and only later turned to the traditional doctrine.

Many of his contemporaries felt that Ignatiev was not in control of the situation, that under him the government was in effect not ruling, that it was behaving as if it were powerless. Both anti-Semites and others felt this way. At a meeting of the Council of Ministers in April 1882, Ignatiev was severely criticized by his fellow ministers who thought that he was either inept or passively supporting the pogroms. This violence, it was pointed out, could only result in very unpleasant economic, diplomatic, and perhaps even political (revolutionary) consequences for Russia.[18]

K. P. Pobedonostsev, influential advisor of Alexander III and director general of the Holy Synod, vigorous anti-Semite though he was, joined in the criticism of Ignatiev. Any violence in the streets was dangerous and should be prevented, he thought; it might turn against the regime. Pobedonostsev "was not an instigator of the pogroms directed against the Jews, if only because the Balkan crisis had taught him that popular movements easily got out of control." He was particularly angered by accusations in the foreign press that he was involved in the riots. He favored restrictions on the Jews and official repression of them, but it was unfair, he thought, to accuse him of supporting the popular violence. So, "in 1882, he denounced the Minister of the Interior for allowing racist demagogues to stimulate riots and demonstrations against the Jews." This is not to say that Pobedonostsev believed Ignatiev planned the pogroms; the director general, like his ministerial colleagues, was criticizing the minister's passivity and ineptitude.[19]

This brings us to the third piece of evidence that Ignatiev was no master planner. One can assume that anyone planning pogroms would have tried to answer beforehand not only the question of how the government would explain their occurrence but also the question of what use it would make of this diagnosis. The fact that during Ignatiev's ministry the government changed its story *and only then* undertook the implementation of an anti-Semitic program demonstrates clearly an absence of forethought about the use that would be made of the rioting, and it can be taken as another strong indication that the pogroms were spontaneous. Only after they had occurred and the government had recovered from its initial shock, did Ignatiev decide how to handle, or perhaps exploit, the situation.

The minister of the interior had no anti-Jewish program sketched out prior to taking office. In fact, he had no anti-Jewish program until the fall of 1881. If he had had such a plan, it would certainly have been reflected in his instructions to Kutaisov when the latter was appointed special emissary to study the causes of the anti-Jewish riots (12 May 1881). As I have shown, while noting the existence of hostile relations between Christians and Jews and expressing the need to clarify the factors contributing to social tension, Ignatiev nevertheless showed himself to be convinced that the pogroms were basically the work of revolutionary socialists, activists who wanted to test the people's capacity for revolutionary agitation and the government's capacity to suppress disorder.[20]

Afterward, when he had decided that it was necessary to institute new Jewish disabilities, Ignatiev felt no compunction about stating his views clearly in his instructions to various bodies dealing with the problem. Had he, already in May, expected Kutaisov to turn in reports supporting an anti-Jewish program, surely he would have said so quite clearly and unambiguously.

On 21 and 22 August 1881, after receiving reports from Kutaisov and other local officials, Ignatiev argued before the tsar that the pogroms were uncharacteristic of the Russian people. They had followed the relaxation of legislative restrictions on the Jews undertaken during the reign of Alexander II.[21] Therefore, they must be taken as a sign that the Jews' new freedoms had enabled them to become increasingly harmful to the Christian population. Ignatiev proposed that the governors of each *guberniia* in the Pale establish special commissions to discuss the Jewish question and means to restrain the Jews' harmful activities. Such *guberniia* commissions (*gubernskie kommissii*) would have the double advantage of producing useful information that would aid the central government in formulating new legislation and, perhaps more important, of calming the population at large and reassuring it that the government was actively engaged in trying to solve the problem.[22]

The notion of *guberniia* commissions fitted in well with Ignatiev's devotion to the Slavophile idea of the unity of the tsar and the people and his desire to enlist popular support for the government while maintaining patriarchal principles in society.[23] Yet the evidence indicates that the idea for establishing the commissions did not come originally from him.

On 9 August 1881, two weeks before Ignatiev proposed and received approval for establishing the *guberniia* commissions, Kutaisov suggested the necessity for a thorough study of the reasons behind the people's hatred of the Jews.[24] Even earlier, on 5 August D. I. Sviatopolk-Mirskii, governor-general of the Khar'kov region, sent a memorandum to the minister of the interior arguing that police measures would not be adequate to prevent further riots in the near future. The government must do something to change the mood of the people. It must clearly demonstrate that it was turning its attention to their problems with the aim of finding just solutions. Then the agitated mob would be calmed, violence would end, and the people would once again rely upon the authorities to protect them from the Jews. The best way to achieve all this, according to the governor-general, would be to investigate the people's complaints publicly. He went on to outline the organization of special commissions that would be under the chairmanship of the respective governors in the

Pale, with representatives of the Ministry of the Interior present, and with the right to invite different "experts" to their meetings. These commissions would be entrusted with the task of reviewing all the laws about Jews and suggesting new measures to protect the lower classes from Jewish economic abuses. A more general commission in St. Petersburg should later review and refine the work of the local commissions. But the work locally was very important, Sviatopolk-Mirskii concluded, first, because the local commissions would establish contact with the local population immediately and assure it that the government was working on the problem, and second, because they would produce experts who could greatly assist in the final elaboration of the project in St. Petersburg. On 1 September 1881, Ignatiev wrote Sviatopolk-Mirskii to acknowledge that his suggestion had been accepted.[25]

In his instructions to the governors establishing the *guberniia* commissions, Ignatiev made clear his hostile views on Jews and ordered the commissions to answer several questions: (1) which economic activities of the Jews were especially harmful to the "native population"; (2) what difficulties officials met when applying existing restrictions on the Jews' economic activities and (3) what new legislation would be useful in restraining the Jews' harmful activities. Ignatiev also asked the *guberniia* commissions to present statistical data on several matters. In other words, the commissions were to assume a priori that the Jews were harmful; their task was merely to determine exactly what the evil was and how to battle it.[26] As for Ignatiev himself, he gave no indication that he had any definite ideas as yet about anti-Jewish legislation.

The *guberniia* commissions were instructed to send their reports to the minister of the interior within two months of the first session of each commission—an exceptionally short period, given the complexity of the issues involved. But Ignatiev thought haste was imperative if the government was to act and thus remove the impetus for further pogroms and the danger that socialist revolutionaries might turn the popular violence to their own ends.[27]

On 19 October 1881, while the *guberniia* commissions were still engaged in their tasks, Ignatiev obtained the tsar's approval and appointed the Committee on the Jews *(Komitet o Evreiakh)*. It reported directly to the minister of the interior and was headed by the assistant minister, D.V. Gotovtsev. Only with the establishment of this committee did Ignatiev finally come forward with a comprehensive anti-Jewish program.[28]

Apart from the contention that the pogroms were part of a long-range plan to promote anti-Jewish legislation, some conspiracy theorists thought that the presumed planners had more immediate goals. According to one view, the hungry masses had every reason to rebel against the regime, which was pervaded by corruption and inefficiency and took no genuine steps to improve the people's lot. Dangerous outbreaks were highly likely in the tense, agitated atmosphere after the assassination of Alexander II. In these circumstances, this view asserts, the alleged patriotic planners of violence found it useful and not very difficult to steer the danger and frustration of the mob away from the authorities and onto the Jews, who became a kind of lightning rod or scapegoat for the sins of the government. The successful pursuit of such a policy, it was thought, would weaken the revolutionaries.[29]

A variation of this view attributed a slightly different line of reasoning to the planners. Once the riots inflamed anti-Jewish feelings, the religious, loyalist, and nationalist passions of the people would be stimulated. Any popular sympathy for the revolutionaries would disappear, and the attention of the people would be distracted from propaganda hostile to the government. The Jews, meanwhile, would be frightened and, fearing the authorities' vengeance, might stop joining the revolutionaries in such large numbers as hitherto. Indeed, no matter whom they thought responsible for the pogroms—the government or the revolutionaries—in either case, Jews would undoubtedly be discouraged from joining the opponents of the regime.[30]

The problem with the views just outlined is that they ignore the genuine anxiety expressed by government officials at all levels concerning the danger of socialist involvement in the pogroms. Officials, even after concluding that the revolutionary socialists were not responsible for originating the spate of pogroms, still felt that they would try to exploit it. If the revolutionaries had at first remained passive, there was no guarantee that they would do so in the future. Such apprehensions could only have been reinforced by another widely held assumption: even if the revolutionaries had had no part in preparing or instigating the pogroms, their propaganda had surely contributed to the excited state of mind of the population in general.[31] Alarming also were the reports about politically dangerous rumors spreading among the people, such as those announcing that violence would begin with the Jews and later turn on the landlords, leading ultimately to a new distribution of the latter's lands.[32] The situation called for severe repressive measures, perhaps including troops firing on the mobs. But such actions, particularly in defense of the Jews, might very well serve only to exacerbate the situation.[33] In these circumstances the real concern of officials was not how to stimulate nationalist passions but how to prevent the mobs' initial loyalist inclinations—as expressed in the rumors about a tsarist *ukaz* to beat the Jews, for example—from turning to their opposite.[34]

Governor-General Drentel'n, anti-Semite that he was, illustrates this point. He was upset because such a large part of the population, including people from the middle and upper classes, sympathized with the anti-Jewish rioters. Only a few understood the possibility of the violence turning, especially under revolutionary socialist influence, from the Jews onto other segments of the population, such as the landlords and the bourgeoisie, and ultimately even onto the government.[35]

Count Kutaisov was afraid that the revolutionaries would learn valuable lessons from the pogroms about how to advance their seditious aims. The riots, said Kutaisov, demonstrated that, while talk of abstract ideals and even of land redistribution could not rouse the simple people to violence, talk of vengeance against the supposedly exploitive Jews could. Given the existing land hunger and the anti-Jewish feelings, the Jewish question might easily pass over into the land question, and anti-Jewish violence might easily become violence against the landlord class. Not only had the revolutionaries now become aware of an easy way to incite the population, but they also had seen the inexperience of the administration and troops in preventing and stopping riots and the absence of smooth working relations between the civil and military authorities. There was no reason to assume, Kutaisov concluded, that the socialists were aware of these lessons before the start of the pogroms. Now the only way to end this new danger was to take measures to remove the sources of Christian-Jewish enmity.[36]

A government that was so acutely sensitive to the potential danger to itself of all turmoil in the streets, even that based on loyalist impulses, would certainly not have encouraged mob violence. Furthermore, pogroms occurred again in the following year, 1882. Insofar as Ignatiev's role in them is concerned, it is highly unlikely that he would have continued to support a policy of pogroms, even had he done so previously, once Kutaisov had revealed the utter incompetence of the police in handling mobs.

Once one takes into account the anxieties besetting the government, its behavior from the summer of 1881 until the promulgation of the May Laws in 1882 becomes perfectly understandable without resort to the notion of planning. The government concluded that the socialists had neither contrived nor taken a very active part in the anti-Jewish riots. But they very well might in the near future. The popular violence had to be ended as quickly as possible.

To emphasize this point, on 4 September 1881 the tsar signed a law instituting extraordinary measures for the maintenance of state order and public tranquility. This law was motivated by general apprehensiveness about the revolutionaries but was also in part a response to the pogroms. All the *guberniias* that had experienced pogroms, as well as St. Petersburg, Moscow, and a few other regions, were placed under a regime of intensified protection *(sostoianie usilennoi okhrany)*. In this state of emergency local officials were given broad extrajudicial and executive powers to fight sedition and public disorders. The law made no distinction between threats to the government and threats to private persons and their property. The special powers it granted included: arrests, fines, and sequestration of property without trial; the transfer of cases from criminal courts to military tribunals; the closing of schools and periodicals; the removal of local officials. At the same time, the rest of the empire was subjected to less extensive extraordinary measures.[37]

The government, of course, felt that it must not appear too blatantly as the protector of the Jews. Therefore, while making some effort to prevent disorders in the streets, the authorities also set about taking what they regarded as manifest and impressive, as well as effective, measures to defend the Christian masses from the Jews' allegedly rapacious and exploitive activities, thereby removing, it was hoped, the major stimulus to pogroms. As I have shown, these were the considerations that lay behind the *guberniia* commissions and the Committee on the Jews in 1881 and the May Laws of 1882.

Ignatiev was not simply exploiting the riots because they happened to fit in with his anti-Semitic prejudices. Almost all Russians—liberals and radicals, as well as conservatives—understood the pogroms as an outburst of economic protest. That is, people at the time construed the pogroms in such a way as to stimulate the minister of the interior's worst fears about the revolutionary socialists and to confirm his worst suspicions about the Jews.

As the 1880s progressed, and anti-Jewish riots ceased and the socialist revolutionaries proved themselves bankrupt, high officials in the Russian government undoubtedly drew other conclusions from the pogroms. First, it seemed that the danger of socialists turning anti-Jewish riots into antilandlord, anticapitalist, and antigovernment revolution had proved itself to be minimal. Second, it was seen that violent attacks on Jews could be accompanied by unwaveringly loyalist attitudes. These lessons may have come in handy after the turn of the century. But prior to 1881 there was no example to reassure anyone who might have thought along these lines. Moreover, the vast majority of officials in the 1880s, even if strongly anti-Jewish, was undoubtedly too timorous, cautious, or conservative even to have begun such a train of thought.

Another difficulty with conspiracy theories that assume scapegoat and patriotic motives on the part of the planners of pogroms is that the Jewish masses lived in only one relatively narrowly defined part of the empire, the Pale, and even there rioting occurred only in the south and southwest. Violent anti-Semitism, then, could hardly have been expected to contribute to solving, or even to diverting attention from, the regime's problems on the imperial plane.

Another view advanced by some conspiracy theorists asserts that anti-Semitic and reactionary circles within and close to the government intended to use the pogroms to show the bankruptcy of even moderately liberal policies.[38] Loris-Melikov had become minister of the interior in 1880. His appointment followed numerous terrorist attempts on the life of Alexander II, to which the educated public had responded with apathy. Loris-Melikov and his supporters set out to reconcile the government with moderate and liberal opinion while at the same time doing everything possible to suppress the revolutionaries. In line with this policy, Loris-Melikov planned to establish a new governmental body made up of elected spokesmen of the public, along with officials. This commission was to have been granted a purely advisory role in the legislative process. Innocuous though it was, the idea met with the approval of Russian liberals and with the hostility of conservatives. In one of history's major ironies, Tsar Alexander II was murdered by the revolutionary socialists just a few hours after he gave his permission for this project, which might have become the first step on the long road from autocracy to constitutional monarchy. Both the assassination of Alexander II and the first outbreaks of anti-Jewish violence took place while Loris-Melikov was in office. Thus it seemed not only that a "liberal" government was unable to protect the life of the tsar but also that it could not even guarantee ordinary law and order. According to some proponents of the conspiracy theory, the planners of the pogroms intended to demonstrate just this point, in order to discredit Loris-Melikov in particular and liberal governmental measures in general. However, there was no need to go to all this trouble. The reactionary Alexander III in any case wanted nothing to do with Loris-Melikov's plan for an advisory commission on legislation. In fact, soon after coming to the throne, he had it shelved; this was on 8 March, over a month before the first pogroms.[39]

Once he became minister of the interior, Ignatiev, in line with his Slavophile style of conservatism, worked for the establishment of a kind of conservative consultative assembly (*zemskii sobor,* "assembly of the land") not too different from the type of commission that Loris-Melikov had wanted to establish. Ignatiev wanted to invite some one thousand peasants and over one thousand representatives of other estates—landowners, merchants, and clergymen—to this assembly. These delegates would presumably demonstrate the nation's unity and loyalty to the tsar and the excellence of Russia's autocratic regime. Taking this project into consideration, some conspiracy theorists argued that the pogroms were intended to demonstrate that only a *zemskii sobor* could bring quiet to the land.[40]

This thesis, of course, directly contradicts the one I cited immediately before it in regard to discrediting Loris-Melikov. Violence in the streets could *either* strengthen *or* weaken "constitutionalist" tendencies; it could not do both.

The two sets of conspiracy theorists came to different conclusions because they emphasized different facts. The first group stressed that the pogroms began during the ministry of Loris-Melikov, who was clearly not an anti-Semite; the second group stressed that the pogroms continued for a long time during the ministry of Ignatiev, who was anti-Semitic and Slavophile in orientation. Both ignored the points of similarity between Loris-Melikov's "liberalism" and Ignatiev's "conservatism." Thus they got themselves into a contradiction.

A final conspiracy theory claims that the pogroms were *intended* to encourage Jewish emigration from Russia.[41] Whether planned or not, they certainly led to this end. Furthermore, Ignatiev is quoted as having said explicitly in January 1882, "The western frontier is open for the Jews." Later, though, he denied making such a statement and even told one Jewish leader that "the endeavors to stimulate emigration [are] 'an incitement to sedition,' on the ground that 'emigration does not exist for Russian citizens.' "[42]

Perhaps the remark attributed to Ignatiev encouraging Jewish emigration was indeed, as he later claimed, a misrepresentation of what he had said. Perhaps, though, it was the true expression of his personal views, and his later denial was the expression of governmental policy, which he was as yet in no position to change. The available documents do not present enough evidence one way or the other. But while the argument that the pogroms aimed at chasing the Jews out of Russia cannot be definitely refuted, it is worth noting that even the most anti-Semitic Russian officials, and not only Ignatiev, showed themselves to be extremely ambivalent about a policy of promoting Jewish emigration.[43] Consequently it is highly unlikely that they would have used pogroms to achieve this end.

In sum, then, none of the aims attributed to the alleged plotters of pogroms holds up under scrutiny. Analysis of the thinking of Russian officials at the time, its development, and the circumstances influencing it, shows that there could have been no anti-Jewish plot. This analysis also shows that the authorities' responses to the pogroms were ad hoc and reflected a genuine concern that the government might lose control of the situation. By its very nature, the Russian government in 1881 could not have even begun to consider, much less execute, a policy of popular violence against the Jews as a means of promoting the government's ends.

# III

## REACTIONARIES AND REVOLUTIONARIES

*Chapter 11*

# THE HOLY BROTHERHOOD

◆ ◆ ◆

A NUMBER OF CONSPIRACY THEORISTS CONCEDED THAT THERE WERE too many problems with an explanation of the 1881 pogroms that made the government responsible for them. Particularly impressive to these writers was the strong condemnation of the anti-Jewish violence by certain high-ranking dignitaries and the successful prevention of rioting by many local officials in the territories under their jurisdiction.[1] Another target was therefore sought upon which to place the blame, some nongovernmental organization with a conservative or reactionary philosophy, whose members were government officials and persons closely associated with officialdom. Such a society was conveniently at hand, the Holy Brotherhood (*Sviashchennaia Druzhina,* sometimes called the Sacred League in English).[2]

The Holy Brotherhood was formed on 12 March 1881, one week before rumors concerning the prospect of anti-Jewish violence began to appear in the newspapers, and one month before the violence itself began. It continued its activities until 3 December 1882, when the tsar, at the insistence of the minister of the interior, Dmitri A. Tolstoi, and the director general of the Holy Synod, K. P. Pobedonostsev, ordered it disbanded.[3]

In the preceding chapters I have described the occurrences that led certain writers to charge that the Russian government was behind the spate of pogroms. Writers who blamed the Holy Brotherhood referred to some of the same phenomena. Some asserted that anti-Jewish rumors were spread systematically or that secret messengers were dispatched to prepare the ground for the rioting and to give instructions to local officials to treat rioters leniently. Some stated that organized roving squads of rioters existed or that the different pogroms were uniform in style.[4]

The aims imputed to the Holy Brotherhood in promoting anti-Jewish violence were similar to those attributed to the government, and just as self-contradictory. For example, the pogroms were supposed to demonstrate the political bankruptcy of Minister of the Interior Loris-Melikov's liberalism; or to undermine the public honor and moral authority—in

179

whose eyes was never explained—of the revolutionaries (who were initially blamed for instigating the rioting); or to inflame the religious, nationalist, and patriotic passions of the people, so that they would forget about the defects in the existing order and turn away from the revolutionaries; or, finally, to frighten the Jews and discourage them from joining the revolutionaries.[5]

The arguments of those blaming the government for planning the pogroms and those blaming the Holy Brotherhood were much the same, so there is no need to repeat here the refutations of those arguments presented in the preceding chapters. In the pages that follow I will examine evidence that indicates that the Holy Brotherhood in particular could not have been behind the anti-Jewish violence.

It will be instructive to examine, first of all, the membership of the society and to focus in on a number of personalities prominent in Russian political life in 1881: Prince P. P. Demidov San Donato; Count Sergei Iu. Witte; the minister of state domains, M. N. Ostrovskii; Count P. A. Shuvalov; Tsar Alexander III; the director general of the Holy Synod, K. P. Pobedonostsev; and the minister of the interior, N. P. Ignatiev. It can be shown that each of these men opposed the anti-Jewish violence. It can also be shown that the Holy Brotherhood had no anti-Jewish legislative program that it wished to promote, never declared itself to be anti-Semitic, and never boasted about inciting pogroms, either at the time or later. Nor did the society have time, from the moment its founders began to get organized until the first outbreaks of rioting, to arrange a large-scale movement such as the pogroms. This is quite apart from the thorough ineptitude of the Holy Brotherhood in the execution of every activity it undertook. A careful analysis of the writings of three Holy Brotherhood insiders will serve to clinch the case for the innocence of this society in fomenting and abetting the spread of pogroms.

Most of the members of the Holy Brotherhood were well-to-do, upper-class, conservative noblemen. Jews, and Poles, even recognizably conservative ones, were not particularly welcome, because they were thought to be insufficiently patriotic and lacking in strong ties to Russian tradition.[6] Nevertheless, there was at least one Jewish member, Isaac Malkiel. Baron Horace Guenzburg, the banker, may also have been a member or a financial backer. In addition, the society had several agents of Russian-Jewish origin working for it in Paris who, incidentally, were evidently not very effective, since they spoke Yiddish but little French.[7] These Jews would surely not have remained in the organization had they known it to be responsible for the pogroms, nor would they have failed to make public such involvement.

Other members of the society are known to have opposed anti-Semitism and anti-Jewish provocations, whether in the form of restrictive legislation or extralegal acts of violence. Such men were Prince P. P. Demidov San Donato, Count Sergei Iu. Witte, who later became a famous minister of finance, M. N. Ostrovskii, minister of state domains in 1881 and 1882, and Count P. A. Shuvalov, a courtier close to the tsar.

In 1881 and 1882, Prince Demidov San Donato used his wealth to support the Holy Brotherhood. In 1883 he published at his own expense and over his own signature a book-length historical and socioeconomic study defending the Jews and pleading for their immediate and complete emancipation from the ramified discriminatory legislation to which they were subject in the Russian Empire.[8]

Count Witte in his memoirs claimed to have been the first to propose the idea that led to the formation of the Holy Brotherhood.[9] There is some circumstantial evidence to support this claim. There is also some evidence supporting Witte's claim that he was appointed head of the organization in Kiev, although his memoirs are silent about the work he did in that capacity.[10] Other sources indicate that he may have asked the longtime chief of the Kiev gendarmerie, a self-proclaimed opponent of the pogroms, V. D. Novitskii, to leave state service and work for the Holy Brotherhood. The latter turned down the suggestion, but in later years he and Witte were good friends and worked well together.[11] Throughout his memoirs, Witte dealt sympathetically with the Jews and the Jewish question. In general he gave the impression that he favored an emancipatory policy.[12]

Particularly interesting is the manner in which Witte described the 1881 pogroms in Kiev and Odessa, which he witnessed. He was certain that the authorities did not incite Christians against Jews and that the outbreaks were spontaneous. "In general the government viewed the matter properly at that time, namely, it would not tolerate any pogroms or disorders against anyone, whether Russian or Jew." For some reason Witte neglected to mention the severity of the rioting in Kiev, though he recalled correctly the speed with which order was restored in Odessa.[13] One may wonder whether the count, having such a viewpoint, would have been so proud of his role in founding the Holy Brotherhood if he had known that it participated in promoting pogroms; and if it had indeed participated, surely a leader in the organization such as himself could not have remained ignorant of this.

Minister of State Domains Ostrovskii, another leading member of the Holy Brotherhood, sharply attacked proposals made by Minister of the Interior Ignatiev in 1882 to increase drastically the restrictions on Russia's Jewish population. This debate in the Council of Ministers ended with the promulgation of the infamous May Laws. But while placing significant new limitations on the Jews, these "temporary regulations" were in fact much less severe than the legislation Ignatiev had originally sought. Thanks, in part at least, for this modification go to Ostrovskii.[14]

Count Shuvalov, one of the most important leaders of the Holy Brotherhood, had a reputation for being "sensible" (blagorazumnyi), that is, moderate and rather liberally inclined, in regard to the Jewish question.[15] The liberal-constitutionalist faction in the brotherhood, to which Shuvalov belonged, surely opposed all popular violence, just as it opposed any activity in the public sphere that would incline the government away from granting a constitution by increasing the need for police-state measures felt by the ruling circles.[16]

Tsar Alexander III never became a member of the Holy Brotherhood, but he did grant it financial support.[17] He would not have rendered this assistance if he had thought the organization supported the pogroms. Not only his public statements regarding the 1881–82 outbursts (see chap. 10) but his private remarks as well lead to the conclusion that the tsar was firmly opposed to the violence. It represented to him a dangerous challenge to public order and authority that must be stopped.

In his marginal notes on reports of the pogroms, Alexander III expressed shock, dismay, and strong disapproval. He wanted order reestablished as quickly as possible. In notes on reports dated 16 and 27 April 1881, Alexander called the riots "very deplorable" (ves'ma priskorbno) and called for immediate steps to restore order. On 28 April he said he was convinced that outside agitators must have incited the people against the Jews. He also called the participation of a military officer in the riots "a disgrace" (bezobraziye). He found "very sad and disturbing" a report of 30 April that troops sent to quell the riots would probably have preferred to attack the Jews. He was "surprised" by a statement in the report about the population's "deep hatred" of the Jews. On a report of 9 May, Alexander wrote, "I am very glad" when told of successful measures being taken to restore calm and prevent further outbreaks in Odessa. He also found it "very comforting" to receive other reports of calm being restored. He praised officers who had punished the rioters swiftly and severely as "energetic and wise." He called the behavior of judges who treated the rioters leniently "inexcusable." As for police inefficiency, which only served to incite the rioters rather than calm them, Alexander more than once wrote, "very distressing" (*ves'ma grustno*). On the report, dated 5 April 1882, of a pogrom, he wrote, "I hope that the disorders will soon cease." Insofar as can be determined from the available evidence, only in a minute scrawled on a report dated 10 May 1883 did he express anti-Semitic opinions. There he wrote in exasperation, "Very sad, but I see no end to this; these Jews [*zhidy*][18] have made themselves too repulsive [*slishkom oprotiveli*] to Russians, and as long as they continue to exploit Christians this hatred will not diminish." Nevertheless, on 11 May 1883 he advised giving the chief instigators of pogroms thorough floggings. In June and July of that same year, he still found the pogroms "very, very unpleasant" and was still anxious for them to end soon. Finally, in the last available remark on a report on a pogrom, dated 23 July 1883, Alexander wrote that he hoped the calm announced by the report would continue.[19]

Alexander's friend, K. P. Pobedonostsev, the influential director general of the Holy Synod and a personality well known for his hostility to the Jews, was frequently accused of being a founder and important supporter of the Holy Brotherhood, at least for a while, as well as a supporter of the policy of organizing pogroms.[20] Evidence is now available that refutes both these charges. According to Pobedonostsev's biographer, Robert F. Byrnes, the director general may have favored the establishment of a conservative political organization in a moment of panic in March 1881, but otherwise he consistently opposed amateur societies of this type. During 1882 he wrote letters to Alexander III denouncing the Holy Brotherhood and recommending its dissolution.[21] As for Pobedonostsev being behind the pogroms, I have already shown that he strongly opposed any violence in the streets and that he actually took steps to help combat the anti-Jewish rioting.

It is more difficult to determine whether N. P. Ignatiev, who became minister of the interior in May 1881, was a member of the Holy Brotherhood, and, if so, for how long.[22]

It is, however, worth noting, the running feud between the organs of the state police, for which the minister of the interior was responsible, and the brotherhood, which tried, rather ineptly, to use conspiratorial and secret police type methods against the enemies of the regime. In general, the official institutions found the society "an annoying source of interference with the smooth and effective functioning of [the] police apparatus." The Holy Brotherhood, for its part, never managed to implement any of its planned activities. It was accused of making efforts to prove the inefficiency of the minister of the interior, Ignatiev, and his police agencies. He in turn complained to Pobedonostsev that "the agents of the Brotherhood are compromising us everywhere." The competition between the society and the police was occasionally colored with comedy, as when they arrested each other's plainclothes undercover agents, suspecting them of being revolutionaries.[23]

We may note here, in passing, that those police officers who vigorously opposed the pogroms—and there were many—would surely have made their suspicions public if they had thought the Holy Brotherhood had a role in the troublesome 1881 disorders.

Perhaps Ignatiev, who was well known to his contemporaries as a liar and conniver, was working both ends against the middle, doubling as chief policeman publicly and pogrom instigator secretly. After all, the brotherhood was forced out of existence only by Ignatiev's successor, Tolstoi.[24] The explanation of the closure of the Holy Brotherhood and Ignatiev's replacement, however, need have nothing to do with the supposed pogrom policies of the minister and society and the antipogrom position of Tolstoi. It has, rather, to do with the "constitutionalist" aspirations of Ignatiev and the society and Ignatiev's evident lack of control of state affairs, on the one hand, and Tolstoi's extreme opposition to any idea of a constitution, as well as his insistence on "order"—officially imposed and policed—on the other hand.[25]

In sum, having taken into account the factors detailed in this chapter, as well as those examined in earlier chapters about the implications of Ignatiev's initial opinion that the pogroms were socialist instigated,[26] we can confidently discount the charge that the minister was behind a policy of fomenting pogroms executed by the Holy Brotherhood.

The Holy Brotherhood never announced itself as being anti-Semitic. A review of its literature and items written about it by former members fails to disclose any strong anti-Semitic sentiments, much less the advocacy, either publicly or secretly, of a pogrom policy. There is one episode, the Holy Brotherhood's sponsorship of the émigré newspaper *Vol'noe Slovo,* that, at first glance, might seem to contradict this claim. However, upon further consideration, this affair really reveals very little about the views of the Holy Brotherhood on the Jews.

The story, as told by Shmuel Galai, is as follows: In the early summer of 1881, the Holy Brotherhood sent its agent, A. P. Mal'shinskii, to Western Europe, where he contacted the prominent Ukrainian nationalist M. P. Dragomanov, who was living in Geneva in self-imposed exile. Mal'shinskii proposed setting up an opposition, revolutionary newspaper, to be funded from Russia, using the printing press that Dragomanov and a few of his supporters owned. Dragomanov agreed, having no idea of Mal'shinskii's Holy Brotherhood connections. Dragomanov also agreed to write for the new paper, named *Vol'noe Slovo (Free Word)*. Its first issue was dated 27 July–8 August 1881. In time, Dragomanov's influence over editorial policy increased, and from mid 1882 he became in practice the paper's sole editor. The last issue was dated 10–22 May 1883, several months after the official closure of the Holy Brotherhood. This right-wing society secretly funded *Vol'noe Slovo* during the whole time of its existence. The cover story used was that a secret, constitutionalist organization in Russia, the "Zemstvo Union," was supplying the financial backing.[27]

Of particular interest here are the clearly anti-Jewish articles, penned by Mal'shinskii and Dragomanov, that appeared frequently in *Vol'noe Slovo*. Galai labels the paper's tone as one of "blatant" and "virulent" anti-Semitism, which increased as Dragomanov gained more influence over editorial policy.[28] One should not, however, jump from this judgment to the conclusion that the Holy Brotherhood was anti-Semitic. There are, in fact, several considerations that prevent us from being able to view *Vol'noe Slovo*'s posture as a reflection of the Holy Brotherhood's approach to the Jews and the Jewish question.

According to Galai, the Holy Brotherhood sponsored this organ as part of a campaign to set up illegal, ostensibly oppositional newspapers with the aim of using them to discredit the terrorist wing of the Russian revolutionary movement. *Vol'noe Slovo*, then, was in no way intended as an expression of the Holy Brotherhood's views, and there is thus no reason to assume any correlation between what was written in the paper and the views of the organization and its members. Insofar as the newspaper was under the control of the brotherhood, it can be assumed that the opinions expressed in its pages were intended to discredit the revolutionaries (many of whom did indeed have anti-Jewish views; in the best case, these socialists thought it would be possible to exploit popular anti-Semitism for revolutionary ends.)[29]

However, Galai never makes clear the degree of control the Holy Brotherhood actually had over *Vol'noe Slovo*. Indeed, he strongly implies that it was minimal. Discussing the question of whether Dragomanov knew that there was no such organization as the "Zemstov Union" and that the brotherhood sponsored his paper, Galai has this to say: in spite of ample reasons for doubt, Dragomanov insisted in his memoirs "that the 'Union' existed and that the newspaper he edited was its official organ."

It is hardly conceivable that, as some historians claim, Dragomanov was simply fooled by [P. P.] "Bobi" Shuvalov, with whom he was in close contact during the first months of 1883. It is much more likely that Dragomanov realized, by early 1883 if not before, that the "Zemstov Union" did not exist, but decided for various reasons to continue as editor of *Vol'noe Slovo* and to cooperate with Shuvalov, of whose position in the Brotherhood he must have been aware. He may have believed, like Pobedonostsev, that Shuvalov was a constitutionalist, who was using the Brotherhood for his own aims. Or else, as one of his followers later hinted, he did not care much about the source of his paper's backing *as long as he had complete editorial control.* In either eventuality, to reveal the truth in his memoirs would have been most embarrassing.[30]

In short, *Vol'noe Slovo* was Dragomanov's instrument as much as, if not more than, the Holy Brotherhood's. Thus the views expressed in that newspaper surely tell much more about the opinions of the famous Ukrainian nationalist than about those of the right-wing organization in Russia.

The final point to be made in regard to *Vol'noe Slovo,* the Holy Brotherhood, and the pogroms of 1881 is that even if certain members of the organization held views hostile to the Jews (perhaps Mal'shinskii, for example, who was the closest link between the society and the paper until the end of 1882),[31] and even if the organization was willing to make use of an anti-Semitic press organ abroad, there is no hint whatsoever in this whole episode that the Holy Brotherhood or any of its members were involved in any way in inciting pogroms.

The difficulty, or even impossibility, of finding any direct expressions of strong anti-Semitic sentiments by the Holy Brotherhood or its members was admitted by some conspiracy theorists, yet they continued to insist on the organization's guilt in causing the pogroms.[32] They evidently felt that anti-Semitism was too good a weapon for the Holy Brotherhood to forgo, so they accepted uncritically the assumption that the society must have used it. But it is difficult to see why the brotherhood would have concealed its anti-Jewish aims so thoroughly, if it did indeed have such aims.

In the absence of direct proof that the Holy Brotherhood as an organization sponsored the pogroms, some conspiracy theorists accused certain elements within the association of being the organizers. It was asserted, for example, that the society was not a unified whole and that among its members were many "blatant and active anti-Semites." Pobedonostsev and Ignatiev in particular were named.[33] Other writers admitted that there was little basis for assuming that the St. Petersburg branch of the brotherhood had a determining influence in arranging the pogroms. They thought that the organizing center was, rather, in Moscow and that at least part of this center was identical with the brotherhood's branch there.[34]

Apart from the problems involved in identifying Pobedonostsev and Ignatiev as Holy Brotherhood members and instigators of pogroms, there are some other very telling questions to be asked of this interpretation: If some members of the brotherhood supported the idea of pogroms, would they not have boasted about its great "success"? Perhaps they kept quiet in order not to arouse opposition within the organization? This claim might hold up for the period 1881–82, when the rioting was actually occurring. But what about later, when the pogroms had ended and the society had become defunct? Furthermore, if the resources and organizational instruments of the brotherhood had indeed been used to promote an anti-Jewish conspiracy, surely those members who objected to the violence would somehow have found out and somewhere expressed their opposition. The society was, after all, organized hierarchically. And the man responsible for setting up the Moscow branch was the "liberal" Count Shuvalov.[35] Would he have been unaware of the conspiracy, if it had existed? And would he have failed to speak out?

Other members with inside information, who touched upon or had occasion to touch upon the Jews and the Jewish question in their writings about the association, never even hinted at a connection between the Holy Brotherhood and the pogroms. Statements made by three insiders vividly illustrate this point. The first of these was the agent sent by the Holy Brotherhood to investigate the disorders soon after the pogroms began. In his report there were no statements to indicate that his fellows had taken part in arranging these events. He, in fact, came to the conclusion that the cause of the anti-Jewish violence was "the outside force of sedition," which, in order to train the people for rebellion against the government, incited them against the Jews.[36]

What has been said earlier in this study about the implications of Ignatiev's blaming the revolutionary socialists for starting the pogroms applies here with equal force.[37] In the circumstances of the spring of 1881, it was only natural to focus on the socialists. But there was nothing in particular to be gained for the conservative cause by blaming them. Such censure could, conceivably, even have brought the socialists added popularity and support. A better explanation, from the conservatives' and reactionaries' point of view, lay ready at hand, namely, the notion of Jewish exploitativeness as the cause of the rioting. This explanation was in fact adopted later, when the government had regained its equilibrium. All these considerations point to the conclusion that the Holy Brotherhood's agent must have blamed the revolutionaries because he really thought they were guilty. If this inference is correct, then the association's noninvolvement in the affair is clearly evident.

The second insider, V. N. Smel'skii, was chief of the Holy Brotherhood's secret agents in St. Petersburg. He had gained considerable experience as a police officer before joining the newly formed brotherhood. Although he was never initiated into the highest spheres of the society, Smel'skii was fully acquainted with its practical activities and had the ear of personages high up in the hierarchy. He kept a diary, which was published in 1916.[38] In his entry for 16 December 1881, Smel'skii reported that he had learned of the government's intention to improve the legal condition of the Jews. In response to this news he had given the leadership of the Holy Brotherhood his views on the matter.

> According to the press it is clear that next February a commission will begin examining the question of giving the Jews full rights. This question is of fundamental importance for Russia. If it is decided according to the wishes of the Jews, then the beating [*pobitie*] of the Jews by the people will be unavoidable; if not, then the Jews will rush to support the revolutionaries. Perhaps any decision is equally pernicious for Russia, especially if taken too soon, that is, before measures to reduce sedition and revolutionary agitation, such as those I have suggested, are implemented.
>
> The Jewish question should be examined leisurely. Meanwhile, a rumor should be spread that the Jews are to be granted various concessions. After two or three years a decision can be reached. This will allow time for calm to be reestablished in Russia. Then, no matter what solution is offered to the Jewish question, it will no longer produce those terrible consequences which can be expected if it is not preceded by the reduction of revolutionary activity.

Smel'skii added that he had explained the matter to his superiors in much greater detail.[39]

Elsewhere Smel'skii expressed the opinion that the rights of the Jews should be increased, but they should not be given full equality. The Jews, and the Germans resident in Russia as well, had "vile principles" that allowed them positively to oppress the peasants. Nevertheless, Smel'skii thought the southwest territories, the area where the pogroms had occurred, should be pacified, and he expressed dissatisfaction with the performance to date of the governor-general of the Kiev region, A. R. Drentel'n, the governor-general of the Novorossiisk region, A. M. Dondukov-Korsakov, and the governor-general of the Khar'kov region, D. I.

Sviatopolk-Mirskii.[40] Smel'skii's incorrect assumption that the government intended in the near future to alleviate the legal condition of the Jews indicates that in the mind of at least part of the public, the government as yet had no fixed policy, and certainly not a violently anti-Semitic one.

What interests us more, however, is Smel'skii's response to his own incorrect assumption. Here was a member of the Holy Brotherhood holding a moderately favorable attitude toward the Jews. He feared the revolutionaries more than anything, and he strongly opposed the unruly anti-Jewish violence in the streets. Like many other brotherhood members, he was willing to use deception (false rumors) to achieve the organization's ends. He assumed or—perhaps more importantly—felt he had no reason not to assume that his views would be well received among the higher echelons of the society.

This man, who was thoroughly familiar with the organization's practical activities, never indicated anywhere in his diary that he had even the least suspicion of his fellow members' involvement in the pogroms. If anyone could have obtained such information, he should have been able to do so, with his network of secret agents. And he surely had no reason to refrain from committing such information, if it had been at his disposal, to his diary. So again we are left not only with no evidence of Holy Brotherhood involvement in the pogroms but, rather, with very strong indications that the organization had nothing whatsoever to do with them.

Perhaps the objection can be raised that Smel'skii was a resident of St. Petersburg and therefore unaware of the activities of the Moscow branch. No such problem exists, however, with the testimony of the third insider, who was writing in 1883, after the Holy Brotherhood had been disbanded and with the express purpose of recounting all the organization's activities, especially its "successes." The document under consideration, according to the editor who published it, was composed with the intention of serving as an official history. It was probably intended for distribution among high government officials, and it evidently reached at least the upper ranks of Holy Brotherhood members. Schematic in structure, the report deals with ideology, organizational structure, methods to be used, and achievements. In the draft two different handwritings were evident: one simply filled in certain facts and was probably that of a "higher brother" who knew secrets the main author did not know.[41] For the present investigation the document is noteworthy more for what it does not say than for what is does say.

The report discusses qualifications for membership in the society: those admitted should be men influential in their communities, wealthy, seriously interested in political and economic matters, of high morals, with conservative family traditions, political maturity, and economic independence. Special efforts were made to assure that members belonged to the "native nationality" of the land and had an interest in preserving the political dominance of this nationality. Thus the society placed little trust in Polish and Jewish conservatism (*evreiskii konservatizm*—note the use of the neutral term *evreiskii* instead of the pejorative *zhidovskii*). It was felt that the political and economic interests of these nationalities diverged too sharply from those of the native Russians.[42]

The reader will recall that the Holy Brotherhood *did* have some Jewish members, in spite of these guidelines (see above). Furthermore, there is no mention of not wanting Jews because they might have hindered the organization's anti-Semitic activities, and no speculation that Jews would probably not have wanted to join anyway because of such activities.

The report says later that members were encouraged to investigate different social questions with the aim of working out solutions. Factual elaboration of the given subject was to be preferred over general considerations, which would merely amount to personal opinions. Among the questions demanding attention were local manifestations of social dissatisfaction, the revolutionaries' sources of support, the circumstances of rioting and lesser disturbances, poverty, and the misappropriation of funds. The research of brotherhood members was supposed to draw an accurate picture of social life. The aim was not only to establish principles, but also to develop a practical conservative program. The society was aware, the report stated, that to undertake such an ambitious project would be difficult, since most writers were liberals or radicals. And, as a matter of fact, during its short existence it admittedly did not get very far, having only just begun to gather information on the condition of Russian society and the political ferment within it.[43]

This description indicates that the Holy Brotherhood, like the government of Minister of the Interior Ignatiev in 1881, had no preconceived solutions for Russia's problems. In fact, the writer of the report makes it clear that the society never got around to formulating a conservative program or defining its policy on numerous topics. Thus it could not decide on the appropriate way to respond to the pogroms (much less had it decided to organize and promote them). Would such popular violence promote conservative goals? The Holy Brotherhood gave no final, definitive answer to this question. A careful reading of the document under consideration, however, reveals that on the whole the society seemed inclined to reject this thesis.

On at least three different occasions the author had an opportunity to sketch the activities of the brotherhood in relation to the Jewish question. He gave a "Short History of the Society," a description of the "Activity of the Society," and a "Short Summary of Information Received by the Society." All the activities he mentioned related to either protecting the tsar, or fighting terrorists and socialists, or discovering the sources of sympathy and power of the revolutionaries and liberals.[44] No mention of Jews was made, no mention of organizing pogroms. Yet why not, if the author wanted to stress the usefulness and achievements of the society? If the anti-Jewish riots were the calculated work of the brotherhood, then they represented a major success, a singular accomplishment, among many false starts, bungled escapades, and outright failures. Would not the author have tried to point out to the government the "wonderful" lesson to be learned—anti-Semitism and pogroms could be used to serve the conservative cause with no fear of the violence turning against the government? This document, however, indicates that the Holy Brotherhood was unaware of this lesson, both before and after the pogroms.

In light of all this, I feel confident in concluding that the writer of the report did not credit his organization with causing the pogroms—because the brotherhood had no part in them. Not only that. As was revealed by this document, the Holy Brotherhood was seriously, almost obsessively, preoccupied with the inability of official governmental institutions to protect the tsar and other dignitaries from terrorist attacks. Men with such concerns surely would not have resorted to popular violence, which could only further expose publicly the weakness of the government's security apparatus, thereby encouraging the revolutionaries and inviting unforeseen, perhaps disastrous, consequences. Rather, the report makes it clear that the Holy Brotherhood, when it was not simply competing with the police, wanted the reestablishment of public order, the calming of the public mood, and a renewal of confidence in the government.

Before leaving this third insider, we must note one more point made by him. During the first several months of its existence, the Holy Brotherhood was "almost exclusively" occupied with internal organizational matters, such as working out the statutes of the society, recruiting members, grouping them according to specialities, and so on.[45] This assertion is easy to accept in view of the society's cellular organizational structure. In theory, each cell of five "brothers," being connected only to the next higher link in the hierarchy, on up to the top, had no knowledge of the membership of other cells. This "was a cumbersome arrangement consuming time and hindering the flexibility and speed of the operations."[46] In other words, there was insufficient time between 12 March and 15 April, or even 15 June, for the society to organize and orchestrate large-scale anti-Jewish rioting.

To judge from the testimonies of the three insiders, Hans Rogger appears to be absolutely correct in his assessment that "anti-Semitism played no part in [the Holy Brotherhood's] programme. What is known of its founders and most eminent members suggests that they feared uncontrolled violence as much as did the Tsar and his government, while the few aristocratic constitutionalists among them . . . were unlikely advocates of pogrom agitation."[47]

With the elimination of the Holy Brotherhood as a suspect in the presumed pogrom conspiracy, one is left to conclude that the rioting occurred spontaneously, for, judging by the historical records, apart from the socialist revolutionaries, the government, and the Holy Brotherhood, there was no other organized group in Russia that could have caused the pogroms. And, as I shall demonstrate in chapter 12, the socialist revolutionaries are easily ruled out as a factor in causing the anti-Jewish violence of 1881.

# Chapter 12

# THE REVOLUTIONARY SOCIALISTS

◆ ◆ ◆

## The Initial Response of the Government

ON 4 MAY 1881, TSAR ALEXANDER III'S BROTHER, GRAND DUKE VLADI-mir, told the Jewish notable Baron Horace Guenzburg that the recent pogroms had not originated as a result of anti-Jewish feelings only, but in the desire to "arouse a general insurrectionary chaos."[1]

On 6 May 1881, Minister of the Interior N. P. Ignatiev handed Tsar Alexander III a note (written on 5 May, the day Ignatiev became minister of the interior) regarding a report he had received from the governor-general of Odessa, A. M. Dondukov-Korsakov. The governor-general had stated that on 4 May several persons, including thirty students known for their political unreliability, had participated in (unsuccessful) efforts to renew riots in Odessa. Ignatiev added: "This supports my supposition *already communicated to you* [Alexander III] that while the immediate cause of the riots in the south was the local population's hatred of the Jews, still, they were provoked by persons hostile to the government who intended to train the masses in revolution by accustoming them to street commotions and overt disorders."[2]

On the same day, Ignatiev informed provincial governors in a memorandum (also written on 5 May) that:

> The movement against the Jews, which manifested itself recently in the south, represents a sad example of how people otherwise loyal to the Throne and the Fatherland can fall under the influence of evil-intentioned persons, who stir up the worst passions of the popular masses. The latter then falls into willfulness and arbitrariness and acts, without being aware of it, according to the plans of the revolutionaries. Such violations of the public order not only should be strictly prosecuted, but carefully prevented. For the first duty of the government is to safeguard the population from all violence and wild arbitrariness.[3]

On 11 May 1881, Alexander III met with a delegation of Jewish notables. He told them that all Russian subjects were equal before him, and added, "In the criminal disorders in the south of Russia the Jews merely serve as a pretext, . . . it is the work of anarchists." The tsar also expressed "the view that the source of the hatred against the Jews lay in their economic 'domination' and 'exploitation' of the Russian population."[4]

On 12 May 1881, Ignatiev wrote Alexander III that information reaching the Ministry of the Interior from the *guberniias* gave grounds for supposing that the disorders in the south, while finding a ready reception in Jewish-Christian relations, were evoked by the activity of evil-intentioned persons who wanted to acquire experience of the popular masses' capacity for engaging in disorders. In order to get more information and further clarify the matter, Ignatiev suggested sending Count P. I. Kutaisov on a fact-finding mission to the pogrom areas. This proposal was adopted the same day. In his instructions to Kutaisov, Ignatiev commissioned the count to clarify the general social causes of the hostile Jewish-Christian relations in southern Russia as well as the immediate causes of the pogroms; their timing indicated that they had occurred under the direct influence of elements hostile to the government, who perhaps wanted to ascertain the capacity of the population for making disturbances and the means available to the government to suppress them.[5]

Until the summer of 1881 most Russian government officials held views such as these about the origins of the pogroms. Then, from August 1881, the Jews alone were blamed for having brought down upon themselves the wrath of the local gentile population.

## The Revolutionary Socialists before 1881

The revolutionary opponents of the tsarist regime during the 1860s, 1870s, and 1880s were known by many names and belonged to many circles and organizations. As a whole they are called *narodniki* in Russian, meaning "populists"; they are also called revolutionary socialists. Sometimes the names anarchist and nihilist were applied to them. The Russian revolutionary movement became a large-scale phenomenon in the 1860s and 1870s. From the beginning, the leading thinkers of the *narodniki* and their followers disagreed among themselves over many issues, and some of these disagreements had implications for the way in which they addressed the Jewish question, though not always in the manner one might have expected.

All the revolutionaries saw the agrarian masses of the Russian Empire as being to one degree or another the repository of essential values—moral purity, integrity, and even truth. The peasant commune was viewed as a sound basis or model for the desired just society of the future. The revolutionaries, who almost all came from the educated classes, tended to feel that their education and well-being had come at the expense of the peasants, so they had a debt to repay to the people. This they would do by leading them to a better future, wherein exploitation, inequality, poverty, and arbitrary rule would be ended.

It is at this point that the disagreements arose. Were the revolutionaries to follow the lead of the people or to guide and educate them, and to what extent in each case? The highly influential anarchist thinker Michael Bakunin (1814–76) and his followers advocated that the revolutionaries should simply spark a popular, spontaneous, elemental revolt, having opened the peoples' eyes to pursue their own natural aims. Peter Lavrov (1823–1900) and his followers advocated that the revolutionaries take control and lead the masses, using education, propaganda, and gradualism, before attempting to overthrow the old order. Revolutionaries debated whether radical social and economic reform and the redistribution of all the land among those who would work it was the only thing needed, or whether political reforms must be pursued as well.

These questions were the subjects of lively debate among the revolutionary youths and students, who were not always clear or consistent in their thinking or committed irrevocably to any one ideological line. Party lines were not firm either, and people moved easily from one camp to the other, or even identified with different camps simultaneously.

This absence of clearly defined lines in matters of general policy was even more evident in approaches to the Jewish question, which was never discussed systematically or thoroughly in the revolutionary literature.[6] Russian socialists generally considered themselves internationalists. For most of them, the question of nationalities as such was not so important. They felt that if the economic and social changes they advocated were implemented, then the problems of the various nationalities large and small would resolve themselves. Peaceful coexistence among the peoples or their gradual assimilation into one large new entity would be the result. Such ideological optimism, of course, was unjustified in light of the practical reality. The Jewish minority in Russia, and the events of 1881 in particular, confronted the Russian revolutionary socialists with some particularly unpleasant dilemmas. I will return to this problem below.

In the early 1870s the *narodniki* tried "going to the people," to encourage, help, educate, or learn from them; later, individual terror against government officials was tried. Those who adopted the latter policy were following the "Jacobin" ideas of Peter Tkachev (1844–85) and Sergei Nechaev (1847–82). These ruthless revolutionary thinkers reasoned that if the peasants would not revolt on their own, then the revolutionaries themselves must act, using the methods of conspiratorial organization, terrorism, and assassination. They adopted the idea that the end justifies the means, and, under the stress of events and continued political failure, many other Russian revolutionaries found it seductive.

The first broad-based populist organization was Land and Liberty (*Zemlia i Volia*). Formed in 1876, it split into the Black Repartition (*Chernyi Peredel*) and People's Will (*Narodnaia Volia*) organizations in 1879. Neither of these groupings maintained complete uniformity in the ideas of their members. They occasionally cooperated with each other and there was some crossing of membership lines. Ultimately both envisioned the establishment of a socialist society in Russia.

Broadly speaking, Black Repartition favored the use of propaganda and gradualism to bring about a popular revolt, its ultimate aims being the redistribution of the land and a federally organized Russian state. These goals, indeed, were thought to be in conformity with the demands of the people themselves. Black Repartition was rather loosely organized, and its ideological position tended to encourage free expression and differences of view.

People's Will, meanwhile, set out to overthrow the absolutist political structure, using individual terror against government officials. This was to be carried out by a revolutionary minority organized in a disciplined, centralized, highly secret organization. It was felt that since the government was so highly centralized, a few assassinations could have a very strong effect, damaging the government to the point where it would make concessions, and at the same time politically educating the whole Russian people. When the members of People's Will decided to kill the tsar, they expected this act to result either in his heir granting a liberal constitution of some sort or in a popular insurrection, and some may have even dreamed of their organization seizing power. While the revolutionaries spoke about their hope that the people would respond to the tsar's death with a violent uprising, they were nevertheless thoroughly surprised by the anti-Jewish rioting that actually broke out, as I shall show.

The attitudes of the *narodniki* toward the Jews, while generally not clearly formulated or stable, tended to divide along the lines of their sentiments toward Michael Bakunin and Peter Lavrov. Lavrov adopted a tolerant and rather positive position on the Jews.[7]

Definite anti-Jewish tendencies can be found in statements by Bakunin—who was an ardent Slavophile and anarchist—as early as the 1840s and 1860s. Anti-Semitic, almost racist expressions became very frequent in his writings from the end of the 1860s, connected to some extent with his bitter feud with Karl Marx and other European socialists of Jewish origin. Bakunin portrayed the Jews—in essence, all Jews—as being innately exploiters and parasites, and supporters of statism, absolutism, reaction, capitalism (and statist socialism), "bankocratia," and so on. In his view, the Jews were enemies of the agrarian Slavs and allies of the expansionist pan-Germans (whom he also despised—tsarist despotism, he thought, was German at root).[8] Note that here, as with other extremely anti-Jewish Russian socialists, the concepts of class interest and class conflict were forgotten when depicting the Jewish people: no distinction was made between rich and poor Jews, exploitative and exploited Jews; they were all viewed as one (particularly harmful) class all by themselves.

Many contemporaries testify to the strong personal influence Bakunin had on the people around him. He was in contact with many Russian political émigrés, some of whom returned to Russia to engage in underground activity. Bakunin's anti-Jewish views found expression in his writings and correspondence. He undoubtedly also expressed them in conversations and discussions with his colleagues, and this surely had some influence on these people.[9]

That many revolutionaries were hostile to the Jews is perhaps surprising only in light of their professed internationalism. In addition to the anti-Jewish attitudes common in Russian culture and society and those inherent in the Russophile, agrarian-oriented populist worldview, the fictional literature popular among the *narodniki* in the 1870s played no small role in creating a negative image of the Jews. All this contributed to the willingness in one degree or another of many revolutionaries to exploit anti-Jewish manifestations.[10]

Without exaggerating the particular influence of Bakunin, in light of the pervasive sources of anti-Jewish prejudice just noted, three parallels may be found between Bakunin's views and those of certain anti-Jewish *narodniki* in Russia in the early and mid 1870s: (1) a perception of the Jews collectively as a social class incarnating bourgeois capitalism; (2) a perception of the Jewish people (or nation) as an exploitative and parasitical entity, necessarily inimical to the working people; and (3) the assumption that the Jews were by nature reactionaries and alien to socialism. In *narodnik* mythology, the Russian people—the peasants, that is—were just

the opposite of these characterizations. The factual basis for this contrast
was, of course, the circumstance that the peasants were agriculturalists
and the Jews had virtually no agricultural class.[11]

It would seem that Bakunin never preached the use of anti-Jewish
violence, unlike some of his followers in Russia, who raised the slogan,
"Beat the *pans* [landlords] and the Jews!" Such agitation received extra
backing in the southern and southwestern regions of the Pale. First of all,
this area was already marked by an excited and violence-prone atmosphere
in general. Second, the residents there preserved the brutal anti-Jewish
traditions of Khmelnitski and the *Haydamaky*. And third, some of the
socialists of Ukrainian origin, both inside Russia and abroad, while remaining members of the Russian *narodnik* circles or close to them, became
ardent Ukrainophiles, sharing and drawing inspiration from the local
traditions. In some cases this meant adopting strongly anti-Jewish views.
All these factors together contributed to making the region where the
pogroms of 1881 occurred a center of anti-Jewish sentiments even within
the revolutionary circles.[12]

Numerous Jews joined the revolutionaries in Russia. Many of them
totally rejected their Jewish origins and set out to identify completely
with their new, "internationalist," gentile milieu. In the best of cases,
these people made a distinction between exploiting and impoverished
classes among the Jews (those impoverished Jews who were perceived as
exploiters—most village tavern keepers or petty peddlers, for example—
presented a special problem) and urged that the exploiters be opposed and
attacked. In taking this line they were no different from their gentile
colleagues, who worked against the possessing classes in general, including
the wealthy of their own people, in many cases their own families. Other
Jewish revolutionaries adopted the strongly negative views of their own
people described above: they saw them as essentially an exploiting nation,
incapable of being receptive to socialist ideas, and they worked with their
non-Jewish comrades solely among the gentile population. Some Jewish
*narokniki* did not even flinch at the idea—at least before they had had any
experience with the reality—of anti-Jewish violence in the service of the
revolution. In their view, only a successful socialist revolution could lead
to a significant improvement in the miserable situation of the Jews in
Russia and change their character for the better.[13]

Opponents of those who lumped all the Jews together as exploiters
were not lacking among the revolutionaries, especially in the circle close
to Peter Lavrov. From items written by them one can gain further insight
into the anti-Jewish thinking and activities of some of the *narodniki*. A

document written in early 1876 entitled "Prejudices of Our Socialist Revolutionaries Against the Jews" and signed "Socialist Revolutionary No. 1" (who has not been identified), had this to say: There are socialist revolutionaries who appeal "to the Russian people in speeches and writings which announce: All the Yids [*zhidi*] should be destroyed." Citing what he called one example among many, "Socialist Revolutionary No. 1" continued, "You write a pamphlet, *Parovaia Mashina* ["Steam-Engine"], which states that the *pans* and the Yids (note, all the Yids like all the *pans,* including the miserable and exploited part of the Jewish people) have taken over all the treasures of the land and condemned the peasants to starvation, distress, and sickness, so it is necessary to rise up and destroy all the Yids and *pans.*"[14]

The pamphlet cited—*Parovaia Mashina*—was perhaps one of the most aggressively anti-Jewish *narodnik* documents to have appeared. It portrayed attacking the Jews not as a concession to popular instincts and rebelliousness, and not as a tactic to be used for turning popular passions into more productive and more general channels, but as an integral part of the struggle the revolutionaries were trying to foment and direct. It ignored the role of economic conditions and pandered to religious and ethnic prejudice, by labeling the Jews a "harmful nation."[15] As I shall point out below, a similar approach was taken in August 1881 by the People's Will activist G. G. Romanenko.

A more moderate approach was taken in 1875 or 1876 in Odessa by a group of revolutionaries (including some Jews) who differed over the question of how to make the revolution but who agreed nevertheless to work together. According to a participant, on one occasion when rumors about possible anti-Jewish violence appeared, the circle discussed what to do. They decided "surely not to incite [anti-Jewish] rioting, but if it occurred, to act together to direct the popular movement to the police station and the jail, where political prisoners were being held." Armed units were formed to carry out this plan.[16]

The decision taken by the revolutionary circle in question indicates that a majority of its members did not view pogroms as something entirely positive or desirable. Noteworthy, however, is the implication that the question of whether or not to "incite" a pogrom was discussed as a real option. In other words, it would seem that there were some Odessa revolutionaries who proposed and perhaps supported such a policy. We do not know from the story presented whether the possibility or desirability of trying to *prevent* a pogrom altogether was raised or discussed. In the end, the view prevailed that a pogrom could serve as a tactical weapon for guiding a spontaneous popular outburst against the Jews into a more general attack against the regime.[17] This approach, like that of *Parovaia Mashina,* also found supporters in 1881, as I shall show below.

The late 1870s were a period of intensified anti-Jewish agitation, both in the legitimate press and among the public. This was especially so during and after the Russo-Turkish War of 1877–78, which aroused strongly chauvinistic and pan-Slavic feelings. As for the revolutionary socialists, however, the Jewish question seems to have been removed almost entirely from the agenda of their publications. The prevailing Judaeophobia was not countered, but neither was it indulged in. However, the Jewish question continued to be among the issues the revolutionaries discussed and around which they developed programs.[18]

The exploitation of Jew baiting and national antagonisms as a means to foment revolution was discussed at the end of 1879 in Black Repartition circles in St. Petersburg. In discussions about how far the revolutionaries were to go in venerating the opinions of the common people, the Jewish *narodnik* Pavel Akselrod asked: "What if the people want to beat the Jews [zhidov]? What if the people want to prevent by force the separation of Poland from Russia?" Akselrod's answer was, "We are with the people insofar as its aspirations are progressive, but we can by no means support the reactionary aspirations of the people."[19] That Akselrod felt it necessary to raise the issue using the terms he did indicates clearly that there were those who did not share his reservations about accepting the people's point of view uncritically and who were not so squeamish about the means to be used to reach the revolutionary goal. Akselrod himself argued that the revolutionaries must remove "from the people's consciousness . . . all superstitions which interfere with the fraternal and equal union of people of different professions, sexes, and religions."[20]

Persons who had participated in the discussions with Akselrod were among those involved in working out the program of the Southern Russian Workers' Union (a revolutionary organization founded in the spring of 1880). They were constantly discussing and rewriting their platform. In one draft version at least, there was the recommendation "to exploit the hatred of the population against the Jews and the Poles in order to inflame quarrels which will bring about disorders, and, finally, to foster revolutionary outbursts." This phrase was appended to the section on "political terror," the rest of which read, "disorganization of the government by any means, in order to compromise its authority with the people and incite them against its officials and the police." The remaining sections of the program dealt with "agrarian," "factory," and "military terror."[21]

Other drafts of the union's platform omitted the phrase about the Jews and Poles. Indeed, it may have been only a passing idea adopted in the eager expectation that a popular revolution was close at hand, or it may have been a view held by only a small minority of the union's leadership. Another union document declared, "Socialism will take up the defense of the Ukrainophiles, Poles, Jews, the native sectarians, and with their help will pull down the rotten pillars of the Russian (or as many would desire) all-Slavic monarchy." What is significant about the draft platform is that a blatantly anti-Jewish policy was seriously entertained by at least some of the revolutionaries. According to Moshe Mishkinsky, "the intent of the . . . clause was unmistakable. It recommended and instructed manipulation of national antagonisms for revolutionary purposes. What is especially remarkable is the directive not only to make capital of spontaneous ethnic upheavals, but also to initiate them." In other words, Jew baiting could be used as a revolutionary tactic: not only could it be exploited when it occurred of itself, but it could also be instigated.[22]

And indeed it was so used. A leaflet in Ukrainian put out by the Southern Russian Workers' Union and dated 30 January 1881 recommended that: "Villages should organize secret councils through faithful people—in order to know from one another what is going [on and] where, things the *pans* [landlords] and the Jews are plotting together, and the tricks they are to take part in. . . . Everywhere it is possible secretly to settle matters with an obstinate *pan,* or a Jew, a policeman-grafter, or a bribed witness—to do it even without any assistance from the Secret Fraternity." Other documents of the union from about the same time do *not* mention the Jews as being among "the social groups inimical to the people that should be targets of agrarian terror. Also, there is no evidence that the Union, which tried to organize protests against the large landowners, was involved in any actions against Jews at the time. Nevertheless, the leaflet of January 30 [undoubtedly] aggravated an [already] intensely anti-Jewish atmosphere."[23]

## The Revolutionary Socialists in 1881

During 1881, Black Repartition had small sections in St. Petersburg, Moscow, and elsewhere, as well as in Minsk (where there was a secret press) and other towns in the Pale. Former Black Repartition members established the Southern Russian Workers' Union in Kiev. Kiev, indeed, "was a center of revolutionary activity, not only locally, but also for the Ukraine and the whole empire, and for the Russian revolutionary movement proper. . . . It is perhaps indicative that Kiev was second only to St. Petersburg in the reports of the *New York Times* about the 'nihilist' movement in the Russian Empire during the late 1870s and early 1880s." The Southern Russian Workers' Union was particularly active among arsenal and railroad workers in Kiev and other southern Russian towns, as is indicated by police and government documents.[24] People's Will, meanwhile, had a press in Moscow and member circles in various places. Most of its leaders were dispersed all over Russia after the assassination of the tsar and unable to work effectively. Both Black Repartition and People's Will had leaders and supporters abroad.

When the assassination of Alexander II failed to produce any political dividends and the government cracked down successfully on the revolutionary organizations, all but destroying them organizationally, a sense of desperation must have come over those revolutionaries who remained free, both within Russia and abroad. Even the members of Black Repartition who disapproved of the methods adopted by People's Will could not help empathizing with the rival group at least to some extent after the fact of the assassination.[25]

The anti-Jewish pogroms that broke out in the spring of 1881, then, came at a propitious time for the revolutionaries. Here at last was perhaps an echo of their activities. The Bakuninist notion of the peasants' instinctive violent rebelliousness joined the populist notion that the revolutionaries ought to identify with and support the aspirations of the people. This enabled many *narodniki,* quite apart from any anti-Semitic sentiments they might have harbored, to escape their frustration over their recent failures by viewing the riots as a genuine expression of popular revolutionary will. This buoyant attitude also enabled them to view the pogroms as the first stage in a wider movement that would ultimately overthrow the whole existing structure.[26] Tsarist officials expressed this same idea. But what was for the officials a menacing specter and a threat, was for the revolutionaries an opportunity and source of hope.[27]

At the same time, for those revolutionaries who had adopted the principle that the end justifies the means, the pogroms could easily be viewed as a handy tactical tool for mobilizing the masses. Perhaps only a very small number of *narodniki* favored instigating anti-Jewish violence, or even saw it as desirable, but many others were ready to exploit it once it occurred.[28]

Other revolutionaries who were clearly not anti-Semites preferred to keep silent about the whole matter, at least in print. This includes the émigré revolutionary leaders affiliated with Black Repartition, men such as Georgii Plekhanov (later known as the father of Russian Marxism), Peter Lavrov, and their Jewish associate Lev Deich. They had behaved similarly in the 1870s in response to anti-Semitic sentiments expressed by fellow *narodniki*. Then as now, they were willing to argue against these in private discussions and correspondence, but not in print. They could not approve of the masses' behavior on higher moral grounds. But to oppose the people by totally and without qualification condemning attacks on the Jews meant to risk generating popular hostility toward the revolutionary movement and losing whatever sympathy and support it may have already managed to acquire among the masses.[29]

Here is how Lavrov formulated this dilemma in April 1882:

> I must admit that I consider the [pogrom-Jewish] question extremely complicated, and, practically speaking, highly difficult for a party which seeks to draw near to the people and arouse it against the government. To solve it theoretically, on paper, is very easy. But in view of current popular passions and the necessity of Russian socialists to have the people wherever possible on their side, it is quite another matter.

Lev Deich added:

> I agree fully with the thoughts expressed by Peter Lavrov. Realistically, in practice, the Jewish question is now almost insoluble for the revolutionaries. What, for example, are they to do now [1882] in Balta where they beat up the Jews? To intercede for them means, as Reclus says, "to call up the hatred of the peasants against the revolutionaries who not only killed the tsar but also defend the Jews." . . . This is simply a dead-end avenue for Jews and revolutionaries alike. . . . Of course, it is our utmost obligation to seek equal rights for the Jews, . . . but that, so to speak, is activity in the higher spheres; and to conduct pacificatory agitation among the people is presently very, very difficult for the party. Do not think that this [situation] has not pained and confused me; . . . but all the same, I remain always a member of the Russian revolutionary party and do not intend to part from it even for a single day, for this contradiction, like some others, was of course not created by the party.[30]

The anti-Jewish, or pro-pogrom, or noncommittal positions taken by the various *narodnik* leaders and groupings made many Jews leave the revolutionary movement in disgust and rejoin their own people in its struggle for survival and a dignified existence. Other Jewish socialists, perhaps the majority, remained loyal to their revolutionary comrades. According to Erich Haberer, "From an initial sense of indifference to . . . or approval of the pogroms, [many] Jewish socialists [underwent] a process of disillusionment which, quite soon after the inception of the riots, caused them to oppose pro-pogrom manifestations—so much so that they played a crucial role in fostering anti-pogrom sentiments in both parties [Black Repartition and People's Will]." "As for [those Jews who remained radicals], the pogroms [tended to heighten] their sense of Jewish self-awareness and [make] them more sensitive to the suffering of their 'own race,' which, in turn, drew them even closer to the revolutionary movement as the only alternative route to win Jewish political and social emancipation in Russia." The Jewish radicals did not, however, manage to get any forthright public condemnation of the anti-Jewish attacks.[31]

This last statement perhaps needs to be qualified somewhat. Moshe Mishkinsky has revealed a short proclamation that appeared in St. Petersburg in mid June 1881. It was signed by the "Land and Liberty Society," a name used by the St. Petersburg Black Repartition organization in its printed materials. This proclamation announced unequivocally that the revolutionary socialists had no part in fomenting the pogroms, on both ideological and practical grounds.

From the Land and Liberty Society

Alexander III informed a delegation of Jews that the beating of their fellow Jews in the south was caused by the agitation of "anarchists." This announcement by the tsar clearly reveals that he has decided to take advantage of the disturbances in the south for the benefit of his reactionary policy.

The Land and Liberty Society finds it necessary on its part to declare that fanning national antagonism stands in complete contradiction to the fundamental principles of the revolutionary socialists, who regard international solidarity as one of the primary conditions for the revolution's success.

Stirring up national passions is almost certainly liable to serve Alexander III, who, like all despots, knows quite well the meaning of the Roman saying, "Divide and Conquer."

The beating of the Jews is the result of the desperate situation of the people and of the medieval policy of squeezing the Jews into the confines of a relatively small territory.

Let, then, the governmental responsibility for the violence that has been caused to the Jewish population in the south fall upon the government and upon the exploiters in general, who through immeasurable oppression have brought the Russian people to express its protest in such fashion.

Signed:The Land and Liberty Society
St. Petersburg, 15 June 1881[32]

The reader will note that this proclamation did not deny entirely the revolutionary potential of the riots. The final paragraph may be understood as meaning that the violence should continue, not against the Jews indiscriminately but only against the exploiters, of whatever nationality, and those responsible for their activities, that is, the government. This idea is expressed rather obliquely, but that may be because the proclamation as a whole was of an explanatory nature, rather than being an inflammatory call to action.

The origins of this document, Mishkinsky shows, are shrouded in mystery, and its existence was hardly known at the time, so it could not have exerted much influence. It is interesting, though, insofar as it came closer than almost any other *narodnik* publication to denouncing completely the anti-Jewish violence.[33] Appearing in St. Petersburg, and not in the Pale, and, as I noted, being of an explanatory nature, it may have been aimed at the Russian intelligentsia and the prominent and educated Jews in the capital. These were people who could be expected to find crude national enmities and ethnoreligious violence completely objectionable. Their sympathy for the revolutionary movement was desirable and worth seeking, since it could conceivably be won. This the proclamation tried to achieve.

As far as is known, the most crude, one-sided, and blatantly anti-Jewish document issued by a socialist revolutionary source in 1881 was the Ukrainian-language proclamation, "To the Ukrainian People," dated 30 August. It was written by G. G. Romanenko, a People's Will activist, who defended his position in the October issue of the party's official journal, *Narodnaia Volia.* Exploiting the party's thorough disarray at the time, Romanenko not only made use of its press but also managed to give the false impression that the party's whole executive committee supported him.[34] The proclamation read, in part:

It is difficult for people to live in the Ukraine and, as time passes, the harder it becomes. . . . The people in the Ukraine suffer worst of all from the Jews. Who takes the land, the woods, the taverns from out of your hands? The Jews. From whom does the *muzhik* [peasant], often with tears in his eyes, have to beg permission to get to his own field, his own plot of land?—The Jews. Wherever you look, wherever you go—the Jews are everywhere. The Jew curses you, cheats you, drinks your blood. . . . It was not always like this in the Ukraine, not in the time of our grandfathers and forefathers. All the land then belonged to the *muzhik;* there were neither *pany* [landlords] nor Jews. . . . But [now] as soon as the *muzhiki* rise up to free themselves from their enemies as they did in Elizavetgrad, Kiev, Smela, the tsar at once comes to the rescue of the Jews: the soldiers from Russia are called in and the blood of the *muzhik,* Christian blood, flows. . . . You have begun to rebel against the Jews. You have done well. Soon the revolt will be taken up across all of Russia against the tsar, the *pany,* the Jews.[35]

Romanenko's view seems to have been that by the incitement of rabidly anti-Jewish sentiments and the encouragement of further pogroms, the revolutionary process would be accelerated.

As soon as the other members of the executive committee learned about Romanenko's proclamation, they rejected it as too morally outrageous. It was one thing to view the pogroms as the first step in the wider revolution, which meant that revolutionary propaganda should emphasize the shifting of the people's wrath from the Jews onto the wealthy exploiters of whatever nationality and their official defenders. It was something else, something morally and politically unacceptable to almost all the People's Will leaders, to inflame further the anti-Semitic violence. They tried to withdraw all the copies of Romanenko's proclamation from circulation. In this they did not succeed, and the reputation of People's Will has suffered ever since. That none of the *narodniki* of any stripe could bring themselves to reject the proclamation publicly (for perhaps the same reasons they could not bring themselves publicly to condemn the rash of pogroms altogether) only strengthened the negative impression it created.[36]

Expressions of the more moderate, or ambivalent, approach are found in publications of the Black Repartition movement. The first I will cite was issued by the Southern Russian Workers' Union on 27 April 1881 in Kiev, as the pogrom there was in its second day. This publication led to the arrest of the leaders of the Workers' Union and the seizure of its press at the end of April.

> Brother workers. You are beating the Jews [*zhidov*], but indiscriminately. One should not beat the Jew [*zhid*] because he is a Jew and prays to God in his own way—indeed, God is one and the same to all—rather, one should beat him because he is robbing the people, he is sucking the blood of the working man. To speak honestly, any merchant or factory owner of our own, more badly than the Jew, robs and ruins the worker, sucks him dry, piles up capital for himself, indeed becomes big-bellied. Then should such a bloodsucker be left in peace while anyone who is a Jew, who perhaps earns his daily bread no more easily than one of our own, at hard work, some trade, or unskilled labor—now, then, is he to be robbed too? It is a sin to hurt a poor worker, even if he be a Tartar. If we are to beat, then let us beat at the same time every kulak-robber who is making capital from our sweat and blood—beat all the authorities who defend those who rob us, who shoot among the people because of some villainous millionaire Brodskii, and kill

innocent people. This is the new state of affairs. Let us, brethren, stand up more staunchly for our just cause.[37]

An article that appeared in June 1881 in *Zerno,* the newspaper for workers put out by the St. Petersburg Black Repartition group, used a similar approach.

What is the background of the pogroms? "Jewish plunder, which has become unbearable for the working people. . . . The Jew operates taverns and inns, rents land from the landlords and leases it to the peasants at triple the price, buys up the peasants' crops before they have been harvested, and deals in usury." In addition, all of the institutions of the regime and its representatives are acting as defenders of the Jews during the pogroms, coming to their aid with whips and rifle butts. The officials are joined by landowners and priests, who fear that the riots might encompass more far-reaching targets than the Jews alone. What the people have done has not helped them in the least; they have merely fallen prey to reprisals by soldiers and Cossacks. Are the people well-off in places where there are no Jews? Are Jews the only exploiters? Why do they beat only Jews? What about the Russian kulaks and usurers? Not all Jews are rich, not all are kulaks. Many Jews work by the sweat of their brow and are exploited; the Jewish kulaks trample upon them no less than upon others. "Why then, we ask, have the miserable huts of Jewish craftsmen been destroyed? Why have their meager possessions, acquired with the few kopeks they have earned by their labor, been plundered and vandalized?" "Desist from hatred toward persons belonging to other peoples and religions. Remember, all those who labor, no matter what their religion or nation, must unite in order to fight the common enemy together. . . . Do not waste your strength in vain; do not hate workers of another people, even Jews."[38]

Another item appeared in the final number of *Zerno* in November 1881, when it may have seemed that the pogrom violence had ended. In its lead article the newspaper repeated the ideas just quoted, in the context of arguing that any rebellion must have preparation and a clear purpose, rather than being simply the pouring out of the people's wrath. The pogroms were the latter type of activity, which brought the people no good and in many cases resulted in punishment by the authorities. Like the June 1881 proclamation article, this article also came close to condemning the pogroms—on the practical grounds that they brought no gains and on the moral grounds that ethnic origin and religious differences were not reasons for hatred and violence. But it also referred to Jewish exploiters, in comparison to whom "the kulaks among the peasants or the landowners" were no better—a backhanded compliment to the Jews.[39]

Other Black Repartition publications expressed a more positive approach to the pogroms. For example, in September 1881 a writer in *Chernyi Peredel,* Black Repartition's theoretical journal published in St. Petersburg, "concluded that the anti-Jewish pogroms were merely a prelude 'to a more serious and purposeful movement' and optimistically added that under present conditions they were an essential stage on the road to an uprising against the regime." An editorial in the same issue expressed an uncharacteristically positive view of terrorist acts. They could defend the legitimate rights of man and citizen and also strengthen and arouse the positive qualities of the people, their "sense of strength, energy, and right, . . . and [their] willingness to defend [their rights] with weapon in hand." The pogroms were a proof that this was the case: in addition to local conditions, the assassination of the tsar had contributed to their occurrence.[40]

A writer in the last issue of *Chernyi Peredel* in December 1881 put together a complex interpretation of the pogroms that expressed very clearly the revolutionaries' ambivalences about the Jews and the anti-Jewish violence.[41] He noted that the violence was an expression of the people's anger over being exploited. Only Jews were attacked, because they were so much more visible than the non-Jewish exploiters. The Jewish exploiters were more crafty than the non-Jewish ones, and all Jews were discriminated against by the state; so those attacking them would presumably face less risk of retaliation by the authorities. In sum, attention could be focused on the Jews easily and they were easier to hurt. The historic "national-religious antipathy" to the Jews also played a role, according to the writer of this article.

However, he did not stop there. He went on to note the anti-Jewish agitation of *Novorossiiskii Telegraf* and the rumors about beating the Jews that spread before the first outbreak. From this he developed a conspiracy theory of the pogroms! He drew the conclusion that the spate of pogroms originated not from the people themselves but from "those who suck their blood" and "elements foreign to the people," that is, business rivals of the Jews who wanted to cripple their competition, and petty officials.

All of these considerations did not stop the author of the article from expressing the opinion that, now that the riots had broken out, they would generate a broader revolutionary movement. He noted various instances of attacks upon landlords and officials to bolster this view. An editorial in the same issue echoed these ideas and stressed the task of the revolutionary socialists in making the people aware of their real enemies, not the Jews, but the tsarist regime and its protégés. One sentence used by this editorialist is particularly revealing for the manner in which it tries to overcome the ambiguities of the situation: "Unresolvable contradictions reside in [the rural environment]; enlightened ideals often take on the monstrous form of dark prejudice."

The support expressed for the pogrom movement in the case of some *narodniki,* at least, must have been an expression of residual or latent anti-Semitism. A contemporary, writing many years later, denied this. In his view, the socialists' response in favor of the people's anti-Jewish outbursts "had nothing in common with anti-Semitism. . . . To the majority of revolutionaries the pogroms appeared not as a manifestation of national hostility, . . . but as a broad popular social movement, as a revolt of the impoverished masses against oppressive exploiters that must be followed by other outbursts culminating in a social revolution."[42]

It would seem that those people who labeled the Jews wholesale as exploiters and worked to inflame and intensify indiscriminate anti-Jewish passions (such as the author of *Parovaia Mashina* and G. G. Romanenko, for example) can safely be labeled anti-Semites. The question may be open in regard to those who rejected the pogroms as an expression of religious-national enmity while approving of them, to one degree or another, insofar as they were (or would become) based upon economic considerations. These people generally distinguished between the so-called exploiting classes among the Jews and the impoverished Jewish masses. Still, most of the agrarian- and peasant-oriented populists probably had greater or lesser prejudices against the Jews as middlemen, petty tradesmen and artisans, liquor dealers, moneylenders, and so forth. That is, in the opinion of these socialists, the Jews were almost by definition exploiters of the common people, in spite of their being among those most sorely oppressed by the Russian government. Jewish *narodniki* often shared this view of their own people. They felt that it was the tsarist regime that forced a parasitic and backward existence on the Jews, and with the overthrow of the present structure, the character of Jewish life would change for the better too.

There were thus *narodniki* of all types and points of view willing to try to exploit the pogroms. Their approaches were based upon a varying and incalculable mixture of irrational anti-Jewish sentiments, populist ideological positions, anti-Jewish biases connected with the position of the Jews in Russian society, and rationalistic (or opportunistic) calculations about how to deal with the existing political reality (in other words, political expediency).

On the whole, the picture unfolding from a review of the revolutionary literature in 1881 indicates that the People's Will publications were generally more willing to exploit or find positive features in the pogroms than were the Black Repartition publications. This is somewhat surprising in light of the ideological viewpoints attributed to the two groups. Since they were more radical and emphasized the role of a politically aware leadership, one might have expected People's Will supporters to be less sympathetic to the peasants' expressions of their "natural instincts" and more insistent on internationalist ideals of ethnic, religious, and national cooperation and brotherhood. Black Repartition, meanwhile, was supposed to be closer to the populism of the 1870s. Yet it tended to be more critical of the peasants' anti-Jewish excesses and stressed the need for a conscious leadership that would set well-defined goals and guide the masses to a clear awareness of their true interests. Such are the ironies of history.

However, we must remember that for most revolutionaries during the period in question, the early Bakuninist notions of Jewish exploitation and spontaneous peasant revolt—with predominantly social and economic goals—continued to have an influence right along with the later emphasis on conscious political action against the regime—with predominantly democratic and constitutionalist goals. Furthermore, positions were not frozen, people's ideas constantly changed and developed, and revolutionaries moved from one group to the other. In sum, a large majority of the Russian socialist revolutionaries demonstrated a high degree of ambivalence as well as revolutionary hopefulness in connection with the pogroms of 1881. Attacking the Jews indiscriminately was "bad," but the rioting could be "good" if it led to a broader insurrection.

The ambivalence here, however, may not have been so evident to the Russian government at the time. For one thing, tsarist officials were surely familiar with the anti-Jewish sentiments expressed in the revolutionary circles during the 1870s and in 1880–81.[43] For another thing, many Russian officials were quite sensitive to the opportunities the situation in 1881 offered the socialists and genuinely feared the spread of the violence beyond the Jews. This is clearly evident in official documents and, in particular, in the incident of the leaflet printed by the Southern Russian Workers' Union on 27 April in Kiev. As Mishkinsky noted:

> [The leaflet's] pronouncements were reflected in the opinions of government officials on the causes of the pogroms and the motives of their perpetrators, and had some effect on immediate official conduct as well as on later inquiries. . . . The police reports exaggerated the story somewhat to demonstrate their own vigilance and efficiency, which certainly prompted the authorities to take greater measures to stop the outrages. . . . The police . . . confiscated

[the leaflet]. They feared that its circulation would widen the scope of the disorders and change their character.[44]

## *The Revolutionary Socialists: "Not Guilty of Organizing Pogroms"*

In spite of the hostile sentiments toward the Jews and the positive attitudes toward the pogroms harbored by many revolutionary socialists, since the summer of 1881 almost no one has assumed that the *narodniki* were responsible for organizing or instigating or even having any significant influence on the several waves of anti-Jewish violence occurring that year. The government adopted and then quickly dropped this explanation.

In theory, the government *could* have changed its story for tactical reasons, even though it knew that the revolutionaries *were* in fact responsible. On the one hand, why risk encouraging the presumably anti-Semitic masses to support socialists acting like anti-Semites? As I shall show, such an idea was already in the air. And on the other hand, why not blame the Jews themselves for their misfortune by referring to their exploitative activities, thereby verifying the government's own anti-Semitic credentials?

This theory is revealed as baseless, though, when one observes that the government never fully dropped its claim that the socialists were implicated in the affair. This leads to the conclusion that the government changed its explanation of the pogroms not for tactical reasons but because its officials really believed that the *narodniki* were not responsible for inciting the violence. Let us look at the matter more closely.

Even after abandoning the notion that the riots *originated* with the *narodniki,* officials still claimed over and over that revolutionaries had taken some part in them, had tried, although so far unsuccessfully, to exploit them after they began, and would surely try to exploit them in the future. The government, then, remained very sensitive to the possibility of the revolutionaries taking part in the pogroms and using them for their own ends. Its representatives, however, never seemed to be very worried that by making such charges against the socialists they might indirectly be encouraging the anti-Jewish masses to sympathize with these enemies of the regime, on the basis of their shared hostility to the Jews.[45]

This thought must surely have crossed officials' minds, and they must have discounted it. Not everyone did, though. The idea was definitely in the air. It was expressed in July 1881 by a member of People's Will writing in the first issue of the organization's bulletin, *Listok Narodnoi Voli.* He argued, rather hopefully and prematurely, that because the socialists were blamed, especially by the Jews, as the instigators of the pogroms, their prestige was already being raised in the eyes of the masses, who until then had treated the educated urban youths with undisguised suspicion. Now the masses would view the revolutionaries as defenders and saviors, which would serve to bring about further revolutionary events in the near future. Members of Black Repartition shared these views, believing that "the prestige of the socialists had been boosted by the general conviction that they were responsible for the pogroms and so they were now in an excellent position to lead a popular uprising."[46]

The *narodniki* themselves, even those willing to support or take advantage of the riots, never claimed responsibility for starting them. Had they indeed been active in causing the lawlessness, one may suppose that they would have been eager to assume credit for such a major success. On the contrary, some revolutionaries admitted being caught completely unawares by the outbreak of anti-Jewish violence. At first they could see no connection between the pogroms and their own activities, apart, perhaps, from the pogroms somehow being linked to the assassination of Alexander II.[47] Later, the most the *narodniki* would say was that "the anti-Jewish movement, which was not originated or shaped by us, is nevertheless an echo of our activity,"[48] since it was directed against a group that, they believed, exploited the masses, acted tactlessly, and linked itself closely to the local authorities. Revolutionary writers labeled the rioting "a purely popular movement" and "a path the people had chosen."[49] Some "concluded that the anti-Jewish pogroms were merely a prelude 'to a more serious and purposeful movement' and optimistically added that under present conditions they were an essential stage on the road to an uprising against the regime."[50] The role of the revolutionaries in all this was to be to turn the popular violence away from the Jews and onto the true source of the people's troubles, the landlords, the non-Jewish bourgeois exploiters, and the officials.

Meanwhile, from the very beginning of the pogroms, there were socialists who disapproved of their colleagues' efforts to play a role in exploiting the Jews' misfortune. I have already discussed the antipogrom proclamation that appeared in St. Petersburg in mid June 1881 signed by the "Land and Liberty Society." During 1881 and 1882 a number of *narodniki* went on to adopt the view that agents of the government and some elements among the Christian bourgeoisie had instigated the rioting, with the aims of distracting the masses from their true interests and grievances and of harming Jewish business competitors.

I have also already examined this assertion among the socialists, combined with a hopeful attitude toward the pogroms, in the article that appeared in the last issue of *Chernyi Peredel* in December 1881. But most *narodniki* who blamed government officials and Christian bourgeoisie for the pogroms saw the rioting as a totally negative phenomenon—as an instrument for promoting reaction and fighting the revolution—rather than as the prelude to a general insurrection that many of their colleagues expected. This was the case with I. Getsov, a Jewish printer of the Black Repartition press in Minsk. He claimed that he presented the "government agents–Christian bourgeoisie" interpretation to a colleague and persuaded him to change the whole tone of an article he had written contending that the pogroms were the beginning of revolution.[51] Meanwhile, members of a revolutionary circle in Vilna issued an announcement in Yiddish (seen affixed to the doors of a local synagogue) at the end of July 1881 in which they declared: "Jews! They try to tell you that we, the nihilists, have been inciting the mobs against you. Do not believe it! We are not your enemies. This has been done by government agents in order to direct the wrath of the agitated people away from the government and against you. Be sure you know who your enemies really are."[52]

The ideas of those who totally opposed the pogroms were at first not widely publicized, on account of the ideological problems that the pogroms forced the *narodniki* to face (involving the whole question of their attitude toward the Jews), and for tactical reasons (so as not to arouse peasant hostility against the revolutionary party by condemning the violence and its perpetrators). But taking such a spineless and disgraceful position was by no means the same as instigating or promoting pogroms. Meanwhile, "the argument that the pogroms had only played into the hands of the regime {was] clearly formulated in the years 1884–6, as a kind of last will and testament, in the final publications of the {People's Will]. Thereafter, this theory became axiomatic in the thinking of the oppositional forces" in Russia.[53]

Historians have refrained from considering the *narodniki* suspects in the "Who caused the pogroms?" inquiry. There is no reason to challenge this consensus. It is instructive, however, to review the arguments that persuaded the Russian government to recognize the revolutionaries' innocence. We know that the government had good reason, insofar as it was aware of the views espoused by the revolutionaries, to assume that they were the ones responsible for instigating the mob violence of 1881. There even seemed to be some hard evidence to support this notion. Upon closer investigation, however, the presumed evidence proved to be misleading and subject to refutation.

Initially it seemed as if there was some element of simultaneity in the rioting. In addition, rumors were heard that the landlords would soon be set upon and their land redistributed among those peasants who joined the attack.[54] Another piece of evidence seemed to be the episode already described of the members of the Southern Russian Workers' Union who were arrested in the act of printing a revolutionary proclamation in Kiev in April while the pogrom there was still under way.[55] There were also reports in various places of students and other persons better dressed than the simple people appearing among the rioting mobs, and these were assumed to be *narodniki*.[56] According to one story popular at the time, a certain young man took time off from leading the rioters in order to play a piece from Gounod's *Faust* on a piano that had been thrown into the street—as only an urban intellectual, and presumably a revolutionary socialist, might have done.[57]

There is evidence that at least a few genuine *narodniki* actually participated in the violence, "watching the mob, studying its mood and doing everything possible to lend the disturbances a revolutionary character."[58] The story was told of a Jewish *narodnik* who, having dressed up peasant-style in a red blouse, joined the *pogromchiks* in the streets of Kiev. He evidently had hopes of seeing the mob turn on its non-Jewish oppressors; he may even have wanted to encourage them to do so. Nothing of the sort in fact occurred. The mobs destroyed the poorest Jewish neighborhoods and then ended their excesses. At this practical lesson in the baselessness of the revolutionaries' high expectations for the pogroms, the Jewish revolutionary was reportedly thrown into deep despair.[59]

However, in at least one instance it would seem that the revolutionaries actually succeeded in diverting the mob away from the Jews, by shouting, "Beat the police and the rich, not the poor Jews!" In response to this call, the rioters began causing damage in non-Jewish neighborhoods and setting fire to Russian-owned shops. According to the story in question, patrolling Cossacks soon forced the mob to desist.[60]

In chapter 7 I have demonstrated that the seeming simultaneity of the pogroms was deceptive. This fact was already recognized in the summer of 1881 by Count P. I. Kutaisov, the special emissary sent by Tsar Alexander III to investigate the pogroms on the spot. He described the riots as moving from place to place consecutively.[61]

Nor was Kutaisov impressed by the uncovering of the Kiev socialists' proclamation in April. He reversed the initial interpretation of this incident and used it to support his contention that the revolutionaries were *not* responsible for the riots. He noted that the proclamation was being printed while the pogrom was in progress and that it criticized the mob for attacking the Jews indiscriminately, the impoverished as well as the wealthy. It encouraged the people to attack their exploiters only, but all of these, including non-Jewish kulaks and landlords, and any government agents who protected the oppressors of the people. Clearly this text, whose ideas were echoed in other socialist publications and newspapers, was written after the violence had begun and in response to it. Kutaisov concluded that the *narodniki,* rather than instigating the riots, showed that they were as surprised as anyone by the phenomenon. [62]

Circulars obviously written after the riots had begun appeared in other instances as well. In some cases, in an attempt to broaden the base of the disorders, isolated proclamations of a generally revolutionary character (not anti-Jewish) were posted by individuals who sympathized with the revolutionaries but clearly had no organized group behind them. These people happened to have some of the revolutionaries' circulars on hand, so they displayed them in public places. In other cases declarations were written by simple, uneducated workmen acting on their own initiative, but evidently under the influence of the *narodniki.* [63]

Kutaisov suspected that in a few cases at least, the Jews themselves had authored the revolutionary proclamations that appeared. He noted that in these instances, the Jews claimed that revolutionaries were involved in the pogroms and referred to handbills they said they had found in the streets. To Kutaisov it was suspicious that only Jews reported having found such proclamations and that in them there were admonitions to the people to stop beating the Jews and to start attacking the landlords. He considered it even more suspicious when reports appeared that some Jews were talking to the peasants and using arguments similar to those in the "revolutionary" circulars, namely: the Jews were by no means as harmful as the landlords, who held all the land; so the landlords should be attacked rather than the Jews. Kutaisov concluded that it was very likely that the handbills had come from the Jews themselves, with the aim of goading the government into giving them greater protection. [64]

The tsarist emissary's anti-Jewish prejudices may have been speaking here more loudly than the circumstantial evidence he cited. To judge by the attitudes and activities of the *narodniki* that I have described through-out this chapter and about which the government surely knew a great deal, it is quite possible that the proclamations in question really did come from the revolutionaries and not from the Jews. More interesting, however, is Kutaisov's further conclusion, that whatever the source of the seditious circulars, they *could not have influenced* the popular masses. As evidence he cited the fact that only Jews, and not landlords or other gentiles, were attacked. Here Kutaisov was undoubtedly on firmer ground. His natural inclination, given the assumptions with which he started his mission, would have been to seek clues indicating the revolutionaries' responsibility. So if he drew the opposite conclusion, he must have had what he felt were fairly strong indications in that direction.[65]

In many places, including Elizavetgrad—the site of the first pogrom in 1881—rioting occurred without having been preceded by political propaganda (that is, printed or written revolutionary notices). Elsewhere officials reported that they had found no evidence that the publicly displayed posters had had any visible effect on the already otherwise agitated population.[66]

Non-Jews were in fact practically never attacked, even in those localities where undoubtedly genuine revolutionary circulars appeared and anti-landlord rumors circulated. Organized revolutionary participation in the riots would surely have altered this state of affairs.[67]

Rarely were outstanding mob leaders and instigators identifiable, and when they were, they almost always turned out to be simple people rather than intellectuals. The latter, though, were the ones most likely to be socialist activists and organizers.[68] In fact, almost no one well known for revolutionary activity was among the rioters arrested.

After what officials declared to be careful investigations, conducted by the police, administrative and judicial authorities, and local civilians, the government concluded that none of the evidence pointed to a revolutionary socialist plot. Indeed, the authorities found that in the circumstances there was no need for such a plot.[69]

# CONCLUSION

◆ ◆ ◆

It is practically impossible to prove a negative assertion ("no one planned the pogroms") since new data implicating some group could always turn up in the future. Nevertheless, the preceding analysis indicates as conclusively as the existing evidence allows that there was indeed no conspiracy behind the pogroms of 1881. The pages that follow attempt to give a coherent account, based entirely upon the evidence documented in the preceding chapters, of the anti-Jewish violence of that year.

Whether we look at the attitude of the Russian government toward its Jewish population or its treatment of that population, the attitudes of the Christian population toward the Jews or the attitudes of Jews toward their Christian neighbors, the role of religion in Christian-Jewish relations or the economic role played by Jews in the Pale of Settlement, we find all kinds of paradoxes and inconsistent tendencies. It is these conflicting strands of historical development that provide the broad and long-term background to the pogroms of 1881. Certain extraordinary developments in 1880 and early 1881 provide the immediate background.

By law, Russian Jews, except for a few privileged exceptions, were crowded into the Pale of Jewish Settlement. The reader will recall that the Pale was not uniform, either geographically, ethnically, or culturally. In light of this, we must note at the outset that the southern and south-western regions where the pogroms occurred (mainly the Ukraine and New Russia), differed from Belorussia and Lithuania, where there were no pogroms, in a number of significant ways that *may* have been factors in where the violence took place.

The local gentile population in the south and southwest had a tradition of active frontier rebelliousness. According to some reports, the "frontier" populations there—with their Cossack and freebooter traditions (people who had fled from centralized authority, serfdom, and military service)—were in general much more deracinated, undisciplined, adventuresome, and independent-minded than the indigenous populations in Belorussia and Lithuania, where the yoke of the nobility and central government authorities had weighed more heavily. Allegedly, from age-old habit or by nature, the Belorussians and Lithuanians were more passive, or submissive, and long-suffering.

In the south and southwest there was also a vivid and active tradition of hatred and persecution of Jews going back to the seventeenth and eighteenth centuries (Bogdan Khmelnitski and the *Haydamaky*). The anti-Jewish rioting in Odessa—itself a "frontier" town—in 1821, 1859, and 1871, also fed into this tradition and popular consciousness.

Belorussia and Lithuania were poorer and less fertile than the south and southwest, which were developing economically much more rapidly, both in industry and agriculture. For this reason many more homeless seasonal workers (that is, rootless, discontented, rough-and-ready men) were to be found in the towns and villages of the Ukraine and New Russia than in Belorussia and Lithuania. Many Jews also moved from the north to the south, to settle permanently; and Great Russians from the interior regions of the empire moved in as settlers as well. This led to heightened tensions and potentially dangerous rivalries between non-Jewish and Jewish business competitors (bourgeoisie) and professionals (intelligentsia), apart from any tensions existing between the non-Jewish lower classes (including the kulaks in the villages) and the Jews.

All this may fit in with the observation made by certain historians and social thinkers that rebellion and popular discontent expressed in violence do not necessarily take place when conditions are at their worst and people most in despair or apathy; rather they tend to occur when conditions begin to improve. The tide of rising expectations tends to promote impatience and the wish to see matters move more quickly. Freed from traditional moorings, the mob's readiness for violence and taking matters into its own hands grows.

The firm attitude against anti-Jewish violence adopted by the local authorities in certain places may also have had some influence. However, it must be noted that even in the regions where there were no pogroms, numerous cases of arson, some very serious in scope, occurred in towns and townlets, and there were instances of individual Jews and even whole families being murdered.

As a final word in this regard, it is worth noting that, even if conditions in the two regions had been very similar, there could still have been different behavior and responses. Pogroms, after all, did not take place everywhere even within the eight *guberniias* affected. Similar conditions (for example, economic hardship, or the presence of harsh or exacting administrators, or anti-Jewish attitudes) could, and did produce different consequences. Historical causality is a very complex matter. The historical process may make certain results possible, but this does not mean that they will necessarily occur.

In the pages that follow, when I talk about the Pale, I have in mind mainly the southern and southwestern areas just described.

In the Pale of Jewish Settlement, the vast majority of Jews suffered grinding poverty. But by the 1880s the Jewish community in the Russian Empire was undergoing momentous changes. The industrialization and modernization process that had begun in the 1860s completely undermined the already precarious economic position of many Jews while at the same time giving a small number the opportunity to become extremely wealthy and socially visible. The Jewish masses remained unassimilated and traditionalist, devoted to Jewish learning and ignoring the outside world for the most part. But the Haskalah (Enlightenment) had reached Russian Jewry. Increasing numbers of Jews were turning to secular education and a secularized life-style, advocating Russification and internal reform, and becoming involved in Russian society at large—or at least preaching such involvement. A small group even joined the socialist revolutionaries. To some Jews the future looked bright and promising; to others there seemed to be no light at the end of the tunnel. Whatever satisfactions they got in this world came from their devotion to the beliefs and practices of their ancestors.

For religious, ethnic, political, social, and economic reasons the Jews as a rule, and the Jewish masses in particular, felt alienated from their Christian neighbors. As always, there were exceptions to the rule. Some Jews and Christians developed genuine friendships. And on an everyday basis the two groups usually got along well together, whether their relations were linked to business or were purely social. But the adversary relationship was always an underlying factor. Because of the poverty and crowding in the Pale, Jews were forced to engage in economic activities that must have seemed even in their own eyes to be exploitative, given the ideas about economics prevailing at the time, and regardless of whether they made a positive contribution to economic activity. Some Jews, of course, were happy to take advantage of non-Jews; others must have felt that they had no choice; still others made every effort to be fair and honest and were acknowledged as being so.

Jews also felt proud of their own distinct religious and cultural tradition and the profound learning that went with it, in contrast to the general ignorance and brutality common in the lives of the surrounding non-Jewish population. Jewish pride, however, was tempered by fear and a sense of dependence: fear that relations with the non-Jewish population might degenerate into primitive violence (before 1881 the main fear was of individual violence, not of mass rioting, although "incidents" were common at Easter); and a sense of dependence resulting from the need to rely upon the grudging mercies of the authorities for protection. This was in addition to the degradation and resentment felt by Jews on account of the legal discrimination to which they were subjected in all areas of life.

Many Jews at the time argued that their relations with their neighbors would be quite good if only there were no outside agitation and if the Jews were equal before the law. Especially destructive to good relations, in this view, was the crowding forced upon the Jewish population by the existence of the Pale.

In the special conditions of 1881, any exceptional Jewish behavior, any manifestation of Jewish pride, self-confidence, vindictiveness, or fear, was liable to contribute to the outbreak of pogroms.

The violence in 1881 was carried out by two categories of people: those from the urban lower classes—poor tradesmen, artisans, and laborers, mainly peasants on their way to becoming an industrial proletariat—egged on by the more well-to-do business and professional competitors of the Jews; and those who were typical peasants and who were drawn into the turmoil when they saw and heard what was happening in the towns. Outsiders coming from the Great Russian interior *guberniias* joined the local people and played an especially important role both in circulating rumors about impending anti-Jewish violence and in spreading the violence itself.

Since the 1860s the southwest region (the Ukraine) had become a job-hunters' paradise. Especially during the spring and summer, unemployed laborers from all over the empire came seeking work. And usually they found it: the railroads, agriculture, and industry were all expanding, and the construction business was booming. But, as I shall describe in greater detail when discussing the immediate factors contributing to the pogroms, 1881 was different: jobs were scarce, yet outsiders continued to flow into the southwest region. Being highly mobile, they were in a position to carry trouble with them wherever they went.

For the most part, peasants and workers in the Russian Empire, the so-called masses, and to some extent the petty bourgeoisie as well, lived impoverished, primitive, and brutalized lives. Discontent was endemic, and outbursts of spontaneous violence were not unusual. One of the most typical sources of dissatisfaction in this period was the chronic land hunger. The peasants thought that acquiring more land was the main, if not the only, key to solving all their problems. Many of those in the urban and industrial work force, who had left their villages only in this or the previous generation and who preserved strong ties with their ancestral homes, felt the same way. Emancipated by Alexander II, the peasants felt that the Great Reforms of the 1860s had cheated them out of property that was rightfully theirs, and true freedom as well. They lived in the constant expectation that a second "Emancipation," a "Golden Charter," or "genuine" Great Reforms, would be promulgated by the tsar. They suspected that only the conniving of the noble landlords (who wanted to go on exploiting the peasants as if there had been no emancipation) and of corrupt government officials (who were from the noble class or who identified with it) prevented the "proper" distribution of the land to the peasants, against the will of the Little Father in St. Petersburg. In other words, while remaining completely loyal to the tsar, the masses in the empire nursed a deep hostility to the ruling classes and the government structure.

The lower classes in the Pale felt they were victimized not only by the nobles and government officials but also by the Jews. That the peasants in the Pale were economically better off than peasants elsewhere in the empire, as was shown by contemporary studies and economic surveys, was largely ignored by almost everyone in Russia. The anti-Jewish press and anti-Semitic publicists, especially from the end of the 1870s, reiterated over and over that the Jews were exploiters of the simple people. This notion was practically a cliché among all but a few non-Jews in the empire. The role played by most Jews as middlemen (peddlers, tavern keepers, wagoners, dealers in standing crops, moneylenders, and so on) and petty artisans, jobs that earned only disrespect in the agrarian-oriented economic thinking of the time, helped reinforce this notion. And it certainly served the interests of the Jews' business and professional competitors, both those who were well-to-do and educated and those who were as primitive and uncultured as the peasants from the nearby countryside.

The Great Russian population lived in places where there were practically no Jews, but this did not necessarily diminish its anti-Jewish feelings. Apart from the contemporary chauvinistic nationalism and anti-Semitic agitation in the press, there were age-old religious antagonisms and prejudices. For the Great Russians, the Jew was mostly an abstract concept, so it was easier to view him as the devil incarnate. There were almost no real human relations, no everyday economic or social intercourse, to temper the image of the Jew held by these people. This held true even for those Great Russians who came to the southwest region every spring and summer as seasonal workers.

Meanwhile, both within and outside the Pale, the few Jews who managed to become fabulously wealthy and the few who met the requirements for receiving permits to move beyond the Pale into the Russian interior tended to provoke even more than the normal measure of envy and animosity among the non-Jewish population. The growing visibility of these Jews contributed to the intense anti-Semitic press campaign that began during the 1870s and played such an important role in the events of 1881. Also contributing to the anti-Semitic press campaign were both the heightened Russian nationalism and xenophobia that accompanied the Russo-Turkish War of 1877–78 and its aftermath and the growing role played by Jews in the revolutionary socialist movement. At the end of the war, the British prime minister, Benjamin Disraeli, who was of Jewish origin, played a prominent role in thwarting Russia's intentions to exploit her military victory. As for the Jewish socialists, their role in the revolutionary movement in Russia was greatly exaggerated by their enemies—not an uncommon occurrence in matters involving the Jews.

As I noted above when describing Jewish attitudes, the Jewish-Christian adversary relationship was usually overshadowed by amicable everyday dealings. Christians generally benefited from their economic intercourse with Jews and were well aware of this. But at the same time they were suspicious that the Jews were taking advantage of them and resentful at their own dependence on these "inferior" aliens. This ambivalence in the Christians' attitudes toward the Jews played an important role in the development of the tendency toward pogroms in southern Russia. On the one hand, it contributed to making the violence possible. On the other, it helps to explain why so many Christians failed to join in the violence or even actively protected Jews, as well as why, after the violence ended in many places, the common people displayed a calm good-naturedness and even goodwill toward their Jewish neighbors whom they had just been attacking.

The popular masses in the Russian Empire had a very poorly developed sense of the rule of law and the inviolability of persons and property. They had little respect for formal legislation and formal legal processes. They were commonly subjected to arbitrary treatment by the authorities, and only during the previous decade or two had this begun to change somewhat for the better. Customary law still predominated in the villages, and the people felt that they had the right to impose their own rough conception of justice (*samosud*, "vigilante justice") whenever the opportunity arose. It was clear to all that Russian imperial law discriminated severely against the Jews: while not pariahs, they certainly seemed to be outside the full protection of the law. This idea, together with the popular notion that the Jews' property did not rightly belong to them since they had used means amounting to theft to acquire it, made it quite easy for the lower classes to attack Jews and their property without feeling that they were doing something essentially wrong. On the contrary, they could assume that their actions met the demands of justice.

Rumors about a tsarist edict instructing the people to beat the Jews—in other words, assurances that legal sanction had been given to anti-Jewish violence—were instrumental in the outbreaks of 1881. These rumors fell on fertile ground prepared long in advance. They fitted in perfectly with the people's conceptions about the Jews and about the law. Furthermore, there was a long historical tradition in Russia of spreading fantastic claims and assertions about matters of concern to the lower classes. This tradition went back at least to the False Tsar Dmitri in the early seventeenth century, and it had found broad expression as recently as the aftermath of the 1861 Emancipation, which the peasants viewed as thoroughly unsatisfactory. The common people's intrinsic naïeveté, or cunning, and stubbornness, together with the government's failure to establish effective lines of communication with them, allowed even the wildest kinds of stories to gain credibility.

The policies of the Russian government were, of course, hostile to the Jews. But this hostility was tempered by the knowledge that, first of all, the Jewish population in the empire could not be eliminated, and second, the economic interests of the Jews and the so-called native or indigenous population were intricately bound together, so that harming the Jews necessarily entailed harming significant numbers of non-Jews. Thus the government adopted contradictory policies. On the other hand, it discriminated against the Jews and kept them isolated in the Pale, allegedly in order to protect the non-Jewish population from Jewish exploitation and cunning. On the other hand, the government encouraged Jewish assimilation, or "fusion [*sliianie*] with the indigenous population," as officials habitually expressed it.

When speaking of the Russian government, one must always keep in mind that it was made up of men holding a wide variety of conflicting opinions. This was true at all levels. Even among officials who were clearly anti-Jewish (probably the majority), there was no uniformity of viewpoints. Opinions ranged all the way from advocating the complete emancipation of the Jews to calling for the severest types of restrictive measures in all areas of Jewish life, with every shade of opinion in between. There were also different degrees of willingness to tolerate popular violence against the Jews. As was demonstrated by events, some local officials were prepared to sit by and watch passively when Jews were attacked, while a few even went so far as to encourage or participate actively in anti-Jewish disorders. But there were also very anti-Jewish officials who consistently opposed any popular outbursts, and others came to this position after the pogroms began. These men may have sympathized with the mobs' motives, but not with their methods, which harbored tendencies dangerous to the government. In short, being anti-Jewish was not the only factor dictating how officials would behave in a crisis involving violence against Jews.

Meanwhile, the central government did not have absolute control over local officials even when lines of authority were clear and well defined. This may have been particularly true under two ministers of the interior: Loris-Melikov (whose career was cut short while he was trying to implement various liberalizing reforms) and Ignatiev (whom contemporaries thought incompetent and not in control of his ministry's affairs in general).

Most responsible people in Russia were aware that the local government structure in the empire was chaotic. Certain aspects of this perennial morass contributed to the development of the pogroms in 1881. As a rule, local officials, the police in particular, were untrained, inefficient, and incompetent. There was little incentive for them to improve their professional qualifications. For the most part they came to their jobs with little or no education. They were poorly paid, and only a select few had any prospects for advancement. Yet even if a local official or policeman had wanted to get professional training, there was practically nowhere for him to do so. Furthermore, the local police had no experience in preventing and suppressing urban riots. Of course, rioting was not unknown in the countryside and the villages, but such disturbances were dealt with by the military, not the police. Also, past disturbances had taken place under different conditions from those in which the pogroms occurred.

It was one thing for the authorities to defend the interests of the landlords and the governing class against disgruntled peasants—this was a matter of protecting the raison d'être of the regime. But it was quite another thing to protect the almost universally despised Jews from the wrath of an essentially loyalist populace, which in 1881 thought it was obeying a tsarist *ukaz*. The dilemmas of the authorities here were quite acute. The more anti-Jewish an official (and the vast majority, of course, held anti-Jewish views to one degree or another), the less interest he had in protecting the Jews. Also, the authorities were fully aware that incautious actions taken in defense of the Jewish victims could provoke the agitated mobs into attacking the government and the propertied classes as well. Meanwhile, from another angle, officials realized that failure to keep the rioters under control could also lead to attacks on the regime. These problems were built into the situation in the Pale of Jewish Settlement, although they only became palpable in the special conditions of 1881.

The physical terrain in the villages and countryside was also different from that in the towns, and so were the economic interests and institutions involved. In both cases the urban environment was much more difficult to deal with when localized disturbances were the problem. An isolated manor house was much more easily defended than the numerous private dwellings, shops, factories, mills, and offices of a town. A village generally had only a few streets, with the peasants' homes spread along them. Towns, of course, were spread over hills and across rivers and contained numerous streets, alleyways, and passages. Fields and forests were not likely to be damaged very badly by the unsophisticated application of force in suppressing a riot; urban marketplaces and businesses were much more vulnerable. So the incompetence and lack of professional training of the forces charged with maintaining law and order, both the police and troops, tended to become much more potent factors when urban rioting had to be handled. On the one hand, in the towns the authorities were likely to be more restrained in general, and on the other, they were likely to find their inexperience a greater hindrance when they actually undertook to act.

Meanwhile, the police forces in the towns of southwest Russia, if not everywhere in the empire, were grossly undermanned. This may seem surprising when one recalls that the tsarist regime in nineteenth-century Russia was popularly known as an authoritarian or police state. But it is nevertheless a fact that there were very few policemen in the towns of the Pale, and thus it was easy enough for them to lose control of the situation. And not only did they have to worry about protecting the Jews; there were banks and, frequently, arsenals in the towns. No chances could be taken with these, so in case of popular violence some of the police forces would have to be drawn off to guard them. Sometimes the troops in the local garrison could be used for this purpose, but then they would not be available to reinforce the police when it was necessary to protect the Jews.

In general, it was no simple matter to call in and employ troops to reinforce the police. First of all there was the matter of what one might loosely call professional pride: the local police chiefs did not want to be thought of as incompetent and unable to control their own bailiwicks. Second, they were often ignorant of the procedure for calling in troops.

Sometimes a local garrison was already on the spot, but in these cases it was generally too small to be of much use, so troops had to be summoned from outside. Local police chiefs often did not know where they should be brought from, how to go about calling them in, or who had the authority to authorize their use for the purpose of putting down disturbances. Then, once troops arrived in a town, the lines of authority between the local officials and the military commanders were not well defined. It was not clear who was to be in charge, the civilians or the military; how orders were to be passed on; or how the tasks were to be divided between the police and the soldiers. These confusions prepared the way for a situation in which no definite instructions would be given to either the police or the soldiers. As a result they would act indecisively, which, in an atmosphere like that of 1881, could only encourage the mob in its belief that what it was doing had the approval of the authorities.

There were other problems as well with using troops for mob control: how they were to be transported and supplied; how many soldiers should be sent to any particular location, especially when riots were happening in many places in the vicinity; how long the troops should remain in a particular place (so as to calm the population, without antagonizing it by overstaying their welcome). Dealing with all these problems would inevitably lead to costly hesitations and mistaken decisions. And even with the best of will and ability (which were painfully rare), officials, when subjected to the pressure of popular violence, were likely to make mistakes in judgement.

Though I am concerned here with depicting the more or less permanent features of the Russian Jewish context, it would not be out of place to mention the government's genuine fear of socialist-inspired popular agitation. This fear went back some years before 1881, perhaps as far back as the end of the 1860s when the populist movement began. It grew as the revolutionaries increased their activities, including direct attacks on government officials (which the government, of course, did not take lying down), and it certainly intensified after the assassination of Alexander II by revolutionary socialists. Quite apart from socialist agitation, there was the peasants' intense and persistent land hunger. These two factors, socialist-inspired popular agitation and peasant land hunger, were associated with the Jewish question in the minds of many officials since they were well aware of the anti-Jewish views held by many revolutionaries. They therefore responded instinctively to the 1881 pogroms by charging that the revolutionary socialists were responsible for them. In this view, the pogroms were intended as a training ground for mass revolt. When this was found not to be the case, officials expressed concern that, if the government did not quickly reassert firm control, the revolutionaries might try to exploit the disorder. Officials also expressed anxiety that the anti-Jewish violence could easily pass over into antilandlord and then antigovernment violence, quite apart from socialist influence. Indeed, one of the government's main concerns during the crisis of 1881 was how to end it without converting the mobs' initially loyalist inclinations (their conviction that they were obeying a tsarist edict by attacking the Jews) into the opposite—anger, hostility, and attacks on the authorities for defending too vigorously the generally despised Jews. In sum, though these apprehensions may not have been expressed prior to the events of 1881, they were already latent well before then.

Such was the unpromising context of Russian Jewish life. Yet in spite of all the unfavorable circumstances, mass violence against Jews was quite rare. How was 1881 different from all the preceding years? Why did the troubled yet relatively quiet waters suddenly become turbulent and stormy?

A large number of elements special to 1881 went into preparing the setting for the initial outbursts of anti-Jewish violence. Then, once the rioting began, new ones entered that invigorated the process and allowed it to continue for almost a year. The assassination of Alexander II looms so large that it is necessary to begin with it, although, as I shall demonstrate, there were other developments that began before this traumatic occurrence.

The importance of the tsar in nineteenth-century Russian national life is undisputed and indisputable. In the eyes of the peasant masses, if not the population as a whole, the tsar was the source of all good. Ignoring revolutionary socialist propaganda, the people retained their age-old faith in the Little Father's genuine concern for their welfare; they thought that only corrupt officials prevented this solicitude from being carried into practice.

When Alexander II met his violent death, the Russian people were sincerely and deeply shocked. They felt lost, overcome by a terribly unsettling bewilderment, not knowing what the future would bring. Would the peasants' position be improved or eroded under the new tsar? Would only the interests of the landlords be served, or would the welfare of the popular masses be promoted? These questions were of real and immediate concern to the population all over the Russian Empire, which had so recently been made to cope with the great expectations, disappointments, frustrations, and dislocations of Alexander II's peasant Emancipation and Great Reforms. Now, with the assassination, the people were brought to new heights of uncertainty, agitation, and unrest. Tensions increased, and officials sensed with foreboding that the people were on the verge of rioting, no matter whether Alexander III ordered new land divisions or decreed the reintroduction of serfdom. The supercharged atmosphere was noted all over the empire. Most of the enmity was directed against the landlords and the authorities; and though this phenomenon was quite distinct from the Christian-Jewish frictions building up in the special circumstances of the Pale of Jewish Settlement, it was also one of the factors contributing to them.

After the assassination of Alexander II, the anti-Semitic newspaper campaign, which had been going on for several years, took on new meaning. The press reported the participation of the Jewish woman Gessia Gelfman in the assassination plot, and the people greatly exaggerated the role of Jews in the affair. When Gelfman, who was pregnant, was not executed along with the other conspirators, as a humanitarian gesture and a bow to Western public opinion, the people attributed her reprieve to Jewish cunning and trickery, which allegedly always enabled Jews to avoid punishment for their misdeeds.

The year 1881, along with everything else, marked the tenth anniversary of anti-Jewish rioting in the town of Odessa, where *Novorossiskii Telegraf,* a veteran and leading anti-Semitic organ, was published. People in the town, it seems, were talking about celebrating this anniversary with renewed attacks on the Jews. *Novorossiskii Telegraf* reported this talk as "rumors of impending anti-Jewish rioting." According to the newspaper, the people were saying that anti-Jewish violence would take place during Easter, as a means of protest and act of revenge against the Jews' exploitative economic activity and their participation in the assassination of Alexander II as well. This news was picked up and reported by other newspapers in southwest Russia, and people elsewhere also began to talk about beating the Jews.

As events unfolded, belief in one rumor in particular became especially important in the genesis and spread of the pogroms. This was the rumor often mentioned in preceding chapters according to which the new tsar had issued an *ukaz* (a decree or edict) calling on the people to beat the Jews. The origins of the story are shrouded in mystery. It could easily have developed out of the items appearing in the anti-Semitic press, or it could have arisen spontaneously and become the basis of some of those reports.

As I have noted, rumors commonly played an important role in public events in Russia, so much so that by the late nineteenth century, this was already a historical tradition. The government had no formal or orderly means for communicating its will and intentions to the people. Apart from the occasional use of village priests and local police officials, word of mouth was practically the only method of spreading news among the largely illiterate population. Items from the press heard secondhand could easily be garbled or misinterpreted, quite unintentionally, and quite apart from deliberate distortions, exaggerations, and so on that might be perpetrated by local agitators serving various ends. Once the common people got an idea into their heads, they held on to it naïvely and stubbornly—especially when it conformed with deeply held prejudices and when it allegedly had the approval of the tsar. Thus Jewish chicanery and bribery were blamed for the fact that the people never saw an official publication announcing the tsar's alleged anti-Jewish *ukaz* and for the many instances when the authorities took resolute steps to prevent or end anti-Jewish violence. Another current contributing to the flood tide and persistence of rumors in general in 1881 was the generally troubled and unsettled atmosphere I have already described resulting from the sudden accession of a new and unfamiliar tsar.

The seeming impunity of the press to preach anti-Jewish opinions, as well as the appearance in the newspapers of reports about Jewish participation in the assassination of Alexander II and reports about approaching anti-Jewish violence, also helped give credence to the rumors about a tsarist *ukaz.* For the people knew that the press in Russia was heavily censored; they therefore believed that whatever appeared there must have the government's approval and support.

Here again a unique situation existed in early 1881 that gave impetus to the pogrom movement. By law, inciting one part of the population against another was a forbidden and punishable act in the Russian Empire. But this was the time of Loris-Melikov's so-called dictatorship of the heart, when the minister of the interior was trying to gain support for the government by cracking down on its avowed enemies while at the same time allowing some liberalization in the treatment of those who supported the regime to any extent. Thus press censorship was virtually nonexistent for those organs that fell into the latter category. Perhaps the liberally oriented Loris-Melikov would have cracked down on the anti-Semitic press too, if he had remained in office long enough to implement his full program. But he was replaced soon after Alexander III became tsar.

As it was, the anti-Semitic Russian press organs never called openly for anti-Jewish violence, just as they never directly accused the Jews of the murder of Alexander II, and they probably never expected such violence to occur, especially on the scale it did in 1881–82. But having said this, I do not mean to excuse the press completely from responsibility for what happened: the inflammatory—or, at least, impassioned—style and content of the anti-Jewish articles appearing during this period contributed a great deal to creating an environment conducive to pogroms.

Once the pogroms began to occur, there were other factors that served to reinforce the belief that the government supported the rioting. One was the tangible example the people now had before them. Witnesses and participants in riots in one place would move to another, spreading the news. What before might have been passed over as mere talk now seemed to be verified by events. In the murky and overcast atmosphere of the spring of 1881, the very occurrence of a pogrom was enough to precipitate conditions that would lead to more steadfast belief in the legitimacy of striking out at the Jews and, consequently, to the outbreak of more pogroms.

Another reinforcement at work in this direction was the behavior of many officials, policemen, military officers, and soldiers. At first most local officials, even when they took steps to prevent the actual outbreak of violence, felt helpless when it came to trying to put an end to the rumors; they therefore did little about them. When the worst actually happened, some continued to be inactive, letting their anti-Jewish sympathies get the better of them. Others hesitated, not knowing how to respond or what to do first. When troops were called in, they sometimes demonstrated their sympathy with the rioters by treating them indulgently or, even worse, joining them (as happened in a few cases). Often the soldiers (or more precisely, their officers) simply failed to act decisively, either because the lines of command were not clear; or because they did not want to hurt any of the many innocent bystanders who were merely watching the "show" (a common feature of the 1881 pogroms); or because they were afraid of antagonizing the mob and provoking a serious insurrection (the government's main concern throughout 1881). However, the people could have had no idea of the authorities' motives, so that in all the cases just mentioned, the rumors about a tsarist *ukaz* prescribing popular attacks on the Jews seemed to be confirmed.

The mobs rarely resisted the authorities actively. When ordered to disperse, they often simply ignored the troops—who, as a rule, were reluctant to use their firearms—or they obeyed, only to reassemble at another spot to continue their outrages. The rioters were convinced they were acting out of loyalty to the regime. Many continued in this faith even when they were later brought to trial, as was indicated by their testimony and the explanations they gave for their behavior. They interpreted the officials' and the soldiers' efforts to stop them as the result of Jewish bribery or as actions taken simply for the sake of form or just to show who was in charge—that is, to verify that the government had not lost control of the situation. Disabusing the people of their firmly held belief in the legitimacy of their anti-Jewish actions was perhaps the most difficult task the government faced in 1881.

The task was made even more formidable by the blatantly inconsistent behavior of Governor Erdeli of Kherson *guberniia* early in the wave of pogroms. Immediately after the first pogrom in Elizavetgrad, Erdeli arranged for public aid to be given to the Jewish victims of the violence; but he also allowed the establishment of a public committee to give aid to indigent families of persons arrested on suspicion of having participated in the rioting. Erdeli may have been motivated by humanitarian considerations, but his action had the effect of reinforcing belief in the rumor of a tsarist *ukaz*. For, in the eyes of the people, it appeared that the families of rioters were being rewarded.

Mention should be made at this point of the large number of Russian officials who were completely successful in preventing pogroms in the places under their jurisdiction or who managed to keep the disturbances down to clashes between individuals. Frequently these officials acted to protect the Jews in spite of their own avowedly anti-Jewish opinions. Many of the common people were undoubtedly dissuaded from believing in the rumor of a tsarist *ukaz* as a result of determined action taken by officials. Unfortunately, though, there was not enough of such action to silence the rumors altogether; and often the action taken was attributed to Jewish bribery, thus allowing the belief in the existence of an anti-Jewish *ukaz* to persist.

A main vehicle for the dissemination of anti-Jewish rumors and the spread of anti-Jewish violence was the mass of unemployed laborers roving all over the region struck by pogroms. They were joined by the rough, rowdy, and mobile railroad workers. Here again 1881 was unique in an unfortunate way. In previous years there had been plenty of jobs available in the spring and summer for anyone wanting to work, and laborers from all over the empire had grown accustomed to coming to the southwest during these seasons. Hosts of them came in 1881 too, but now there was little work to be found, whether agricultural or industrial. During 1880 and 1881 local crop failures had brought on near famine conditions in some areas. And from the winter of 1880 on into 1882, all of Russia suffered an industrial depression. This meant not only that jobs were scarce but also that more people were competing for the few that were available. Thus the ranks of the unemployed and discontented swelled, and a roving and prolific source of anti-Jewish activities emerged.

The spring of 1881 was a time of public mourning for Alexander II, and the government decreed that none of the amusements customary at Easter were to take place. This became another element in the tense atmosphere in the Pale. The common people got the impression that the normal public festivities had been banned on account of the Jews, who allegedly had bribed the authorities in hopes of preventing attacks upon themselves. In Elizavetgrad in particular incautious remarks by some Jews contributed to this impression. So the already excited anti-Jewish feelings were exacerbated further, and rumors flew more furiously.

When Easter week of 1881 arrived, religious feelings, as usual, ran high, often abetted by heavy drinking. Many people took a holiday from their work, and they were joined by the many unemployed. This year it was exceptionally hot, and people were unusually irritable. Many spent their time strolling in the streets. The air hung thick with tension. Only a small seed, like a quarrel in a tavern or the marketplace, was needed to precipitate a storm. An excited crowd was likely to gather quickly at the first sign of trouble and turn a minor incident into a full-fledged pogrom. This is what happened in Elizavetgrad on 15 April 1881.

Once the first storm had broken, the waves it created moved in torrents from town to town and from the towns to the surrounding villages. As I have noted, the violence was spread mostly by migrant unemployed laborers and the highly mobile railroad workers. Peasants returning from the towns to their home villages also contributed to the spread of the violence. These people had no plan or deliberate goals. They were not anyone's agents. They acted spontaneously and in response to the highly charged atmosphere of the time.

There were undoubtedly some individuals who tried to take advantage of the situation and deliberately engaged in spreading rumors or directing rioters on the spot on an ad hoc basis. Business and professional competitors of the Jews (the more well-to-do, of course, would not deign to participate personally in the violence), merchants, industrialists, shopkeepers, artisans, intellectuals, or even an occasional socialist-influenced laborer or peasant could have become involved in this. Their organizing activities, however, were only a minor eddy in the troubled and stormy waters of 1881. The dynamics of the flood of pogroms were already in motion. These would-be "organizers" simply tried to give it an additional push.

There were well-to-do and educated Christians who stood idly by and watched as the Jews were attacked. They may have sympathized with the rioters, but they had no inclination to join or direct them. In contrast to the positive or passive responses of many Christian businessmen, others were quite alarmed by the rioting; they foresaw the blow it would deal to business interests in general and were afraid that it might get completely out of hand, with the mobs turning on the propertied classes directly. And they made these concerns known to the government, calling upon it to take more forceful action to restore quiet.

The outbreak of massive anti-Jewish violence took the revolutionary socialists, like almost everyone else in Russia, quite by surprise. A few of them tried to hitch a ride on the disorder and turn it in a direction compatible with their own idea of revolutionary action, but they suffered a notable lack of success.

The death of Alexander II was the culmination of numerous efforts by one small group of revolutionary socialists who thought that their little band could spark a total revolution in Russia by putting a dramatic end to the life of the tsar. As was proved by subsequent events, this political conception was erroneous. The pogroms were the only mass uprising to occur having any connection with the assassination, and they were by no means a revolutionary or antigovernment phenomenon.

However, in April 1881 the government had no way of knowing the weakness of the revolutionary movement or the depths of loyalty, to the tsar at least, of the Russian masses. Thus it was only natural for officials, surprised by events like everyone else, to place the blame for the pogroms initially on the socialists, some of whom were known for their anti-Jewish views. Only as evidence accumulated that the revolutionaries had practically no part in the disorders did the authorities revert to their temporarily forgotten, traditional explanation of Jewish-Christian relations. Now officials explained that the Jews incessantly exploited Christians, until finally the latter had been provoked to rise up in rage against their oppressors. Yet even after the adoption of this explanation, officials continued to take quite seriously the idea of possible socialist influence over the masses. Over and over they expressed concern that if the disorders were not ended quickly, then the revolutionaries might succeed in exploiting them.

As I have emphasized repeatedly, the government's main concern in regard to the pogroms of 1881 was to reinstitute order while at the same time avoiding any measures that might dispel the mobs' originally loyalist inclinations. Officials feared that to do otherwise would be to fall into a socialist trap and provoke a revolution. This balancing act explains much about the way the authorities behaved during the course of the year, for example, the general reluctance to use firearms, to employ harsh repressive measures, or to administer severe punishments.

In the end, the series of pogroms dissipated more or less of themselves, the several cases of violence in 1882, 1883, and 1884 being merely an echo of 1881. Order was finally restored, and the masses remained loyal. The government once again felt firmly in control and turned to legislative means of dealing with the Jewish question and the possibility of anti-Jewish violence in the future.

Meanwhile, the Jews of Russia were traumatized. Many of those who had considered themselves progressives now began to have serious doubts about the efficacy of enlightenment and assimilation. They were thoroughly disillusioned by the failure of "enlightened" Russians to rise to the defense of their people during the time of its distress. Large masses of Jews, for the first time in the long history of their settlement in Eastern Europe, turned to emigration. The small stream that had begun to flow in the previous decade or so led, in the years 1881–1914 alone, to nearly two million Jews leaving the Russian Empire. The vast majority were drawn to the promising shores of the New World, especially the United States. Some hardy pioneering spirits, over fifty thousand by 1914, opted for settlement in their ancestral homeland, *Eretz Yisrael* (then called Palestine).

Among those Jews who remained in the Russian Empire, many organized in support of a Zionist solution to the Jewish problem. Others imagined that a solution could still be found on Russian territory, whether along the path of reform and liberal democracy or in a more radical direction. A disproportionate number of young Jews, blaming the Russian government for all the troubles of their people, including the pogroms, or simply allured by the universalist-internationalist idealism of socialism, joined their non-Jewish comrades who were intent on overthrowing the hated tsarist regime by revolutionary means.

Thus the pogroms of 1881 contributed in a very direct way to the enormous growth of the Jewish community in the United States, the rise of modern Zionism, and the large numbers of Jews in the Russian revolutionary movement. All of these phenomena proved to have far-reaching implications of major significance for the history of the world in the twentieth century.

The picture presented in the preceding pages makes it very clear that the anti-Jewish violence of 1881 can be understood only in its whole Russian context. The events were part of an intricate web woven from many dynamic strands. There was no single force or factor that caused the pogroms. There was no conspiracy. Indeed, it would not be wrong to say that the pogroms resulted from weaknesses and powerlessness that pervaded all aspects of the tsarist regime and Russian society rather than from a show of power. The Russian government was marked by divided counsels, dilemmas, ineptitude, and lack of control over people and events. The gentile population suffered from numerous worries, frustrations, ignorance, and massive poverty; it nourished deep prejudices and animosities, which significantly weakened the bonds of social stability. The dependency, powerlessness, and almost universal poverty of the Jewish population were also facts of Russian life, even if anti-Semites refused to recognize them. The pogroms of 1881 took place in a context of general cultural primitiveness, social tensions, economic dislocations, and political disarray. It took the appearance of certain exceptional circumstances—themselves also manifestations of weakness—to amalgamate all the factors and produce the unprecedented anti-Jewish tides we have been studying.

When this movement eventually died down, the weaknesses and powerlessness of the Russian regime and society remained. But in some significant ways a completely new context for Russian Jewish history had been created. The Russian government on its part, and many Jews on theirs, set out to find new solutions to the empire's Jewish problem. The endemic weaknesses of each side, however, thwarted their efforts.

NOTES

BIBLIOGRAPHY

INDEX

◆ ◆ ◆

# NOTES

## Introduction

1. Rogger (II). In 1980 I myself published a "revisionist" article, in the *Russian Review* (see bibliography), which is incorporated in revised form in chap. 7.

2. Slutsky (III), 444.

3. Ettinger (I), 881–83.

4. Pincus, *The Jews,* 28–29; Pincus, *Yehudei,* 111–12.

5. Practically anyone writing today about Russian Jewry must confront the historiographical problem of the political and nationalist commitments and biases of the classic Jewish historians. See, for example, Klier (II), xiii, and Stanislawski, 3–5, where these authors address this issue directly. As Klier concisely noted, the Jewish historians of Russian Jewry "were, for the most part, men of action as well as scholarship, and their research was a weapon in their struggle for human and political rights for Russian Jewry." I will try to make explicit some of the implications of this observation for the study of the 1881 pogroms in the pages below. It goes without saying that for the Russian officials and others who studied the pogroms for purely practical reasons, "their research was a weapon in their struggle" to define and implement policies regarding Russia's Jewish population.

6. Klier (II), xiii–xiv. Also see Stanislawski, xiii, 3–5.

7. For examples, see Maor (I) and (II) (1952, 1969); Slutsky (I), (II), and (III) (1962, 1963, 1971); Vishniak (1942). The fine studies by Linden (1910) and Goldberg (1933) came very close to rejecting the conspiracy theory but did not do so altogether. Even Berk (II) (1985) is not entirely free of this interpretation.

8. In a slightly different context, Jonathan Frankel stated that "the inner turmoil engendered by the pogroms starting in April 1881 reached a climax in the months from January to May 1882, when the Jewish people appeared to be living in expectation of an imminent and massive emigration. The image of a new *exodus,* a going-out from the *land of bondage* to a promised land, came to dominate, however momentarily, every aspect of Jewish public life in Russia." Frankel, 49, my emphasis.

9. The Jewish National Library at the Hebrew University in Jerusalem has a copy of this work, inscribed and signed, in Russian, "To the Jewish National Library in Jerusalem, from the author, E. B. Levin, St. Petersburg, 8/21 December 1902." The book contains the following chapters: (1) Laws; (2) Accusations Refuted; (3) Pogroms, *Guberniia* Commissions (this chapter was published by Dubnow in *Evreiskaia starina,* 1909, cited here as Levin [I]—Dubnow stated in his introductory

remarks that he did not know who wrote the work); (4) Causes of Pogroms, Criticism of D. M. Tolstoi as Minister of the Interior (this chapter was translated into Hebrew and published by Slutsky in *Heavar,* cited here as Levin [II]—see below); (5) Solutions to the Jewish Question.

The book in Jerusalem is indeed as Dubnow described it in *Evreiskaia starina:* no author's name printed on it; entitled, *Evreiskii vopros i anti-Evreiskoe dvizhenie v Rossii v 1881 i 1882 g.;* folio; 248 numbered and 15 unnumbered pages; hectographed, written at the end of 1882. Dubnow may have known that it was written by Levin but may have needed to protect him for some reason (in 1909, not in 1916; Levin died in 1913).

When Dubnow said that the author "speaks about all this in a bold tone for those times, but at the same time so objectively that it is difficult to guess [his] nationality," he probably did not intend to imply that the work was by a non-Jew. On the contrary: he evidently wanted to say that it was written by a Jew, yet it was nevertheless very reliable. Dubnow asserted several times that in his opinion the conclusions of the anonymous author could be trusted.

Slutsky stated in his introductory remarks in *Heavar* (cited herein as Levin [II]) that the chapter he was presenting (chap. 4 of the book) was a translation from the copy found in the Jewish National Library. He gave the same title as Dubnow. Slutsky also noted that it was written in the summer of 1882, and he stated that the copy he used was signed by the author, E. B. Levin, and intended for high government officials.

Dubnow in *Golos minuvshago,* 1916, cited herein as Levin (III), stated that the item being reprinted there was written by Levin (in July 1881) and distributed to high officials in answer to a request for information made by Alexander III, who received a Jewish delegation on 11 May 1881. This was evidently an early version of *Evreiskii vopros i anti-Evreiskoe dvizhenie v Rossii v 1881 i 1882 g.*

Curiously, in *Evreiskaia starina* 8 (1915), cited here as Dubnow (II)—which is the Russian version of the last part of Dubnow's three-volume *History of Russian Jews* in English, cited here as Dubnow (I)—on pp. 279–80, n. 2, (missing from the English—see Dubnow [I], 2: 261–62), Dubnow stated that the memorandum to Alexander III was written by M. G. Margulis and that Ignatiev would not allow it to be presented to the tsar.

In his article on the pogroms in *Evreiskaia entsiklopediia,* vol. 12, cited here as *Evr. ents.* (IV), Iu. Gessen summarized Levin (I) and accepted its arguments. So did Dubnow (I), Greenberg, and others.

10. Levin (I), 93, my emphasis.
11. Levin (I), 97, my emphasis.
12. Levin (I), 97–98.
13. Dubnow (III), 200–14.
14. Dubnow (III), 201, my emphasis.
15. Dubnow (III), 202, 204, my emphasis.
16. Dubnow (III), 212.

17. I do not think it is necessary here to explore at length the psychological aspects of belief in conspiracy theories. My intention is merely to indicate possible biases of those who employ this explanation, with the aim of being able to understand their position better and interpret it accordingly. For expert treatment of this subject see the works by Billig; Lipset and Raab; Graumann and Moscovici; Nelson, Megill, and McCloskey; Potter and Wetherell. A topic for research in this regard may be the connection, if any, between the anti-Semitic belief in a world Jewish conspiracy and the belief of many Jews in a tsarist conspiracy against their people.

18. Apart from the case of Dubnow, discussed above, an explicit example of this is given below, chap. 6.

19. See Aronson (VI).

## *Chapter 1. The Russian Context*

1. The description that follows is, of course, by no means exhaustive. Its aim is simply to give the reader an awareness of the salient features of Russian life that prepared the way for the anti-Jewish violence of 1881. Economic factors are also dealt with in chap. 7 below. For a thorough recent treatment of the major interpretations and learned debates about tsarist economic history, see Gatrell.

2. Gatrell, xii–xiii, 100–02, 119, 122–24, 128, and passim. Citing Gregory and others.

3. Gatrell, 59, 119; Gregory (I), 148; Gregory (II), 130–31, cited in Gatrell, xiii, 44, 138.

4. Gatrell, 137. Citing Gregory (I).

5. Gatrell, xiii, 200–02, and passim.

6. Gatrell, 137–38. Also see Gatrell, 46–47, 198–203.

7. Gatrell, 203, 268, n. 28.

8. For details on Russian population growth, see Gatrell, 49–61.

9. See Gatrell, 154–56.

10. See Gatrell, 156–57.

11. Gatrell, 86.

12. Gatrell, 86.

13. Gatrell, 67.

14. For some diverse opinions on these points, see Gatrell, 64, 248, n.41. Also see Gatrell, 67, 68, 84–97.

15. Bazhan, 90; Marinich, 118.

16. Kubijovyč, 697; Bazhan, 90; Gatrell, 103, 130–32, 139–40; Marinich, 120.

17. Kubijovyč, 698; *Bol. sov.,* 577; EKO, 57–58.

## *Chapter 2. The Jews in 1881*

1. See Lestchinsky; Zipperstein, chap. 1.

2. See Klier (II); Rogger (VI), chap. 9; Stanislawski.

3. Stanislawski, 125, 127.

4. See Stanislawski, 127–54. For a discussion of the reasons why the 1844 law only partly abolished the *kahal,* see Stanislawski, 124–27.

5. See Kahan, 45–46.

6. See Slutsky (III), 450. Also see Greenberg, 1:163; Kahan, 1–69.

7. Slutsky (III), 435, 450–51. Also see Kahan, 6–17.

8. Kahan, 6.

9. Kahan, 15.

10. A. Kahan perceived a "secular decline of the [Jewish] death rate, which during the second half of the century was coupled with a stable birthrate, thus resulting in an increase of the population growth rate." Kahan, 4.

Elsewhere Kahan wrote: "It is clear from the available data that during the period 1881–97 not only was the total Jewish population increasing, but the size of its urban sector grew at an even higher rate. In fact, the rate of growth of the urban Jewish population was higher than the rate of growth of the non-Jewish population." He accounted for this not only by the natural increase of the urban population but also by migration from less densely settled areas to more densely populated centers. "Thus, taking migration into account, one would expect the Jewish population of the larger towns to grow at a higher rate than the total urban Jewish population and to observe the process of population concentration." Kahan, 28–29. "The migration process was caused by the differences in the availability of employment opportunities between regions [of the Pale], with the Southwestern and Southern regions offering the best opportunities for expanding employment." Kahan, 33. This is the area where the 1881 pogroms took place. Kahan's research makes clear the socioeconomic flux characteristic of the period under discussion.

J. Silber, who admittedly used approximation methods extensively because of the errors known to be contained in the available data, came to the following conclusions: Russian Jews at the end of the nineteenth century had a fertility rate lower than that of non-Jews, and they tended to be older (*sic*) at the time of marriage, but at the same time their mortality rate was relatively low, which allowed for their increase in numbers. Silber, 269–80.

Hans Rogger, meanwhile, stated that in spite of laws approved during the reign of Nicholas I restricting early marriages among Jews, the Jewish growth rate was 150 percent between 1825 and 1880, while the general rate was 87 percent. Rogger (V), 16. Also see Rogger (V), 235, n. 38, which cites Silber.

11. Kahan, 39–41.

12. Kahan, 41. Also see Kahan, 98.

13. Kahan, 10.

14. Greenberg, 1:161; Kahan, 21.

15. Greenberg, 1:161.

16. See esp. Greenberg, 1:165.

17. Kahan, 15, 66, n. 22.

18. Kahan, 16. Also see Kahan, 97–98.

19. See esp. Greenberg, 1:168–71.

20. See Kahan, 17–18.


## *Chapter 3. The Coming of the Pogroms*

1. The description of Elizavetgrad is based upon *Bol. sov.; Encyclopaedia Judaica; Evr. ents.;* and K.-A.

2. Ruud, 201–02.

3. Ruud, 229.

4. I will have more to say below about the population's readiness to believe and spread rumors.

5. My description of the organization of the Russian Empire is based upon Rogger (VI), chap. 4, 5; Clarkson, chap. 17; Florinsky, chap. 33; and others. The matters mentioned here are touched upon throughout the pages that follow and are discussed in detail in chap. 8 below.

6. The description of the Elizavetgrad pogrom in this chapter is based upon: Dubnow (I), 249–51; Dubnow (II), 271–72; *Evr. ents.* (IV), 612; Goldberg, 25; K.-A., 1–6, 20–26, 226–32, 241–49, 260–86, 471–77; Kherson, 1180–81; *Obshchaia zapiska,* 84–85; Sonin, 207–10; Sosis, 177, 181–82. These sources include testimonies and reports by official government investigators, police chiefs, governors, governors-general, and eyewitnesses, Jewish and non-Jewish.

7. The description of the flow of the pogroms is based on K.-A., passim; and Slutsky (I), 16–18.

8. See Klier (V) for a recent account of a discussion that took place in 1882 concerning this matter. The documents in K.-A. tend to support the assertion of those who claim that very few Jews were killed. As I have noted in the text, a number of rioters were also killed in different places when troops fired on them.

9. See the recent full-length study, Berk (II).

10. Noteworthy are Dubnow, Greenberg, Dinur, Maor, and Slutsky. Even Berk (II), does not rule out completely the possibility that there was a conspiracy behind the pogroms. See esp. Berk (II), 40–44, 75–76.

11. See Klier (III) for a decisive refutation of the notion that German anti-Semites might have played a role in the 1881 pogroms.

See Pritsak, 8–43, for a vain attempt to show that "Moscow merchants" organized the pogroms of 1881, using the "highly mobile railroad workers" as their hired instruments to execute their plans. Pritsak's essay is scholarly but idiosyncratic, strenuously apologetic (for the Ukrainian people), and sometimes misleading. The author presents much information on the geography of the areas where pogroms occurred, but he also gives very forced interpretations of the available evidence and states as proven and firm conclusions, assertions for which there is no real evidence at all. Pritsak also fails to take into account the petition submitted by a number of Moscow trade firms to the government on 5 May 1882, expressing the hope that decisive measures had been taken to prevent future pogroms. The petition stressed that by harming Jewish tradesmen, the pogroms harmed *all* Russian commerce, and especially the interests of Moscow merchants and industrialists who had extensive ties with the Pale of Jewish Settlement. For details see *Russkie Liudi o Evreiakh,* 322–24, and Aronson (VI), 169–71.

12. Rogger (II), 45.

13. See, for example, Maor (I), 224.

14. See K.-A.

15. Zaslavskii, 295. For the Stalinist use of this method of interpreting evidence, see Solzhenitsyn, 386–87.

## Chapter 4. The Press, the Government, and the Pogroms

1. Rogger (II), 47.

2. J. Klier has shown that although the *Kievlianin* did indeed receive a government subsidy, it was by no means simply an official mouthpiece. See Klier (VII), 83–101, esp. 85–86.

3. Dinur (I), 411; Dinur (II), 14; Dubnow (I), 247; Dubnow (II), 269; Klier (I), 264; Levin (I), 91–92; *Sistematicheskii ukazatel',* passim; Sosis, 93, 178–79. I will have more to say on censorship below.

4. Dubnow (I), 247; Dubnow (II), 269; Goldberg, 20; K. -A., xxv, xxxi–xxxii; Klier (I), 264; Klier (IV), 202–04; Levin (III), 244; Sosis, 177–79.

5. K.-A., xxv–xxvii, xxxii, 428; Lukashevich (II), 102–03; *Sistematicheskii ukazatel',* passim; Sosis, 177; Vital, 55.

6. *Razsvet,* no. 16, 1881. Cited by Dinur (I), 409; Klier (IV), 202. Also see below, chap. 5, sec. 1.

7. See Berk (II), 54–55; Klier (IV), 199–221.

8. Greenberg, 20.

9. Goldberg, 20–22; Yarmolinsky, 263–64, 273, 275–77. Also see Dinur (I), 409; Dubnow (I), 247; Dubnow (II), 269; K.-A., xxxi–xxxii, 75, 236, 277–78, 396; Sosis, 178–79; Vital, 55. Klier (IV), 203. P. 203 n. 14, tends to dispute the claim that Gelfman's Jewishness was exploited by the press: "Even after the trial, press reports tended to de-emphasize the Jewishness of Gelfman and her ties to Judaism. It was widely reported in the press that she refused to give the child she bore in confinement to her parents 'because they were fanatics.' "

10. K.-A., 75, 395–96, 418, 461.

11. Dinur (I), 411–13; Dinur (II), 14; Ekaterinoslav, 363–64; Heilbronner, 521–22; K.-A., xxix–xxxii, 230, 236, 274, 428; Levin (III), 244; Linden, 65, 73; Mogilev, 97–98; Peretts, 131–32; Shvabakher, 4–5; Sosis, 93, 179; Subbotin, 153.

12. Dinur (I), 409–10; Dinur (II), 12; Dubnow (I), 247; Dubnow (II), 269; *Evr. ents.* (IV), 612; K.-A., xxxii, 230, 236, 277, 468; *Obshchaia zapiska,* 85.

13. Zipperstein, 114–28. Apart from the violent anti-Jewish altercations and

scuffles which occurred almost annually after 1821 during Holy Week ("almost always initiated by Greek sailors . . . in front of the city's major Orthodox church," p. 119), Odessa witnessed major anti-Jewish rioting (pogroms) in 1821 (one day), 1859 (three days), and 1871 (four days). For the most part, this strife was an expression of the rivalry between Greeks and Jews, although persons of other nationalities were also involved.

Zipperstein makes several points which are of particular interest insofar as they indicate parallels with the events of 1881. First, "the immediate cause of the riot [of 1871] was the *rumor* . . . that Jews had desecrated the Greek Orthodox church and cemetery" (p. 121, emphasis added).

Second, "on the first day of the riot, the pogromists limited their attacks to the houses adjacent to the church. The next day . . . [they attacked] the middle-class Jewish neighborhoods, shattering windows of houses and businesses." "By the third day the pogrom was citywide. Pogromists began to enter Jewish homes and to destroy property." "When the authorities finally resisted the rioters on the afternoon of the *third* day—perhaps in response to the intercession [that morning] of the Jewish communal leaders—the pogromists abandoned the city center for Moldavanka [a poor Jewish neighborhood]. Rioting continued through the night and into the next morning. . . . On the morning of the fourth and last day, the pogrom intensified, fueled by *the rumor that the St. Petersburg authorities had condoned it* so long as no bloodshed occurred. . . . Rioting broke out again in the city center. . . . By the time the authorities finally quelled the pogrom, on the afternoon of its fourth day, thousands of Jews were left homeless" (p. 122–23, emphasis added).

Third, "the rioters had generally *preferred to destroy property rather than steal,* thereby revealing the depth of their antipathy toward Jews" (p. 123, emphasis added).

Finally, in light of the rioting in 1871, "the local [Jewish] intelligentsia began to lose their optimism about [the presumed advantages which would accrue from] eventual Jewish acculturation." "Try as they might to assure themselves that the disturbance was an isolated one, precipitated by the envy of local Greeks, [Jewish] intellectuals felt . . . the growing conviction that anti-Jewish sentiment was far more tenacious than they had previously assumed, several . . . lost confidence in institutions that they had established earlier on the basis of a more optimistic appraisal of the non-Jewish world." In the local Jewish community at large, however, acculturation and the abandonment of tradition proceeded apace (p. 115, 127, and also 119, 124–28).

14. See K.-A., 277, 394; *Obshchaia zapiska,* 85; Sosis, 179.

15. Dinur (I), 410, cited the *Odesskii Listok* and "other newspapers" of 1881 as his sources. Also see K.-A., 230; Levin (III), 244–45; Tsherikover (I), 344; Tsherikover (II), 447.

16. Dinur (I), 409; *Evr. ents.* (IV), 612; Gessen (II), 217; K.-A., xxxi–xxxii; Shvabakher, 4–5. Also see Goldberg, 23; Kherson, 1179–80; *Obshchaia zapiska,* 85.

17. Article 1036 of the Criminal Code of 1866 was Paragraph D9(2) of the April

1865 "Regulations on the Press," which read: "Whoever makes an appeal in the press which incites one segment of the population of the state to animosity against another, or one class against another is subject to incarceration in a detention center or in a prison for the term defined in vol. 15, pt. 1, arts. 40–42, or to detention from 4 days to 3 months, or to a fine not exceeding 500 rubles." Ruud, 249.

18. Levin (I), 91; Levin (III), 244, 253.

19. Ekaterinoslav, 363–64; *Evr. ents.* (IV), 612; K.-A., xxx–xxxii, 230, 235–36; Levin (I), 92; Levin (III), 244; Linden, 39; Maor (I), 225; Peretts, 131–32; Shvabakher, 43–44; Turtel, 43.

20. See Dahlke, 425.

21. Goldberg, 44; K.-A., 241, 268, 274, 276, 391, 445–46.

22. K.-A., 226–27.

23. K.-A., 230.

24. John Klier was able to investigate the way the Russian press dealt with the Jewish question during lengthy study tours in the Soviet Union in 1978–79 and 1980–81. He most graciously provided me with the specific information on *Novorossiiskii Telegraf* presented here. Also see Klier (IV), 199–221. In the précis that follows, direct quotations are noted.

25. Klier (IV), 203–08 passim, 216.

26. Personal communication; Klier (IV), 199–221.

27. K.-A., 236.

28. Levin (I), 91.

29. Shvabakher, 4–5. Also see Linden, 25, 73; Lukashevich (II), 102–03.

30. *Evr. ents.* (III), 740–41. Also see Tsherikover (I), 344; Tsherikover (II), 447.

31. See Dinur (I), 409; K.-A., 236. Also see Dubnow (I), 247; Dubnow (II), 269; K.-A., xxxi–xxxii.

32. See Linden, 25.

33. See n. 13 above. Also see Dubnow (I), 191–93.

34. See Aronson (I), 3; Aronson (IV), 352, 358–60; Byrnes, 202–09, and passim; Rogger (II), 44; Rogger (III), 26–28; and below, chaps. 8 and 11.

35. Pobedonostsev (I), 55; Pobedonostsev (II), 343–44. Kantor, as editor of Pobedonostsev (I), cites the letter to Ignatiev, which, unlike the one to the tsar, did not clarify the content of the offending newspaper article. Consequently, Kantor *mistakenly* states that Pobedonostsev was calling for censorship of a liberal newspaper that had published a too radical *protest against* pogroms. This statement, of course, makes Pobedonostsev appear to support the outbreak of pogroms. The letter to the tsar and other evidence thoroughly refute any such interpretation.

36. Dinur (I), 411; Dinur (II), 14; Ekaterinoslav, 353–64; K.-A., 230, 428; Levin (III), 244; Mogilev, 97–98.

37. On the 1865 press regulations and their implications, see Ruud, passim, esp. 145–46, 237–52; Florinsky, 1055–56. In 1878, a special division was created within the imperial censorship authority to handle provincial periodicals separately from the press of the capitals. Balmuth, 77.

38. See Ruud, 181–206. Also see Balmuth, esp. 103–07.

39. See Klier (I), 257–68, esp. 260, 264.

40. Zaionchkovskii (II), 261–62, 314–15. Also see Baluev, 20; Klier (I), 263–64.

According to D. Balmuth, even before the time of Loris-Melikov, throughout the 1870s, the censors rarely rejected more than 5 percent of the manuscripts and proofs they read, and often only about 2½ percent. These figures, of course, do not reflect the authors' own self-censorship, undertaken as a matter of precaution before submitting their works to the critical review of the censors, but they do give a rough statistical idea of the situation. Balmuth, 78, 189, n. 18. Also see Balmuth, 84–85, 192, n. 19.

Under Minister of the Interior N. P. Ignatiev, who followed Loris-Melikov in May 1881, circulars were issued restricting press comment on delicate subjects, such as the pogroms and peasant disturbances. During Ignatiev's ministry of twelve months, sixteen administrative penalties were imposed on periodicals and five publications were banned without prior warning. Balmuth, 93; Baluev, 34–35, 37, 39; Zaionchkovskii (II), 410–11.

41. Baluev, 38.

42. Balmuth, 91; Baluev, 33; Golitsyn, 181; Heilbronner, 399; Zaionchkovskii (II), 354.

43. K.-A., 391.

44. Ben-Ami, 18–49; Dubnow (I), 257–58; Dubnow (II), 277; K.-A., 1, 63–67, 233–39, 385–95; Kherson, 1221–22; Linden, 70–71; Sosis, 176–77, 184–85; Shvabakher, passim.

45. Dubnow (I), 248, 251; Dubnow (II), 270, 272; Goldberg, 20; Levin (I), 92; Turtel, 43.

46. See Aronson (IV), 351–52; and below, chap. 11.

47. Shvabakher, 4.

48. K.-A., 49.

49. Cf. K.-A., 105 with K.-A., 49.

50. K.-A., 105.

51. K.-A., 126.

## Chapter 5. *Rumors, Handbills, and Posters*

1. Demidov (II), 97–98; Dubnow (I), 251–52, 257; Dubnow (II), 272–73, 276–77; *Evr. ents.* (I), 826; *Evr. ents.* (IV), 612; Frederic, 126; Goldberg, 22; K.-A., 243, 277–78, 387, 395–97, 401, 445–46, 506; *Obshchaia zapiska,* 91–92; Ettinger (II), 169.

2. Shvabakher, 4; *Obshchaia zapiska,* 86.

3. K.-A., 9. Similar skullcap stories appeared in the sixteenth century in the West in regard to Ivan the Terrible, and in Russia in regard to Vlad Dracul of

Wallachia. I thank John Klier for this information. Perhaps there was some hoary folk tradition at work here during the 1881 pogroms.

4. Kherson, 1180. The *zemstvo* board, part of the *zemstvo* system of *guberniia* and district assemblies and boards, was a popularly elected, all-class institution of local government ultimately subject to the control of the governor of the *guberniia*.

5. K.-A., 443–44.

6. K.-A., 459.

7. For examples, see K.-A., 10–13, 95–96, 124, 286, 289–92, 401, 404, 459–60; *Papers,* 41:452; Sosis, 91.

8. The Russian press in April 1881 reported attacks by Christians upon Moslems in the Azerbaidzhani city of Baku, an oil-producing center and port on the Caspian Sea. The press referred to these events as a pogrom. I thank John Klier for this information. The Christians involved may have been Armenians and not Russians. In the early twentieth century, the Baku area was marked by serious labor troubles, verging on a state of civil war between Moslem Tatars and Armenians. See Clarkson, 376, 377–78, 403, 633–34.

9. For examples concerning landlords see Gelber (I), 470–72; K.-A., 68, 70–72, 451–56; *Papers,* 40:1020; "Proscriptive Edicts," 52–53; Slutsky (I), 19. For examples concerning socialists see Heilbronner, 521–22; K.-A., 13, 52, 79, 83, 445–47; Peretts, 132–33; Sosis, 91.

10. Bloch, 4; Dubnow (I), 251; Dubnow (II), 272; *Evr. ents.* (IV), 612; Gessen (II), 217; Goldberg, 26; K.-A., 83, 113, 154, 278, 397, and passim; Kherson, 1204; *Obshchaia zapiska,* 65–66.

11. K.-A., 251.

12. K.-A., 261–63. This incident, or concern over the possibility of something like it happening, may have influenced the governor-general of the Warsaw region in Poland in December 1881, when he refused to allow the organization of a civil guard to fight the then-raging pogrom. Dubnow (I), 283, and Dubnow (II), 293–94, thought the idea was to demonstrate to European public opinion that anti-Jewish rioting was not an exclusively Russian phenomenon.

13. K.-A., 206.

14. K.-A., 242, 260. Also see K.-A., 25. Kutaisov gave no dates for these events. For other reports of Jews being insolent and making mocking remarks when special measures to protect them had been instituted, see K.-A., 74, 80–81, 416, 435–36, 442, 525.

15. K.-A., 25, 74, 76, 96, 148, 416, 435–36, 525; *Obshchaia zapiska,* 81.

16. Ben-Ami, 28; K.-A., 126, 241, 277, 435–36, 492–93; Kherson, 1180; *Obshchaia zapiska,* 85. For other examples of the Jews' panicky reactions, see Drentel'n, 181–82; K.-A., 12, 14, 19, 35, 42, 74–75, 80–81, 355, 412–13, 462, 490.

17. The irrational nature of the notion of the Jews getting rich is obvious when one remembers that the population of the Pale saw everyday at every turn the extreme poverty of the mass of their Jewish neighbors.

18. Demidov (II), 99, 103; Dubnow (I), 294–95; *Evr. ents.* (IV), 614, 616–17; Gessen (II), 215, 218; Gradovskii, 216; *K ist. Evr. pog.*, 41; Klier (IV), 212, 213–14, 220; Mogilev, 98–103; *Obshchaia zapiska*, 94; *Papers*, 40:1020; Peskovskii, 382; Subbotin, 152.

19. K.-A., 242.

20. See Bloch, 3; *Evr. ents.* (I), 826; *Evr. ents.* (IV), 612, 614; Gessen (III), 154; K.-A., 395–96, 452; Mogilev, 98; *Obshchaia zapiska*, 81, 82, 86; Sosis, 178–79, 181; Subbotin, 152. Conspiracy theorists argue that the organizers of the pogroms intentionally exploited this atmosphere, in order to turn the anger and confusion of the masses into a channel not dangerous to the ruling classes, who had been so corrupt and inept as to be incapable of protecting the beloved tsar. See esp. Levin (II), 80–81; Levin (III), 247–48; Slutsky (I), 19, 25; Tsherikover (I), 344; Tsherikover (II), 446–47.

21. Zaionchkovskii (II), 391–92.

22. See *K ist. Evr. pog.*, 41.

23. Dubnow (I), 257; Dubnow (II), 276–77; Field, 208; K.-A., 126, 184; *K ist. Evr. pog.*, 41; *Obshchaia zapiska*, 69–70.

24. K.-A., 205.

25. Ekaterinoslav, 362.

26. K.-A., 468.

27. Dubnow (I), 257; Dubnow (II), 276–77; *Obshchaia zapiska*, 69; Sosis, 184.

28. K.-A., 432; Shvabakher, 6.

29. See Field; Venturi, 214–17, 581–84; Yarmolinsky, 195–97.

30. Field, 210, 214. Also see Bushnell, 226–27.

31. Zaionchkovskii (II), 313–14.

32. Goldberg, 19–21; Heilbronner, 480–81; K.-A., 13, 17–18, 75, 492, 506; Valk, 153–63; Venturi, 713–14; Yarmolinsky, 279–80; Zaionchkovskii (II), 391–92.

33. Zaionchkovskii (II), 389.

34. Zaionchkovskii (II), 391.

35. K.-A., 184.

36. K.-A., 259–61, 264–65, 441. Also see Dinur (I), 410; Goldberg, 22.

37. K.-A., 264.

38. Yaney, 57–58. Citing *Raboty*, 1:73–75.

39. K.-A., 209, 441.

40. See Demidov (II), 97–98; Dinur (I), 409–10, 413; Dinur (II), 12, 14; Dubnow (I), 252, 257; Dubnow (II), 272–73, 276–77; Ettinger (II), 169; *Evr. ents.* (I), 826; Frederic, 126; Goldberg, 22, 39–40; Levin (I), 91; Linden, 43–44; *Obshchaia zapiska*, 91–92; Tsherikover (I), 345; Tsherikover (II), 448; Vital, 55.

41. See Dinur (I), 411; Levin (I), 91–93.

42. See *Evr. ents.* (IV), 612; K.-A., 20; and esp. Sonin, 208–09.

43. Dubnow (I), 252; Dubnow (II), 272–73. Also see K.-A., 76.

44. Ben-Ami, 28.

45. *Papers,* 40:1020; "Proscriptive Edicts," 52–53; Sosis, 176–77, 179; Tsherikover (I), 344–45; Tsherikover (II), 447.

46. K.-A., passim. See esp. K.-A., 14–15, 35, 427. It is interesting to note at this point that the "Temporary Regulations" of 3 May 1882, which were justified as preventive measures against pogroms, included a provision forbidding Jews to open their places of business on Sundays and Christian holidays. See Aronson (II); Aronson (V); Gessen (I).

47. K.-A., 56, 61, 63, 116, 158–59, 452.

48. On the proclamations as the product of some organized body within or supporting the government, see Linden, 43–44; Tsherikover (I), 345, 355; Tsherikover (II), 448, 456–57; Vital, 55. Also see Goldberg, 20–21, 39–40; Kantor, 149.

49. K.-A., 447.

50. See K.-A., 412–13.

51. K.-A., 203–04, 270–71, 370.

52. For examples, see K.-A., 7, 56, 88, 97, 370; Kantor, 149; Sosis, 183–84. See esp. K.-A., 83, 202–04, 273–74, 370, 393–94, 416–17, 447; Sosis, 180.

53. K.-A., 36, 80, 83, 95–96, 203–04, 270–73, 287, 416; Kantor, 153.

54. See K.-A., 83, 416–17.

55. K.-A., 7, 158–60, 272–73, 364; Linden, 46–66 passim.

56. Tsherikover (I), 355; Tsherikover (II), 457.

57. K.-A., 36, 83, 95–96, 272–73, 287.

58. K.-A., 80, 225, 415. Also see below, chap. 12.

59. See K.-A., passim; Linden, 46–66; and below, chaps. 10 and 12.

60. K.-A., 268–71, 274, 413; Sosis, 183–84. Not even Tsherikover, who emphasizes the significance of the manifestos, could cite any appearing before 15 April 1881.

61. See K.-A., 80, 203–04, 272–73, 364, 393–94, 416; Tsherikover (I), 355; Tsherikover (II), 457.

62. See above, n. 53.


*Chapter 6. Mysterious Messengers and Great Russian Raiders*

1. Dinur (I), 411–14; Dinur (II), 12, 14–15; Dubnow (I), 247–48, 256–57; Dubnow (II), 270, 276; Ettinger (II), 169; Frederic, 116; Gelber (I), 484, 491; Goldberg, 39–40; Levin (I), 92–93, 267; Levin (III), 245–46; Linden, 37, 43–44; Rogger (II), 45; Tsherikover (I), 346; Tsherikover (II), 448; Turtel, 43.

2. See Aronson (I); Aronson (IV); Klier (IV), 214, 218–19; Rogger (IV); and below, chaps. 10 and 11.

3. K.-A., 80.

4. Sonin, 207–11.

5. Sonin, 212–13, 215, 216–17, 218.

6. See Ekaterinoslav, 362; *Evr. ents.* (IV), 612; Gelber (I), 478–81; K.-A., 79, 397–98. Also see *Obshchaia zapiska,* 67; Sosis, 182.

7. Gelber (I), 478–81.

8. The anti-Semitism of the Jews' business competitors and of the intellectual classes is discussed in greater detail in chapter 7. The most relevant sources are: Ben-Ami; Demidov (II), 98–99; Ekaterinoslav, 361–62; K.-A., 159–60, 299–300, 405; and Subbotin, 153. Also see above, chap. 3, n. 11. On the anti-Semitism of Ukrainian intellectuals, see Berk (I), esp. 32–35; Ettinger (II), 169; Galai; Maor (III); Mishkinsky (I).

9. Dubnow (I), 253; Dubnow (II), 274, citing *Razsvet,* 1881, pp. 741–42.

10. K.-A., 412–14.

11. K.-A., 476–77; Kherson, 1181–82.

12. K.-A., 80; Kherson, 1204.

13. K.-A., passim, esp. 44, 531–41. Dinur (I), 411; Dubnow (I), 256; and Dubnow (II), 276, are mistaken when they state that the Great Russians disappeared without a trace.

## Chapter 7. *The Geographical Pattern and Socioeconomic Factors*

1. The list of towns struck by pogroms was compiled from K.-A., Slutsky (I), and others. The information on the size of the towns was taken from Fedor, 183–203. Also see Fedor, 1–17, 99–102, and passim; Rozman, 50, 58, 212, 285.

2. For examples of conspiracy theorists not only expecting simultaneity but also mistakenly asserting that this was indeed the case, see Dubnow (I), 248–49; Dubnow (II), 270; Ellenberger, 136; K.-A., 79, 128, 278, 412, 447; Tsherikover (I), 345–46; Tsherikover (II), 448; Vishniak, 130–31; Vital, 55. These writers, it seems to me, were led into error because of their a priori assumption of planning and their failure to pay careful attention to the movement of the pogroms on the map.

3. Bazhan, 90; Marinich, 118, 120.

4. Bazhan, 90, 290; Kubijovyč, 697, 829; Marinich, 119.

5. Bazhan, 90; Kubijovyč, 697; Marinich, 120.

6. On the economic difficulties in 1880–81, see K.-A., xiv–xvi; Tugan-Baranovsky, 265–68. Nonresident and unemployed laborers were mentioned in many sources dealing with conditions in 1881. For examples see: Ben-Ami, 39; Bloch, 6; Boyarsky, 146–47; Demidov (II), 98–99; Dinur (I), 411–12; Dinur (II), 28; K.-A., ix–xvi, 35–36, 39–40, 44, 61, 79–80, 117, 207–09, 439, 452, 456; *K ist. Evr. pog.,* 38; *Obshchaia zapiska,* 94–95; Slutsky (I), 21–22; Slutsky (II), 148; Sosis, 184; Subbotin, 152; Tsherikover (I), 343–44; Tsherikover (II), 446–47; Tugan-Baranovsky, 265–68.

7. Dinur (I), 411–13; Ettinger (II), 169; Linden, 46; Slutsky (I), 21–22; Tsherikover (I), 343–44; Tsherikover (II), 446–47.

8. Boyarsky, 146–47; Demidov (II), 98–99; K.-A., xiii–xvi, 44, 117, 452,

456–57; *K ist Evr. pog.,* 38; Slutsky (I), 21–22; Sosis, 184; Tsherikover (I), 343–44; Tsherikover (II), 446–47.

9. See Aronson (II); Dinur (I), 411–13, 416; Dinur (II), 28; Ettinger (II), 169; Goldberg, 23; Gradovskii, 135; K.-A., xxx, 117, 159–60, 299–300, 390, 452, 455, and passim; Slutsky (I), 22–24; Sosis, 181–82, 184; *Trudy,* passim.

10. See Aronson (II); Dinur (II), 28; Dubnow (I), 250; Dubnow (II), 271–72; Ekaterinoslav, 361; K.-A., 471, 531–41; *Obshchaia zapiska,* 63–64.

11. See Dahlke, 425; Ekaterinoslav, 361–62; K.-A., 21, 23, 77–78, 80, 102, 163, 239, 247, 354, 428–29; Subbotin, 153. Dinur (I), 416, claimed that well-to-do urban "organizers" acted as agents of the Holy Brotherhood, in order to serve their own economic interests. Pritsak, 8–43, claimed that Moscow business interests sent hired agents to the south and southwest regions to organize the pogroms. See above, chap. 3, n. 11.

12. K.-A., 159–60, 299–300.

13. Demidov (II), 98–99.

14. See Dubnow (I), 256; Dubnow (II), 276; Goldberg, 22; K.-A., 54–55, 209, 219, 222–24, 402–03, 414.

15. See Bloch, 3, 6; Dubnow (I), 266; Dubnow (II), 282; K.-A., 8–9, 15, 213, 222–24, 249, 402–03, 414, 417–18, 431, 474, and passim; *Obshchaia zapiska,* 94–95; *Obzor,* 95–96; *O neobkhodimosti,* 9–10; Poltava, 864–65; Slutsky (I), 22–23.

16. Dinur (I), 411; Dubnow (I), 250; Dubnow (II), 271–72; Levin (I), 92; Levin (III), 246; Turtel, 43.

17. Kherson, 1180. The governor-general of the Odessa region reported simply that the pogrom began when a Jewish tavernkeeper hit a customer who had smashed a glass. K.-A., 20, 25, 244.

18. Ben-Ami, 28–29; Bloch, 3; Drentel'n, 181; Dubnow (I), 252; Dubnow (II), 272–73; K.-A., 25, 79, 96, 104, 117, 204, 209, 239, 356–57, 442, 489–90.

19. *Evr. ents.* (IV), 613; Gessen (II), 217; K.-A., passim; Slutsky (I), 17–18, 22; Slutsky (II), 148. Also see Levin (I), 92; Levin (III), 245–46.

20. K.-A., 362–63.

21. See K.-A., 57, 117, 128, 272, 455; Slutsky (I), 22.

22. Kantor, 152; K.-A., 44, 117, 128–29, 208, 272, 362–64, 430, 452, 455; Slutsky (I), 17–18.

23. I could not discover the given name and patronymic of this governor.

24. K.-A., 362–63.

25. See Berk (I), 22–39; K.-A., passim; Yarmolinsky, 294–98; and below, chap. 12.

26. Boyarsky, 146–47.

27. Ulam, 9–42.

28. K.-A., 132, 252.

29. Fedor, 84, 98, 101–02, 115, 129, 140.

30. *Obshchaia zapiska,* 94–95. Also see *O neobkhodimosti,* 9–10.

31. See *Obshchaia zapiska,* 94–95; *Obzor,* 95–96, 99–100. Also see Rogger (I), 171–211.

32. Aronson (III), 167–82; Aronson (VI), passim.

33. Aronson (III), 167–82; Aronson (V), 59–74; Aronson (VI), passim; Rogger (I), 180–86; Roger (III), 22–26.

34. *Obzor,* 95–96. Also see *O neobkhodimosti,* 9–10.

35. *Obzor,* 99–100.

36. See Zaionchkovskii (II), 313–15. Also see Bushnell, 24, 34, 226–30. Bushnell, 26, notes "peasant dependence on the urban world" as a factor in the impulse to violence over the question of land repartition. For a detailed study of the paradoxes of peasant violence and passivity, see Field.

37. Gessen (I), 1632; Gessen (III), 154; K.-A., 512. Ignatiev's attribution of this "uncharacteristic" outburst to Jewish exploitation was, of course, a gross oversimplification of the forces at work in 1881.

38. Dubnow (I), 257; Dubnow (II), 276–77; Ekaterinoslav, 361–62, 377; Goldberg, 38–39; Gradovskii, 243–44; K.-A., 41, 106, 118–19, 123–24, 296–97, 354, 366, 432; Levin (I), 273; Linden, 46; *Obshchaia zapiska,* 69, 95; *O neobkhodimosti,* 9–10; Sosis, 182, 184; Subbotin, 152; Shvabakher, 5–6.

39. K.-A., 402–03. Also see K.-A., 73–74, 118–19, 124, 126, 248, 366, 370, 383, 441–42, 458–59, 478; *Evr. ents.* (IV), 613.

40. Frierson, 55–69.

41. See above, n. 29.

42. Kahan, 24, my emphasis.

43. Aronson (VI), 224; Demidov (II), 65–67; Gessen (I), 1680; Leskov, 31–33, 36–38, 43; *Obshchaia zapiska,* 135, 293–94; Subbotin, 116, 148–49; Vilna, 110–11; von Laue, 103–04.

44. See esp. K.-A., 126. Also see *Trudy,* passim; Aronson (VI), 141–273, passim.

45. Dubnow (I), 283. These sentences were blanked out by the censor in the Russian version, Dubnow (II), 294. Also see Dinur (I), 411; Dinur (II), 13; Dubnow (I), 249; Dubnow (II), 270; Goldberg, 39–40; Maor (I), 225; Sonin, 218; Sosis, 179; Tsherikover (I), 345–46; Tsherikover (II), 448; Turtel, 43; Vital, 55.

46. A reading of the *Report of the U.S. National Advisory Commission on Civil Disorders* (1968) will suggest parallels to the findings of the present study. Also see Dahlke.

47. See Boyarsky, 145–54; Dubnow (I), 358; Dubnow (II), 367; Ettinger (II), 170; Kantor, 156. Also see Slutsky (II), 148–49, on the similar circumstances in the town of Ekaterinoslav in 1883.

48. *Obshchaia zapiska,* 86.

*Chapter 8. Action and Inaction in Defense of the Jews*

1. Levin (I), 92–93; Levin (III), 244–45.

2. Dinur (I), 410; Dinur (II), 12; Maor (I), 224–25. Also see above, chap. 3.

3. Dinur (II), 12; Levin (I), 93; Zaslavskii, 294–95.

4. See, for example, Gelber (I), 491; Kherson, 1204; Maor (I), 224–25.

5. Sonin, 207–18. See above, chap. 6.

6. K.-A., 20, 468. Similar orders may have been given elsewhere, but I found no written evidence of this. For other instances involving the governor-general of the Odessa region, see K.-A., 1–2, 4, 20, 247, 262, 389; Kantor, 151.

7. K.-A., 3–4, 407.

8. K.-A., 488–89, 494–95.

9. K.-A., 20. Also see K.-A., 226–27, where the testimony of Jewish witnesses confirms the essential elements in this description.

10. K.-A., 74, 207, 264. Also see K.-A., 76, 251–52, 263; Kantor, 154.

11. K.-A., 406.

12. K.-A., 407. Also see *Hatsfira* (Warsaw), year 8, no. 22, 2–14 June 1881, p. 170, cited somewhat misleadingly by Dinur (II), 12.

13. Dubnow (I), 252; Dubnow (II), 272–73; K.-A., 75–77.

14. Dubnow (I), 254; Dubnow (II), 274; Gelber (I), 478; K.-A., 8, 397.

15. Gelber (I), 483. The report was based upon the testimony of witnesses at the trial of the Kiev rioters.

16. Novitskii, 185–86. V. D. Novitskii was chief of police in the town of Kiev. In his account of the pogrom there he attempted to shift all the blame for what happened onto Drentel'n while himself denying any responsibility. Nevertheless, his remarks tend to confirm the picture of Drentel'n drawn here. Novitskii quoted him as saying at the start of the pogroms that the Jews deserved a good beating in order to restrain their impudence and greed. However, in describing Drentel'n's behavior after he was knocked down, Novitskii quoted the governor-general as saying that he was sorry, when he saw how much damage had been done in the town, that he had not given orders on the first day to shoot the rioters.

17. K.-A., 219–20, 399–400; Novitskii, 186–87.

18. Chapter 11, below, on the Holy Brotherhood, demonstrates that Drentel'n could not have been acting secretly as an agent for that organization.

19. K.-A., 80–81.

20. See Dubnow (I), 253–54; Dubnow (II), 273–74; K.-A., 398; Levin (I), 93; Levin (III), 244–45; Novitskii, 180–83; Slutsky (I), 19.

21. K.-A., 398–400.

22. Fuller, 84–86.

23. Fuller, 90.

24. On this last point see Linden, 31–32.

25. Golitsyn, 180–82; Heilbronner, 398. Also see Fuller, 101.

26. In addition to the two reports cited below in nn. 27 and 28, see K.-A., 18, 131, 165, 261–63; Fuller, 101–02.

27. K.-A., 50–53.

28. K.-A., 488–89, 494–95.

29. See Dubnow (I), 249–50, 281–82; Dubnow (II), 271–72, 292–93; Gelber (I), 471–73; K.-A., 13–14, 18, 20–23, 76–77, 106, 118, 176–77, 192, 209–10, 224, 245–47, 266, 282–83, 290, 397–98, 431, 457, 489–90; Kherson, 1180–81.

30. See esp. Drentel'n, 181–82; Gessen (I), 1681; K.-A., 19, 35–36, 42, 60, 207, 288, 398–400, 413, 521; Kantor, 154; Zaionchkovskii (II), 391. Also see K.-A., 113–15, 174, 262–63, 285–86, 357, 402.

31. Fuller, 79–81.

32. See *Evr. ents.* (IV), 613; K.-A., 13–14, 19–20, 96, 117, 210–11, 237, 262–63, 282–86, 290, 407, 438; Kantor, 151; Levin (III), 244.

33. See Ben-Ami, 37–38; Bloch, 4; Dubnow (I), 249–50; Dubnow (II), 271–72; *Evr. ents.* (IV), 612; Gessen (II), 217; Goldberg, 44; K.-A., 21–23, 63, 101, 200–01, 237, 245–46, 262, 266–67, 282–83, 356–57, 385–86; Levin (I), 93; Sosis, 182.

See K.-A., 388–89 and 391–92, for the example of Odessa, where police and troops, having been given clear instructions beforehand by local officials, acted decisively and stopped the budding riot at its very beginning.

34. Fuller, 99.

35. K.-A., 21–22, 245–46, 266, 282–83.

36. Fuller, 94, 99.

37. See Ben-Ami, 45–46; Bloch, 4; Dinur (I), 413; Dubnow (I), 249–50; Dubnow (II), 271–72, 285–86; Ekaterinoslav, 362; Ettinger (II), 169; *Evr. ents.* (I), 826; *Evr. ents.* (IV), 612, 614; Gelber (I), 491; Gessen (II), 217; K.-A., 107, 230, 236–37, 244–46, 249, 262, 265, 277–79, 398, 401–03, 414, 417–18, 433, 445–47, 477; Maor (I), 224–25; Maor (II), 117; *Obshchaia zapiska,* 85; Sosis, 182.

38. See Boyarsky, 151–52; Dinur (I), 413; Dubnow (I), 267; Dubnow (II), 283; Gelber (I), 470–71, 491–92, n. 33; Goldberg, 26; K.-A., 4, 9, 25, 74, 76, 128, 154, 168, 207, 352–53, 356, 385, 399, 417, 520; Kherson, 1222; Zaionchkovskii (II), 313–14.

39. Fear of harming innocent bystanders, almost always Christians, also played a role. See Boyarsky, 151–52; Dinur (I), 413–14; Dinur (II), 12; Gelber (I), 470–71, 491–92, n. 33; K.-A., 7–8, 77–78, 133, 141, 207, 245–46, 282–83, 397, 399, 520; Kantor, 151. In a number of cases the troops fired only when they felt themselves to be threatened by the mob. See Dubnow (I), 255–56, 267; Dubnow (II), 275, 283; *Evr. ents.* (IV), 613; Gelber (I), 474; Gessen (II), 217; K.-A., 9, 21–22, 78–79, 99–101, 154, 198–201, 207, 246, 349–53, 356, 399–400; Kantor, 151–52; Linden, 73–74; Slutsky (I), 17–18; Tsherikover (I), 342; Tsherikover (II), 445.

40. Fuller, 106. Bushnell, 28–29, also deals with this proposal.

41. Bushnell, 28–29, 32–33; Fuller, 94–95.

42. Fuller, 108. Also see Fuller, chap. 3, esp. 94–95, 105, 108–10.

43. See Baron, 52; Drentel'n, 181; Dubnow (I), 282; Dubnow (II), 293; Gelber (I), 491; Gessen (II), 217; Goldberg, 39; K.-A., 24, 48, 118, 245, 402, 433–34; Kantor, 152; Sosis, 182; Vishniak, 133; Vital, 53–54.

44. See Heilbronner, 521–22; K.-A., 23, 24, 116–30, 224, 237, 356, 434; Linden, 27; *Obshchaia zapiska,* 95; Peretts, 130–33.

45. Ministerstvo, xiii.

46. Dubnow (I), 263; Dubnow (II), 280; Greenberg, 25; K.-A., 231; Levin (I), 98–99; Levin (III), 245.

47. K.-A., 78, 124, 220–21, 248, 255, 366, 401, 403, 419.

48. K.-A., 26. Contrast this account with Dubnow (I), 263; Dubnow (II), 280; Greenberg, 23.

49. K.-A., 23, 248, 264, 472–73.

50. K.-A., 264. Also see above, chaps. 3 and 5, sec. 1.

51. K.-A., 36–37, 45–46, 103, 201, 213, 436–37, 442.

52. Demidov (II), 98; Dubnow (I), 257; Dubnow (II), 276–77; Goldberg, 37; K.-A., 119–30 passim, 288–89, 291–92, 359, 367–68, 378, 408–09, 432–33, 440, 452, 457–58; *Obshchaia zapiska,* 69–70; *Papers,* 53:533; Sosis, 83.

53. See K.-A. citations in n. 52 above.

54. K.-A., 359, 378; Zaionchkovskii (II), 391.

55. Heilbronner, 519–20; Pobedonostsev (I), 53–56 (the reader must remember to discount Kantor's incorrect editorial remarks. See above, chap. 4, n. 35); Pobedonostsev (II), 344.

56. K.-A., 408–09; *Razsvet,* no. 25, 1882, cited in Goldberg, 37, and in Linden, 67.

57. K.-A., 23–30.

58. K.-A., 12–13.

59. Dubnow (I), 299. Also see Dinur (II), 10; Dubnow (II), 8; Klier (V), 18–19, 25–26. (Klier cites *Pravitel'stvennyi Vestnik,* no. 82, 18/30 April 1882, and *The Times* of London, 10, 21, and 22 April 1882.)

60. Dubnow (I), 299.

61. K.-A., 391.

62. K.-A., 116–17, 452–56, 461. Also see Dinur (I), 409–10; Sosis, 91.

63. K.-A., 439, 456–57.

64. Rostov-on-the-Don formed part of Ekaterinoslav *guberniia* until 1887, when it was excluded from the Pale, transferred to the Don Cossack Oblast (region), and closed to new Jewish settlement. Dubnow (I), 346; Greenberg (II), 38–39.

65. K.-A., 38–39, 116–30.

66. See Ellenberger, 136–37; Levin (I), 93; Slutsky (I), 19; Turtel, 43.


*Chapter 9. Punishing the Rioters*


1. Dubnow (I), 256; Dubnow (II), 275; K.-A., 42, 247; Gelber (I), 476; Gruenbaum, 146.

2. Ben-Ami, 38–39, 45–46; Boyarsky, 153–54; Dinur (I), 413–14; Dubnow (I), 256–57, 264, 315; Dubnow (II), 18–19, 276, 281; Gelber (I), 473, 481–85 passim; Goldberg, 26, 34–35; Greenberg, 25; Levin (I), 92–93; Levin (III), 244–45; Linden, 70–71; Maor (I), 225; Maor (II), 116–17; Sosis, 86, 185; Tsherikover (I), 342; Tsherikover (II), 445; Vital, 54; Zacek, 423.

3. Dubnow (I), 315–16; Dubnow (II), 18–19; Sosis, 86–87.

4. Florinsky, 903–06.

5. Florinsky, 903–06. Also see Kucherov.

6. K.-A., 251–52, 263. Also see K.-A., 113.

7. K.-A., 113.

8. K.-A., 42–45, 60, 62, 113, 118, 126, 163, 288; Kantor, 154, 156; Sosis, 86–87.

9. K.-A., 18–19, 74, 291; Kantor, 156; Kherson, 1204.

10. K.-A., 187.

11. Dubnow (I), 264; Dubnow (II), 281; Gelber (I), 482–83.

12. See "Napadenie," 530. The original text was unavailable for use in this study. For more on the boomerang effect, see below.

13. "Napadenie," 530. Also see Sosis, 86.

14. Goldberg, 26; K.-A., 223, 250–52, 390–91; Sosis, 86.

15. K.-A., 101, 106; Kantor, 154, 156.

16. K.-A., 216–17. Also see K.-A., 251–52, 263, 288, 290–91, 411–12.

17. K.-A., 23, 74, 207.

18. Fuller, 86–87.

19. For examples see K.-A., 70, 106, 118–24, and esp. 73–74.

20. K.-A., 44, 411. The law referred to is Article 179, *Stat'ia o nakazaniiakh nalagaemykh mirskimi sud'iami.*

21. Goldberg, 34; K.-A., 25, 43, 60, 62, 67, 73–74, 113, 128, 399, 410; "Napadenie," 530. Also see Dinur (I), 413; Gelber (I), 470–71, 484–85; Goldberg, 26; Kantor, 156.

22. See Aronson (IV).

23. Dubnow (I), 257; Dubnow (II), 276; K.-A., 20–21, 244.

24. See Ben-Ami, 30, 38–39, 45–47, 49. Also see Dubnow (I), 257–58; Dubnow (II), 277; Linden, 70–71; Sosis, 184–85.

25. Dubnow (I), 256–57; Dubnow (II), 276; Levin (I), 92.

26. K.-A., 370, 382–83, 458–59.

27. K.-A., 42–45; Gelber (I), 472. Also see K.-A., 288, 291, 409–10.

28. K.-A., 59–60, 62.

29. K.-A., 410–11.

30. K.-A., 419–20.

31. Dubnow (I), 264–65; Dubnow (II), 281; Gelber (I), 482–83; Goldberg, 34–35; Greenberg, 25; Sosis, 86.

32. Goldberg, 35; Kantor, 154. Strelnikov was slain by the *Narodnaia Volia* (People's Will) organization in 1882. As the town's military prosecutor, he had sent numerous revolutionaries to the gallows, so their comrades decided to kill him. His assassination was reported in the press at the time. I thank John Klier for this information.

33. Fuller, 121–22, 126–27.

34. K.-A., 410–11.

35. Gelber (I), 485.

36. Gelber (I), 481, 484–85. Some contemporary Jews also thought that local

officials had received instructions from above prohibiting them from taking energetic measures to suppress the riots. See Levin (I), 93. Strelnikov was mistakenly called Strelnitskii by Tsingaria. Perhaps this error is an indication of the care with which the consul checked his information in general.

## Chapter 10. The Aims of the "Conspirators"

1. Dinur (I), 408, 413; Dinur (II), 15, 17; Levin (II), 80; Pritsak, 8–43; Sosis, 179; Vital, 50–51.

2. See Aronson (VI); Rogger (I).

3. Baluev, 37, citing *Russkii Kur'er,* 1 Aug. 1881; K.-A., 53, 58, 82, 451–52, 457–58, 486–87, 508.

4. Dinur (I), 416; Dinur (II), 15, 18, 24, 28, 30; Dubnow (I), 247–48, 269–71; Dubnow (II), 270, 284–85; Greenbaum, 26–37; Joseph, 59–60, 63; Linden, 65–66; Levin (II), 81; Levin (III), 245; Zaslavskii, 296.

5. See Aronson (I), 5–6; Dinur (II), passim, esp. 18–19, 24; Heilbronner, 521–22; Peretts, 132; Rogger (IV), 28–29; Zaionchkovskii (II), 335, 380; Zaionchkovskii (III), 126.

6. See Zaionchkovskii (II), 335–82 passim.

7. See K.-A., 105, and esp. K.-A., 6. Also see Gelber (I), 469–83; *Papers,* 40:1020; and "Proscriptive Edicts," 52–53 for comments by representatives of foreign governments concerning the Russian authorities' initial surprise and their slowness in realizing the "widespread and deeply-seated character" of the spate of pogroms, as well as their concern to end the phenomenon once they woke up to the danger.

Kutaisov's opinion was that officials got so used to hearing the anti-Jewish rumors that they did not consider it possible to combat them or to prevent a "misfortune" (*beda*). They viewed it as an "unavoidable evil" (*neizbezhnoe zlo*), and so, beforehand, took measures aimed only at fighting the rioting if and when it occurred. K.-A., 259–60.

This opinion of Kutaisov's does not necessarily contradict the statements of the foreign observers. Officials could have expected trouble, but not on the scale on which it actually occurred. They had no experience of large-scale anti-Jewish rioting prior to 1881. As Kutaisov himself stated, some local officials, judging by the historical tradition, thought rioting could occur only in Odessa. K.-A., 261. Also see above, chap. 5, sec. 1.

8. Dubnow (I), 259–60; Dubnow (II), 277–78; *Evr. ents.* (IV), 614–15; Kantor, 153; Linden, 29; Rogger (II), 44–45; Rogger (III), 18; Zaionchkovskii (II), 384–85.

9. Kantor, 153.

10. K.-A., 46–48.

11. Kantor, 152; *Obshchaia zapiska,* 82.

12. K.-A., 58–59. Also see Gelber (I), 486; and above, chap. 5, sec. 3, and below, chap. 12.

13. Zaionchkovskii (II), 389. Also see Rogger (II), 44–45; Rogger (III), 18.

14. The first part of the tsar's statement was published in *Razsvet,* 1881, no. 20, cited in *Evr. ents.* (I), 826. Dubnow (I), 260–61, and Dubnow (II), 278–79, report the whole incident. Also see Dinur (II), 16; Goldberg, 42; Kantor, 151, 153.

15. See Dubnow (II), 270, n. 2; Gelber (I), 476; K.-A., 51–52, 56, 128, 202–03, 231, 362–64, 412, 443–44; Kherson, 1204; *Obshchaia zapiska,* 82; Sosis, 93, 180.

16. See Ignatiev's circular of 22 August, establishing the *guberniia* commissions, in Gessen (I), 1632–33; or K.-A., 512–14. Also see K.-A., 384–86.

17. See below, chap. 12; Berk (I); Yarmolinsky, 298.

18. Heilbronner, 522–23, 544; Miliutin, 69; Peretts, 130–33.

19. Byrnes, 207–08. Also see Aronson (IV).

20. K.-A., 47–48.

21. In Ignatiev's words, "For the past twenty years the government has tried to assist the fusion [*sliianie*] of the Jews with the rest of the population by a whole series of measures and almost made the Jews equal in rights to the native population." This, of course, was a gross exaggeration of Alexander II's achievement with regard to the Jews. Gessen (I), 1632; Gessen (III), 154; K.-A., 512.

22. Gessen (I), 1632–33; K.-A., 168–69, 384–86, 512–14; Rogger (III), 18–19.

23. See Rogger (III), 17; Zaionchkovskii (III), 126–39.

24. K.-A., 385–86.

25. K.-A., 168–69.

26. K.-A., 513; *Obshchaia zapiska,* 251.

27. K.-A., 385–86, 510, 514, 516.

28. Cf. Dubnow (I), 309; Rogger (III), 19–20; Sosis, 89; Zaionchkovskii (II), 413–15; and esp. K.-A., 520, 527–28; with Gessen (I), 1633; and Gessen (III), 185. Also see Aronson (IV); Aronson (V).

29. Dinur (I), 413; Dubnow (I), 247–48, 280; Dubnow (II), 270, 292; Goldberg, 23; K.-A., vi–vii, xxx; Levin (II), 80–81; Levin (III), 247–48, 251; Maor (I), 226, 228; Maor (II), 118, 122; Rogger (II), 44; Slutsky (I), 19, 25; Vital, 49–50.

30. Berk (I), 29–32; Dinur (I), 413; Dinur (II), 13; Ettinger (II), 169–70; Gruenbaum, 145; K.-A., vi–vii; Linden, 42–43, 65–66; Maor (I), 226, 228; Maor (II), 118, 122; Rogger (II), 44; Sosis, 179–80; Zaslavskii, 296.

31. See Dubnow (I), 260; Dubnow (II), 278–79; *Evr. ents.* (IV), 614; Gelber (I), 470–71; Gessen (II), 219; K.-A., 44, 79, 272, 362–64, 406; Mogilev, 97–98.

32. See above, chap. 5, sec. 1, and chap. 5, n. 7.

33. K.-A., 128, 416–17, 520; cf. Gelber (I), 491–92.

34. Dubnow (I), 260, 279; Dubnow (II), 270, 278–79, 291; *Evr. ents.* (IV), 614; Gessen (II), 219; Heilbronner, 519–20; K.-A., 7, 25, 36, 51–52, 56, 67, 70–72, 82–83, 95, 184–85, 273–74, 289–92, 362–64, 385–86, 394–95, 416–17, 446–47; Kantor, 152–53; Kherson, 1222–23; Miliutin, 68, n. 369; Peretts, 130–33; Rogger (II), 44, 47; Slutsky (I), 19; Sosis, 91; Tsherikover (I), 350–51; Tsheri-

kover (II), 452; Vital, 49–50; Zaionchkovskii (II), 313–14, 389, 415–17, 419; Zaslavskii, 295–96.

35. Kantor, 152. Also see Dubnow (I), 260; Dubnow (II), 278–79; Gelber (I), 470, 472; K.-A., 273–74; Zaslavskii, 295.

36. K.-A., 385–86, 394.

37. Florinsky, 1091; Zaionchkovskii (II), 402, 407–9.

38. Ignatiev, who is often accused of being the master planner behind the pogroms, became minister of state domains on 25 March 1881. He held that position until he replaced Loris-Melikov as minister of the interior on 5 May 1881.

39. Dinur (II), 13; Greenbaum, 26–33. Also see Ettinger (II), 169; Linden, 42–43; Slutsky (I), 19.

40. Dinur (II), 18, 24; Slutsky (I), 19. Also see Goldberg, 22; Maor (II), 118; Rogger (III), 22.

41. Dinur (II), 18, 24. Also see Dinur (II), 21–22, 25, 28.

42. Dubnow (I), 285, 306; Greenberg, 62; K.-A., 526.

43. See Aronson (I); Rogger (IV).

## Chapter 11. The Holy Brotherhood

1. Dinur (I), 414; Levin (I), 93; Linden, 26–27, 43–44; Tsherikover (I), 346–47; Tsherikover (II), 449; Vital, 55–56.

2. Baron, 52; Dinur (I), 408, 414, 416; Dinur (II), 12–15; Dubnow (I), 248–49; Dubnow (II), 270; Ettinger (II), 169; Greenberg, 24; Levin (I), 91–93, 97; Levin (III), 244–46; Maor (I), 225–26, 232–33; Maor (II), 116–18; Slutsky (II), 145; Tsherikover (I), 346–49, 355–56; Tsherikover (II), 449, 451, 457; Vishniak, 133; Vital, 55–56. Also see Linden, 25–27, 43–44, 46. Linden thought there was a strong likelihood that a secret organization prepared to use violence against Jews was active. He said it was perhaps a patriotic pan-Slav group, counting on the active assistance, or at least helpful passiveness, of the many bureaucrats who sympathized with its aims. He does not name the Holy Brotherhood, but no other similar organization on such a large scale has been discovered.

3. Byrnes, 208; Dinur (II), 12–13; Galai, 44, 53–54; Lukashevich (I), 506–09; Maor (II), 117–18; Sadikov, 204.

4. See Dinur (II), 12–13; Dubnow (I), 248–49; Dubnow (II), 270; Ettinger (II), 169; Levin (I), 92; Levin (III), 244–46; Linden, 43–44; Maor (I), 225–26; Maor (II), 116–17; Tsherikover (I), 345–46; Tsherikover (II), 448; Vital, 55.

5. Dinur (II), 13; Levin (II), 80–81; Levin (III), 247–48; Maor (I), 226, 228; Maor (II), 118, 122; Slutsky (I), 19; Sosis, 179–80; Vital, 55.

6. Sadikov, 211. Also see Dinur (II), 14; Lukashevich (I), 495; Tsherikover (I), 349–50; Tsherikover (II), 451–52.

7. Lukashevich (I), 493, 495, 504; Rogger (II), 45; Smel'skii, no. 2, 143–44; Smel'skii, no. 3, 165–66. Also see Bogucharskii (I), 305–06; and Tsherikover (I),

350, n. 36; or Tsherikover (II), 452, n. 36, where *Narodnaia Volia,* February 1882, nos. 8–9, concerning Baron Guenzburg, is cited.

8. Demidov (I) or (II). On Demidov's membership in the Holy Brotherhood, see Bogucharskii (I), 305–06; Heilbronner, 489; Lukashevich (I), 491, 493; Miliutin, 112, 167, n. 80; Smel'skii, no. 1, 232–33; Smel'skii, no. 2, 143–44, and passim.

9. Witte (I), 129–30, 522–24, n. 29, 30. Also see Lukashevich (I), 491; Tsherikover (I), 348–49; Tsherikover (II), 451.

10. Witte (I), 129–30, 522–24, n. 29, 30; Lukashevich (I), 491. For a contrary view see Galai, 44, n. 49.

11. Witte (I), 524, n. 30. Also see Witte, 527, n. 38; Novitskii, 180–87.

12. See Witte (I), 154, 302, 430; Witte (II), 210–15; Witte (III), 393–94; Aronson (I), 3; Aronson (IV), 351.

13. Witte (I), 153–54, 527, n. 38.

14. Aronson (V); Gessen (I), 1631–37, 1678–84; Gessen (III), 156–61, 185; Zaionchkovskii (II), 413–19. On Ostrovskii's membership in the Holy Brotherhood, see Bogucharskii (I), 305–06; Tsherikover (I), 348; Tsherikover (II), 450.

15. Peretts, 141; Dinur (II), 14. On Shuvalov's membership in the Holy Brotherhood, see Bogucharskii (I), 305–06; Dinur (II), 14; Lukashevich (I), 491–509; Maor (II), 118, Miliutin, 167, n. 80; Witte (I), 129–30, 522–24.

16. See Lukashevich (I), 505–09; Rogger (II), 45. The view presented here is in conflict with that of Maor (II), 118, who thought constitutionalism and anti-Semitism *could* go together. This claim may be true in certain instances, but it is very doubtful in regard to the 1881 pogroms.

17. See Lukashevich (I), 491, 493, 506–09; Rogger (II), 45.

18. On the use of the term *zhid,* see Klier (VI), 1–15; Mishkinsky (II), 210–12.

19. K.-A., 2; and esp. Kantor, 149–58. Representatives of the U.S. government in St. Petersburg in 1881–82 reported that in the capital it was generally believed that Alexander III himself, and his government, opposed the pogroms and were promoting energetic measures to put an end to them. *Papers,* 40:1020; 41:452–55.

20. Bogucharskii (I), 273–367 passim, esp. 273, 305–06, 367; Galai, 53; Greenberg, 24; Maor (II), 119; Pobedonostsev (II), 392–96; Pobedonostsev (III), 95, 248; Tsherikover (I), 348, 350; Tsherikover (II), 450, 452.

21. Byrnes, 208; Galai, 53–54; Pobedonostsev (II), 392–96; Pobedonostsev (III), 247–48. Byrnes cites Lukashevich (I) (see esp. Lukashevich (I), 493–94, 506–09), who found no evidence to link Pobedonostsev with the Holy Brotherhood, and a Soviet thesis (Evenchik, 49–54) based in part on archival materials of the Holy Synod, which concluded that all the available evidence shows that Pobedonostsev opposed the society's existence. Also see Vital, 56.

22. Bogucharskii (I), 305–06; Dinur (II), passim, esp. 12, 14–15, 18, 21, 24, 26–27; Galai, 44 and n. 52; Greenberg, 24; Linden, 27, 44; Lukashevich (I), 493–94, 504; Maor (II), 119; Slutsky (I), 19; Slutsky (II), 144–45; Tsherikover (I), 350–51; Tsherikover (II), 452; Vital, 56.

23. Galai, 44; Lukashevich (I), 504–05. Also see Maor (II), 119.

24. Lukashevich (I), 504, 506–09; Maor (II), 119; Slutsky (I), 19.

25. According to Zaionchkovskii (II), 464, cited by Galai, 44, n. 52, Ignatiev and the Holy Brotherhood came to an agreement by which Ignatiev would allow the society to continue to exist and it would support his proposal to convene a *zemskii sobor* (a type of consultative assembly). Also see Aronson (IV), 360–61; Bogucharskii (I), 367; Lukashevich (I), 506–09; Miliutin, 167, n. 80; Rogger (III), 21; Zacek, 419; Zaionchkovskii (III), 126–39.

26. See above, chap. 10. Also see the report, cited below, of the Holy Brotherhood agent on the origin of the pogroms.

27. Galai, 35–55.

28. Galai, 47, 48, n. 81, 51.

29. See below, chap. 12; Galai, 49.

30. Galai, 55, my emphasis. Pavel (Bobi) Petrovich Shuvalov, not to be confused with Petr Andreevich Shuvalov, mentioned above, was the Holy Brotherhood's agent in Russia who maintained contact with *Vol'noe Slovo*.

31. Galai, 53. A case can be made that Mal'shinskii's views on the Jews, as expressed in *Vol'noe Slovo* and cited by Galai, 47, simply echoed those prevalent both in Russia's ruling circles and in the socialist camp at the time. It was common wisdom by the summer of 1881 that the Jews themselves were responsible for the pogroms, because of their exploitative activities. Mal'shinskii, at least, distinguished between (good) Jewish laborers and (bad) Jewish exploiters. His assertion that Jewish moneylenders were worse than their gentile counterparts because they belonged to a different, distinctive national group resembles V. N. Smel'skii's views on Jews and Germans cited below. Smel'skii, it will be seen, can by no means be labeled an anti-Semite.

32. Dinur (II), 14–15; Maor (I), 226; Maor (II), 118; Tsherikover (I), 347–57; Tsherikover (II), 449–58. Also see Zaslavskii, 294–95. Baron, 52, states that the Holy Brotherhood engaged in large-scale anti-Jewish propaganda but provides no references to support this contention.

33. Tsherikover (I), 349–50; Tsherikover (II), 451–52.

34. Dinur (II), 12, 14–15, 18, 21, 24, 26–27; Slutsky (I), 19; Slutsky (II), 144–45.

35. Lukashevich (I), 494–509 passim.

36. Dubnow (II), 270, n. 2.

37. See chap. 10. Also see Tsherikover (I), 350–51; or Tsherikover (II), 452. Tsherikover thought Ignatiev was the source of the idea expressed in the Holy Brotherhood report that the revolutionaries were responsible for the pogroms. As I have shown, this view is incorrect, since the minister of the interior, Loris-Melikov, in the first days of the first pogroms, had already raised this possibility. See K.-A., 6; above, chap. 10.

38. Smel'skii, no. 1, 222–25, and passim.

39. Smel'skii, no. 4, 107–08. Reprinted in *Evreiskaia starina* 9 (1916): 332–33.

40. Smel'skii, no. 3, 163.

41. Sadikov, 201, 203.
42. Sadikov, 211.
43. Sadikov, 211–12.
44. Sadikov, 204–16.
45. Sadikov, 204.
46. Lukashevich (I), 494.
47. Rogger (II), 45.

## Chapter 12. The Revolutionary Socialists

1. The Russian Jewish newspapers *Hamelits,* no. 17, 5 May 1881, 354–55; and *Razsvet,* no. 19, 754. Cited by Mishkinsky (III), 9. Also cited by Dubnow (I), 260; Dubnow (II), 278–79.

2. Cited by Kantor, 153, my emphasis.

3. Cited by *Evr. ents.* (IV), 614–15. Also cited by Dubnow (I), 259–60; Dubnow (II), 277–78; Kantor, 153.

4. Cited by Dubnow (I), 261; Dubnow (II), 279–80.

5. K.-A., 46–48.

6. See Mishkinsky (I), 41, 55–57.

7. See Mishkinsky (I), 55–57.

8. See Mishkinsky (I), 41–48. Mishkinsky deals at length with the issue of Bakunin's anti-Semitism, its context, sources, influence, and so on.

9. Mishkinsky (I), 42, n. 11.

10. On the literature of the 1870s, see Mishkinsky (I), 40, n. 8.

11. See Berk (II), 22–23, 85–89; Frankel, 34, 40, 97–107, 112–14, 132, 138–39; Mishkinsky (I), 45.

12. See Mishkinsky (I), 46, 49–54, 58–61, 63–66.

13. See Mishkinsky (I), 47–48; Haberer, 22, 24–25.

14. Mishkinsky (I), 52, my trans. from the Hebrew. Also see Mishkinsky (I), 53, n. 63. *Parovaia Mashina* was a popular propaganda pamphlet written in Ukrainian by the Ukrainophile *narodnik* Sergei Podolynsky (1850–91). For more on the anti-Semitism of Podolynsky and the Ukrainophile *narodniki,* see Mishkinsky (I), 58–60. According to Haberer, 61, n. 95, some Jewish revolutionaries at the time contended that "the complaints of the author [of 'Prejudices'] against the Russian socialists were completely exaggerated."

15. See Mishkinsky (I), 52–53 and n. 68.

16. Mishkinsky (I), 54, my trans. from the Hebrew.

17. See Mishkinsky (I), 54.

18. See Mishkinsky (I), 40, n. 8, 59–66.

19. Voitinskii, 343. Cited by Mishkinsky (I), 63; Mishkinsky (II), 201; Mishkinsky (III), 16. Akselrod emigrated in June 1880.

20. Mishkinsky (II), 201–02. Akselrod's own ambivalences about the revolution-

ary potential of the pogroms are brought to light in Galai, 49, which should be read together with Frankel, 97–107, esp. 104–06.

21. Mishkinsky (II), 199. Mishkinsky discusses the murky background of this document in detail, 198–203.

22. Mishkinsky (II), 200, 203.

23. Mishkinsky (II), 204.

24. Mishkinsky (II), 193–95.

25. See *Chernyi Peredel*, no. 3, March 1881. Cited by Maor (III), 108.

26. See Haberer, 9–12; Mishkinsky (III), 3–4, 10.

27. The reader will perhaps notice that there were other curious and ironic parallels between the anti-Jewish views of persons on the right and the left regarding Jewish exploitation, the causes of the pogroms, their revolutionary potential, and so on.

28. See Haberer, 10; Mishkinsky (I), 209.

29. See Haberer, 15–19. Also see Mishkinsky (I), 54–61.

30. Voitinskii, 30–31. Cited by Haberer, 17, 35; Frankel, 106–07. Elisée Réclus was a French geographer and anarchist.

31. Haberer, 3, 29, 43. This whole issue is discussed by Haberer, 20–43. Also see Frankel, 101–07; Yarmolinsky, 298.

32. Mishkinsky (III), app. 2.

33. See the Vilna proclamation described below for an even more unequivocal denunciation of the pogroms.

34. Haberer, 13, n. 26, and passim. Also see Berk (II), 87.

35. Cited by Frankel, 98. Also cited by Berk (II), 87–88; Haberer, 12; and others.

36. Mishkinsky (III), 4; Haberer, 6, 12–14 and n. 25, 16–17, and passim.

37. K.-A., 225, quoted as translated by Mishkinsky (II), 206–07. Mishkinsky (II), 205–16 analyzes this document. Also cited by Berk (II), 90; Frankel, 100; Haberer, 14; and others. Brodskii was a wealthy Jewish businessman living in Kiev.

38. Quoted and paraphrased from Mishkinsky (III), 16–17; and Frankel, 100. Also cited by Haberer, 15.

39. Mishkinsky (III), 18, and app. 3.

40. *Chernyi Peredel*, no. 4, September 1881. Cited by Mishkinsky (III), 21–23.

41. *Chernyi Peredel*, no. 5, December 1881. Cited by Mishkinsky (III), 23–25, and n. 57.

42. Voitinskii, 215. Cited by Haberer, 7.

43. See Frankel, 100–01.

44. Mishkinsky (II), 207–08.

45. Berk (II), 59; *Evr. ents.* (IV), 614; Gelber (I), 471; Gessen (II), 219; Goldberg, 43; K.-A., 36, 58–59, 67, 80, 83, 170–72, 270–74, 354–55, 362–64, 414–17, 446; Linden, 46–66 passim; *Obshchaia zapiska,* 82; Sosis, 92–93, 180–81, 183–84.

46. Berk (I), 25–26; Berk (II), 86–87; Frankel, 99–100.

47. Voitinskii, 215. Cited by Haberer, 5, n. 6.

48. *Listok Narodnoi Voli,* the bulletin of the People's Will terrorist organization. Cited by Yarmolinsky, 295. Also see Heilbronner, 519–20; Bogucharskii (I), 221–22; Mishkinsky (III), 11.

49. Bogucharskii (II), 219, 337. Cited by Berk (I), 28; Berk (II), 89. Also see Berk (II), 85–99; Klier (IV), 212.

50. *Chernyi Peredel,* no. 4, September 1881. Cited by Mishkinsky (III), 21.

51. Cf. Haberer, 25–26 with Mishkinsky (III), 19–20. The article referred to by Getsov may be the one that appeared in *Zerno* in June 1881 and that, as I pointed out above, was quite ambivalent about the pogroms; or it may be an article that appeared in *Zerno* in November that contained an unequivocal antipogrom statement. The point here is that Getsov, by his own account, was not ambivalent.

52. Ruelf, 73–75. Cited by Haberer, 28; Mishkinsky (III), 35–36, n. 32.

53. Frankel, 138. Also see Yarmolinsky, 297–98 for a short review of *narodnik* writings after 1881 about the pogroms.

54. K.-A., 51–52, 79, 83, 128, 412, 443–44.

55. For a primary source on this episode, see K.-A., 59.

56. Dubnow (I), 256; Dubnow (II), 275; Kantor, 153; Klier (IV), 210; K.-A., 52, 79, 83, 392, 412. Berk (II), 44, suggests that the students involved in the rioting may have been members of the Holy Brotherhood.

57. Klier (IV), 210, citing the contemporary Russian press.

58. Cahan, 362–63. Cited by Haberer, 14. Also see Kantor, 153.

59. Tsherikover (III), 177. Cited by Haberer, 24.

60. Sukhomlin, 80. Cited by Haberer, 51, n. 28.

61. K.-A., 414.

62. Berk (I), 29; Berk (II), 90–91; Frankel, 100 ff., 112–14; Haberer, passim; K.-A., 80, 225, 270, 415. Frankel and Haberer discuss at length the problems that the pogroms presented for the *narodniki.*

63. K.-A., 271–73, 413. Also see K.-A., 203; Sosis, 92–93.

64. K.-A., 203–04.

65. K.-A., 203–04.

66. K.-A., 146, 202–04, 268, 270–71, 273–74, 370, 393–94, 413, 415–17, 445; *Obshchaia zapiska,* 94; Sosis, 92–93, 180.

67. Haberer, 11, and n. 19; K.-A., 79–80, 203–04, 219, 268, 273, 413, 445–56; *Obshchaia zapiska,* 82, 86; Sosis, 180.

68. K.-A., 146, 202–03, 219, 268–69, 392, 414, 443–44; Linden, 46–66 passim.

69. Berk (I), 22–39; Berk (II), 85–99; Klier (IV), 210–12; K.-A., 25, 79, 202–03, 268, 272, 354–55, 370–71, 392–94, 413–14, 443–46, 512; Linden, 46–66 passim; *Obshchaia zapiska,* 82; Sosis, 180; Zaionchkovskii (II), 385, n. 20.

# BIBLIOGRAPHY

The author wishes to thank Mr. Zvi Sheier, the late Mr. Moshe Springer, and Dr. Avraham Greenbaum for assisting in the translation of the works written in Yiddish.

Amburger, Erik. *Geschichte der Behoerdenorganisation Russlands von Peter dem Grossen bis 1917.* Leiden, 1966.

Aronson, I. Michael. "The Attitudes of Russian Officials in the 1880s toward Jewish Assimilation and Emigration." *Slavic Review* 34:1 (March 1975): 1–18. Cited as Aronson (I).

———. "Geographical and Socioeconomic Factors in the 1881 Anti-Jewish Pogroms in Russia." *Russian Review* 39:1 (January 1980): 18–31. (Appears in a revised form in chap. 7 of the present book.)

———. "Industrialization, Pollution, and Social Conflict in the Ukraine: The Case of Pereiaslav in 1881." *Societas* 8:3 (Summer 1978): 193–204. Cited as Aronson (II).

———. "Nationalism and Jewish Emancipation in Russia: The 1880s." *Nationalities Papers* 5:2 (Fall 1977): 167–82. Cited as Aronson (III).

———. "The Prospects for Jewish Emancipation in Russia during the 1880s." *Slavonic and East European Review* 55:3 (July 1977): 348–69. Cited as Aronson (IV).

———. "Russian Bureaucratic Attitudes toward Jews, 1881–1894." Doctoral dissertation, Northwestern University, Evanston, Ill., 1973. Cited as Aronson (VI).

———. "Russian Commissions on the Jewish Question in the 1880s." *East European Quarterly* 14:1 (Spring 1980): 59–74. Cited as Aronson (V).

Balmuth, Daniel. *Censorship in Russia, 1865–1905.* Washington, D.C., 1979.

Baluev, B. P. *Politicheskaia reaktsiia 80-X godov XIX veka i Russkaia zhurnalistika.* Moscow, 1971.

Baron, Salo W. *The Russian Jew under Tsars and Soviets.* New York, 1964. (The 2d edition of this book, 1976, contains no revisions of the material on the 1881 pogroms, although its pagination is slightly different.)

Bazhan, N. P., ed., et al. *Ukrainskaia Sovetskaia Sotsialisticheskaia Respublika.* Kiev, 1967.

Ben-Ami [pseud.]. "Odesskii pogrom 1881 goda i pervaia samooborona." *Evreiskii mir,* pt. 1, no. 5 (May 1909): 18–49.

Berger, David, ed. *The Legacy of Jewish Migration: 1881 and Its Impact.* New York, 1983.

Berk, Stephen M. "The Russian Revolutionary Movement and the Pogroms of 1881–1882." *Soviet Jewish Affairs* 7:2 (1977): 22–39. Cited as Berk (I). (Republished as chap. 4 of *Year of Crisis, Year of Hope*.)

———. *Year of Crisis, Year of Hope: Russian Jewry and the Pogroms of 1881–1882.* Westport, Conn., 1985. Cited as Berk (II).

Billig, Michael. *Arguing and Thinking: A Rhetorical Approach to Social Psychology.* Cambridge, 1987.

———. "Rhetoric of the Conspiracy Theory: Arguments in National Front Propaganda." *Patterns of Prejudice* 22:2 (Summer 1988): 23–34.

Bloch, Jan Gotlib [Ivan S. Bliokh]. *Sravnenie material'nago byta i nravstvennago sostoianiia naseleniia v cherte osedlosti Evreev i vne eia.* Vol. 1. St. Petersburg, 1891.

Boguharskii, V. Ia. [V. Ia. Iakovlev]. *Iz istorii politicheskoi bor'by v 70-kh i 80-kh gg. XIX veka.* Moscow, 1912. Cited as Bogucharsky (I).

———. *Literatura partii Narodnoi Voli.* Moscow, 1907. Cited as Bogucharskii (II).

Bol'shaia sovetskaia entsiklopediia. 65 vols. Moscow, 1938. "Mukomol'no-krupianaia promyshlennost'," 40: 577–78. Cited as *Bol. sov.*

Boyarsky, Joseph. *The Life and Suffering of the Jew in Russia.* Los Angeles, 1912.

Bushnell, John. *Mutiny amid Repression: Russian Soldiers in the Revolution of 1905–1906.* Bloomington, Ind., 1985.

Byrnes, Robert F. *Pobedonostsev: His Life and Thought.* Bloomington, Ind., 1968.

Cahan, Abraham. *The White Terror and the Red. A Novel of Revolutionary Russia.* New York, 1905.

Clarkson, Jesse D. *A History of Russia.* 2d ed. New York, 1969.

Dahlke, H. Otto. "Race and Minority Riots: A Study in the Typology of Violence." *Social Forces* 30 (May 1952): 419–25.

Demidov, Pavel Pavlovich, Prince of San Donato. *Evreiskii vopros v Rossii.* St. Petersburg, 1883. Cited as Demidov (I).

———. *The Jewish Question in Russia.* Translated from the Russian by J. Michell. 2d ed. London, 1884. Cited as Demidov (II).

Dinur, Ben-Tsion [B-Ts. Dinaburg]. "Hamishim shana lapraot." *Ahdut haavoda* 2:5–6 (March–April 1931): 407–16. (Hebrew.) Cited as Dinur (I).

———. "Tokhniyotav shel Ignatiyev l'pitron shailat hayehudim v'v'idot netsigai hakehilot b'Peterburg b'shnot 1881–1882." *Heavar* 10 (Iyar 5723): 5–60. (Hebrew.) Cited as Dinur (II).

Drentel'n, A. R. "Iz proshlogo: Drentel'n i anti-Evreiskie pogromy 1881 g." Edited by I. V. Galant. *Evreiskii vestnik,* 1928, 180–82.

Dubnow, Semen [Simon] Markovich. *History of the Jews in Russia and Poland.* Translated from the Russian by I. Friedlaender. Vol. 2. Philadelphia, 1918. Cited as Dubnow (I).

———. "Iz istorii vos'midesiatykh godov." *Evreiskaia starina* 8 (1915): 267–95, 9 (1916): 1–30, 353–79. Cited as Dubnow (II).

———. *Nationalism and History, Essays on Old and New Judaism.* Edited by Koppel

S. Pinson. Philadelphia, 1958; reprint New York, 1970. Cited as Dubnow (III).

Ekaterinoslav. Ekaterinoslavskaia gubernskaia komissiia. *Trudy Ekaterinoslavskoi gubernskoi komissii.* Sec. 2, pt. 2 of *Trudy gubernskikh komissii po Evreiskomu voprosu.* St. Petersburg, 1884.

EKO. Evreiskoe kolonizatsionnoe obshchestvo. *Sbornik materialov ob ekonomicheskom polozhenii Evreev v Rossii.* Vol. 2. St. Petersburg, 1904. Cited as EKO.

Ellenberger, Heinrich. *Die Leiden und Verfolgungen der Juden.* Budapest and Prague, 1882.

*Encyclopaedia Judaica.* 16 vols. Jerusalem, 1972.

Ettinger, Shmuel. "The Modern Period." In *A History of the Jewish People,* edited by H. H. Ben-Sasson, pt. 6, 725–1096. Cambridge, Mass., 1976. Cited as Ettinger (I). (Translated from the 3-volume Hebrew edition of 1969.)

———. *Toldot Yisrael B'ait hahadasha.* Vol. 3 of *Toldot am Yisrael.* Edited by H. H. Ben-Sasson. Tel Aviv, 1969. (Hebrew.) Cited as Ettinger (II).

Evenchik, S. L. "Reaktsionnaia deiatel'nost' Pobedonostseva v 80-kh gg. XIX-go veka." Thesis for candidate degree in history, Moscow University, 1939.

*Evreiskaia entsiklopediia.* 16 vols. St. Petersburg, 1906–13.

"Aleksandr III, " by Iu. Gessen and S. Pozner, in 1: 825–39. Cited as *Evr. ents.* (I).

"Aksakov, Ivan S.," by S. Tsinberg, in 1: 659–61. Cited as *Evr. ents.* (II).

"Antisemitizm v Rossii," by Iu. Gessen and S. Lozinskii, in 2: 730–52. Cited as *Evr. ents.* (III).

"Pogromy v Rossii," by Iu. Gessen, in 12: 611–18. Cited as *Evr. ents.* (IV).

Fedor, Thomas S. *Patterns of Urban Growth in the Russian Empire during the Nineteenth Century.* University of Chicago, Department of Geography, Research Paper no. 163. Chicago, 1975.

Field, Daniel. *Rebels in the Name of the Tsar.* Boston, 1976.

Florinsky, Michael T. *Russia: A History and An Interpretation.* Vol. 2. New York, 1953.

Frank, Stephen P. "Popular Justice, Community and Culture among the Russian Peasantry, 1870–1900." *Russian Review* 46:3 (July 1987): 239–65.

Frankel, Jonathan. *Prophecy and Politics: Socialism, Nationalism and the Russian Jews, 1862–1917.* Cambridge, 1981.

Frederic, Harold. *The New Exodus: A Study of Israel in Russia.* New York and London, 1892.

Frierson, Cathy. "Crime and Punishment in the Russian Village: Rural Concepts of Criminality at the End of the Nineteenth Century." *Slavic Review* 46:1 (Spring 1987): 55–69.

Fuller, William C., Jr. *Civil-Military Conflict in Imperial Russia, 1881–1914.* Princeton, N.J., 1985.

Galai, Shmuel. "Early Russian Constitutionalism, *Vol'noe Slovo* and the 'Zemstvo

Union.' A Study in Deception." *Jahrbuecher fuer Geschichte Osteuropas,* N. F. 22:1 (1974): 35–55.

Gatrell, Peter. *The Tsarist Economy, 1850–1917.* New York, 1986.

Gelber, N. M. "Di Rusishe pogromen onhaib di 80ker yoren in shein fun Estreichisher diplomatisher korespondents." In *Historishe shriften,* edited by E. Tsherikover, 466–96. Vilna, 1937. (Yiddish.) Cited as Gelber (I).

————. "Hapraot b'Varsha, 1881." *Heavar* 10 (5723): 106–23. (Hebrew.) Cited as Gelber (II).

Gessen, Iulii I. "Graf N. P. Ignat'ev i 'vremennyia pravila' o Evreiakh 3 Maia 1882 goda." *Pravo* no. 30 (27 July 1908): 1631–37; no. 31 (3 August 1908): 1678–86. Cited as Gessen (I).

————. *Istoriia Evreiskogo naroda v Rossii.* Vol. 2. Leningrad, 1927. Cited herein as Gessen (II).

————. *Zakon i zhizn.* St. Petersburg, 1911. Cited as Gessen (III).

Goldberg, Mina. "Die Jahre 1881–1882 in der Geschichte der Russischen Juden." Doctoral diss., Friedrich-Wilhelms-Universitaet zu Berlin, 1933.

Golitsyn, N. V. "Konstitutsiia grafa Loris-Melikova." *Byloe* 10–11:4–5 (April–May 1918): 125–86.

Gradovskii, Nikolai Dmitrievich. *Zamechaniia na zapisku kniazei Golitsynykh o cherte osedlosti Evreev.* St. Petersburg, 1886.

Graumann, C. F., and S. Moscovici, eds. *Changing Conceptions of Conspiracy.* New York, 1987.

Greenbaum, Yitshak [I. Gruenbaum]. "L'ahar shmonim shana (historiyon Polani— Y. Kukharzhevsky—al hapraot b'Rusiya b'1881–1882)." *Heavar* 9 (5722): 26–37. (Hebrew.)

Greenberg, Louis. *The Jews in Russia.* 2 vols. New Haven, Conn., 1944–51.

Gregory, Paul R. "Grain Marketings and Peasant Consumption in Russia, 1885–1913." *Explorations in Economic History* 17 (1980): 135–64. Cited as Gregory (I).

————. *Russian National Income, 1885–1913.* Cambridge, 1982. Cited as Gregory (II).

Gruenbaum, I. "Die Pogrome in Polen." In *Die Judenpogrome in Russland,* edited by A. Linden [Leo Motzkin], 1: 134–86. Cologne and Leipzig, 1910.

Haberer, Erich. "Cosmopolitanism, Anti-Semitism, and Populism: A Reappraisal of the Russian and Jewish Socialist Response to the Pogroms of 1881–1882." Manuscript.

Heilbronner, Hans. "The Administrations of Loris-Melikov and Ignatiev, 1880–1882." Doctoral diss., University of Michigan, Ann Arbor, Mich., 1954.

Ingerflom, Claudio Sergio. "Idéologie révolutionnaire et mentalité antisémite: Les Socialistes russes face aux pogroms de 1881–1883." *Annales: Economies, Sociétés, Civilisations* 38:3 (May–June 1982): 434–53.

Joseph, Samuel. *Jewish Immigration to the United States from 1881 to 1901.* Vol. 59, no. 4, whole no. 145 of *Studies in History, Economics, and Public Law.* Edited by the Faculty of Political Science of Columbia University. New York, 1914.

K.-A. Krasnyi-Admoni, Grigorii Iakovlevich, ed. *Vos'midesiatye gody, 12 aprel' 1881–29 fevral' 1882.* Vol. 2 of *Materialy dlia istorii antievreiskikh pogromov v Rossii.* 2 Vols. Petrograd-Moscow, 1923. Cited as K.-A.

Kahan, Arcadius. *Essays in Jewish Social and Economic History.* Chicago, 1986.

Kantor, R. M. "Aleksandr III o Evreiskikh pogromakh 1881–1883 gg. (Novye materialy)." *Evreiskaia letopis'* 1 (1923): 149–58.

Kherson. Khersonskaia gubernskaia komissiia. *Trudy Khersonskoi gubernskoi komissii.* Sec. 9, pt. 2 of *Trudy gubernskikh komissii po Evreiskomu voprosu.* St. Petersburg, 1884.

*K istorii Evreiskikh pogromov i pogromnykh protsessov v Rossii. Rechi po pogromnym delam.* Kiev, 1908. Cited as *K ist. Evr. pog.*

Klier, John Doyle. "1855–1894 Censorship of the Press in Russia and the Jewish Question." *Jewish Social Studies* 48:3–4 (Summer–Fall 1986): 257–68. Cited as Klier (I).

———. "*Kievlianin* and the Jews: A Decade of Disillusionment, 1864–1873." *Harvard Ukrainian Studies* 5:1 (March 1981): 83–101. Cited as Klier (VII).

———. *Russia Gathers Her Jews: The Origins of the "Jewish Question" in Russia, 1772–1825.* De Kalb, Ill., 1986. Cited as Klier (II).

———. "Russian Judeophobes and German Antisemites: Strangers and Brothers." Manuscript. Cited as Klier (III).

———. "The Russian Press and the Anti-Jewish Pogroms of 1881." *Canadian-American Slavic Studies* 17:2 (Summer 1983): 199–221. Cited as Klier (IV).

———. "*The Times* of London, the Russian Press, and the Pogroms of 1881–1882." *Carl Beck Papers,* No. 308 (1984), 1–26. Cited as Klier (V).

———. "Zhid: The Biography of a Russian Pejorative." *Slavonic and East European Review* 60:1 (January 1982): 1–15. Cited as Klier (VI).

Kubijovyč, V., ed. *Ukraine, A Concise Encyclopaedia.* Vol. 2. Toronto, 1971.

Kucherov, Samuel. *Courts, Lawyers, and Trials under the Last Three Tsars.* New York, 1953.

Leskov, N. S. *Evrei v Rossii, neskolko zamechanii po Evreiskomu voprosu.* Petrograd, 1919 (1884 ed.).

Lestchinsky, Jacob. *Dos Yidishe folk in tsifern.* Berlin, 1922. (Yiddish.)

Levin, [Lewin] E. B. "Anti-Evreiskoe dvizhenie v Rossii v 1881 i 1882 gg." Edited by S. M. Dubnow. *Evreiskaia starina* 1 (1909): 88–109, 265–76. Cited as Levin (I).

———. "Mitokh tazkir al hapraot b'shnot 1881–1882." Edited by Y. Slutsky. *Heavar* 9 (5722): 78–81. (Hebrew.) Cited as Levin (II).

———. "Zapiska ob antievreiskikh pogromakh 1881 goda." Edited by S. M. Dubnow. *Golos minuvshago* 4:3 (March 1916), 243–53. Cited as Levin (III).

Linden, A. [Leo Motzkin]. "Prototyp des Pogroms in den achtziger Jahren." In *Die Judenpogrome in Russland,* edited by A. Linden [Leo Motzkin], 1: 12–96. Cologne and Leipzig, 1910.

Lipset, S. M., and E. Raab. *The Politics of Unreason.* London, 1971.

Lukashevich, Stephen. "The Holy Brotherhood: 1881–1883." *American Slavic and East European Review* 18 (December 1959): 491–509. Cited as Lukashevich (I).

―――. *Ivan Aksakov, 1823–1886: A Study in Russian Thought and Politics.* Cambridge, Mass., 1965. Cited as Lukashevich (II).

Maor, Yitshak. "Hakesher bain haantishemiut hagermanit ubain hapraot b'y'hudai Rusiya b'shnot hashmonim l'maia hat'sha-esrai." *Proceedings of the Fifth World Congress of Jewish Studies, 1969.* 2:224–38 (Hebrew section). Jerusalem, 1972. (Hebrew.) Cited as Maor (I).

―――. "70 shana l'sufot banegev' (Haantishemiut hagermanit k'goraim b'pogromim b'rusiya)." *Niv hak'vutsa* 1:3 (June 1952; Sivan 5712): 116–30. (Hebrew.) Cited as Maor (II). (Maor (I) and (II) attempt to establish a link between some German anti-Semites and some members of the Holy Brotherhood.)

―――. "Hakruz haantishemi shel 'Narodnaya Volya.' " *Zion* 15 (1950): 150–55. (Hebrew.)

―――. *Sheelat hayehudim batnua haliberalit vehamahpkhanit berusya (1890–1914).* Jerusalem, 1964. (Hebrew.) Cited as Maor (III).

Marinich, A. M., ed., et al. *Ukraina, obshchii obzor.* Moscow, 1969.

Miliutin, D. A. *Dnevnik D. A. Miliutina, 1881–1882.* Vol. 4. Moscow, 1950.

Ministerstvo Vnutrennikh Del. *Istoricheskii ocherk.* Vol. 2. St. Petersburg, 1901.

Mishkinsky, Moshe. "Al emdata shel hatnua hamahpekhanit harusit legabe hayehudim bishnot ha–70 shel hamea ha–19." *Heavar* 9 (1962): 38–67; 10 (1963): 212–13. (Hebrew.) Cited as Mishkinsky (I).

―――. "The Attitude of the Southern-Russian Workers' Union toward the Jews (1880–1881)." *Harvard Ukrainian Studies* 6:2 (1982): 191–216. (Revised translation of " 'Igud hapoalim hadrom-rusi.' ") Cited as Mishkinsky (II).

―――. " 'Chernyi Peredel' and the Pogroms of 1881." Manuscript. Cited as Mishkinsky (III).

―――. " 'Igud hapoalim hadrom-rusi' vehapogrom bekiev bishnat 1881." *Shvut* (Tel Aviv) 1 (1973): 62–73. (Hebrew.)

Mogilev. Mogilevskaia gubernskaia komissiia. *Trudy Mogilevskoi gubernskoi komissii.* Sec. 5, pt. 1 of *Trudy gubernskikh komissii po Evreiskomu voprosu.* St. Petersburg, 1884.

"Napadenie odnoi chasti naseleniia na druguiu." In *Entsiklopedicheskii slovar',* 20-A: 530. St. Petersburg, 1897. (Published by F. A. Brokgauz i I. A. Efron.)

Nelson, J. S., A. Megill, and D. N. McCloskey, eds. *The Rhetoric of the Human Sciences.* Madison, Wisc., 1987.

Novitskii, V. D. *Iz vospominanii zhandarma.* Leningrad, 1929.

*O neobkhodimosti nekotorykh izmenenii i dopolnenii nyne deistvuiushchikh zakonov o prave zhitel'stve Evreev.* [St. Petersburg?], [1888?].

*Obshchaia zapiska vysshei komissii dlia peresmotra deistvuiushchikh o Evreiakh v imperii zakonov (1883–1888).* [St. Petersburg?], [1888?].

*Obzor postanovlenii vysshei komissii po peresmotru deistvuiushchikh o Evreiakh v Imperii zakonov (1883–1888: Prilozhenie k "obschei zapiske" vysshei komissii.* [St. Petersburg?], 1888.

Orbach, Alexander. "The Pogroms of 1881–1882: The Response from St. Petersburg Jewry." *Carl Beck Papers in Russian and East European Studies,* no. 308 (University of Pittsburgh, 1984).

*Papers Relating to the Foreign Relations of the United States.* Vols. 40 (1881), 41 (1882), 50 (1891), 51 (1892), 53 (1894). Washington, D.C., 1882, 1883, 1892, 1893, 1895.

Peretts, Egor Abramovich. *Dnevnik E. A. Perettsa (1880–1883).* Edited by A. A. Sergeev, with a preface by A. E. Presniakov. Moscow-Leningrad, 1927.

Peskovskii, Matvei Leontevich. *Rokovoe nedorazumenie. Evreiskii vopros, ego mirovaia istoriia i estestvennyi put' k razresheniiu.* St. Petersburg, 1891.

Pincus, Benjamin. *The Jews of the Soviet Union: The History of a National Minority.* Cambridge, 1988. Translation from the Hebrew of *Yehudei rusya uvrit hamoatsot.*

————. *Yehudei rusya uvrit hamoatsot. Toldot miut leumi.* Jerusalem, 1986. (Hebrew).

Pobedonostsev, K. P. *K. P. Pobedonostsev i ego korrespondenty. Pis'ma i zapiski.* Vol. 1, pt. 1. Moscow, Petrograd, 1923. Cited as Pobedonostsev (III).

————. *Pis'ma Pobedonostseva k Aleksandra III.* Vol. 1. Moscow, 1925. Cited as Pobedonostsev (II).

————. "Pis'ma K. P. Pobedonostseva k grafu N. P. Ignat'evu." Edited by R. M. Kantor. *Byloe* 27–28 (1924, [1925]: 50–89. Cited as Pobedonostsev (I).

Poltava. Poltavskaia gubernskaia komissiia. *Trudy Poltavskoi gubernskoi komissii.* Sec. 7, pt. 2 of *Trudy gubernskikh komissii po Evreiskomu voprosu.* St. Petersburg, 1884.

Potter, J., and M. Wetherell. *Discourse and Social Psychology.* London, 1987.

Pritsak, Omeljan. "The Pogroms of 1881." *Harvard Ukrainian Studies* 11:1–2 (1987): 8–43.

"Proscriptive Edicts Against Jews in Russia." *United States Congress, House of Representatives, Executive Documents.* Vol. 37 (1st Session, 51st Congress, 1889–90), Executive Document no. 470, pp. 1–142. Washington, D.C., 1890.

*Raboty komissii ob uezdnykh uchrezhdeniiakh.* 2 vols. St. Petersburg, 1859.

Rogger, Hans. "Government, Jews, Peasants, and Land in Post-Emancipation Russia." *Cahiers du Monde Russe et Soviétique* 17:1 (January–March 1976): 5–25; 17:2–3 (April–September 1976): 171–211. Cited as Rogger (I). (Reprinted in Rogger (V).)

————. *Jewish Policies and Right-Wing Politics in Imperial Russia.* Oxford, 1986. Cited as Rogger (V).

————. "The Jewish Policy of Late Tsarism: A Reappraisal." *Wiener Library Bulletin* 25:1–2 (1971): 42–51. Cited as Rogger (II). (Reprinted in Rogger (V).)

————. *Russia in the Age of Modernization and Revolution, 1881–1917.* London, 1983. Cited as Rogger (VI).

————. "Russian Ministers and the Jewish Question, 1881–1917." *California Slavic Studies* 8 (1975): 15–76. Cited as Rogger (III). (Reprinted in Rogger (V).)

————. "Tsarist Policy on Jewish Emigration." *Soviet Jewish Affairs* 3:1 (1973): 26–36. Cited as Rogger (IV). (Reprinted in Rogger (V).)

Rozman, Gilbert. *Urban Networks in Russia, 1750–1800, and Pre-modern Periodization.* Princeton, N.J., 1976.

Ruelf, J. *Drei Tage in Juedisch-Russland.* Frankfurt-am-Main, 1882.

*Russkie liudi o Evreiakh.* St. Petersburg, [1891].

Ruud, Charles A. *Fighting Words: Imperial Censorship and the Russian Press, 1804–1906.* Toronto, 1982.

Sadikov, P. A., ed. "Obshchestvo 'Sviashchennoi Druzhiny.' ('Otchetnaia zapiska' za 1881–1882 gg.)." *Krasnyi arkhiv* 21 (1927): 200–17.

Shvabakher, Simeon Leontevich, Odessa Municipal Rabbi. *Zapiska o prichinakh bezporiadkov na iuge Rossii, predstavlennaia grafu Kutaisovu.* Translated from the German by S. I. Sychevskii. Odessa, 1881.

Silber, Jacques. "Some Demographic Characteristics of the Jewish Population in Russia at the End of the 19th Century." *Jewish Social Studies* 42:3–4 (Summer–Fall, 1980): 269–80.

*Sistematicheskii ukazatel' literatury o Evreiakh na russkom iazyke so vremeni vvydeniia grazhdanskogo shrifta 1708 g. po dekabr 1889 g.* St. Petersburg, 1892. (Edited, anonymously, by Vladimir I. Mezhov.)

Slutsky, Yehuda. "Hagaiografiya shel praot 1881." *Heavar* 9 (Elul 5722): 16–25. (Hebrew.) Cited as Slutsky (I).

————. "Hapraot b'shnot 1882–1884." *Heavar* 10 (Iyar 5723): 144–49. (Hebrew.) Cited as Slutsky (II).

————. "Russia." In *Encyclopaedia Judaica,* 14:433–506. Jerusalem, 1972. Cited as Slutsky (III).

Smel'skii, V. N. "Sviashchennaia Druzhina." *Golos minuvshago,* no. 1 (January 1916): 222–56; no. 2 (February 1916): 135–63; no. 3 (March 1916): 155–76; no. 4 (April 1916): 95–112; nos. 5–6 (May–June 1916): 86–105.

Solzhenitsyn, Alexander. *Gulag Archipelago 1918–1956.* Translated from the Russian by Thomas P. Whitney. New York, 1973.

Sonin, P. "Vospominaniia o iuzhnorusskikh pogromakh 1881 goda." *Evreiskaia starina* 2 (1909): 207–18.

Sosis, I. D. "K istorii anti-Evreiskogo dvizheniia v tsarskoi Rossii." *Trudy Belorusskogo gosudarstvennogo universiteta v gorode Minske. (Pratsy),* nos. 6–7 (1925): 176–88; no. 12 (1926): 82–94.

Stanislawski, Michael. *Tsar Nicholas I and the Jews: The Transformation of Jewish Society in Russia, 1825–1855.* Philadelphia, 1983.

Subbotin, Andrei Pavlovich. *Obshchaia zapiska po Evreiskomu voprosu.* St. Petersburg, 1905.

Sukhomlin, V. I. "Iz epokhi upadka partii 'Narodnaia Volia'." *Katorga i Ssylka,* bk. 24 (1926): 80.

*Trudy gubernskikh komissii po Evreiskomu voprosu.* 2 parts. St. Petersburg, 1884.

Tsherikover, Eliahu. "Homer hadash l'toldot hapraot b'rusiya b'raishit shnot hash-monim." *Yehudim b'itot mahapaikha.* Pp. 341–65. Tel Aviv, 1957. (Hebrew.) Cited as Tsherikover (I).

———. "Neie materialn di pogromen in Rusland onheib di 80er yorn." In *Historishe shriften,* edited by E. Tsherikover, 2:444–65. Vilna, 1937. (Yiddish.) Cited as Tsherikover (II).

———. *Geshikhte fun der Yidisher Arbeter-Bavegung in di Fareynikte Shtatn.* New York, 1945. Cited as Tsherikover (III).

Tugan-Baranovsky, Mikhail I. *The Russian Factory in the Nineteenth Century.* Translated from the Russian, 3d edition (1907) by A. Levin, C. S. Levin, and G. Grossman. Homewood, Ill., 1970.

Turtel, Hasiya. "Pulmus hahagira mairusiya aharai 'hasufot banegev' b'shnat 1881." *Heavar* 21 (5735): 43–65. (Hebrew.)

Ulam, Adam. "The Historical Role of Marxism and the Soviet System." *The New Face of Soviet Totalitarianism.* Pp. 9–42. New York, 1963.

U.S. National Advisory Commission on Civil Disorders. *Report of the National Advisory Commission on Civil Disorders.* New York, 1968.

Valk, S., ed. "Posle pervogo marta 1881 g." *Krasnyi arkhiv* 45 (1931): 147–64.

Venturi, Franco. *Roots of Revolution.* Translated from the Italian by F. Haskell. London, 1960.

Vilna. Vilenskaia gubernskaia komissiia. *Trudy Vilenskoi gubernskoi komissii.* Sec. 1, pt. 1 of *Trudy gubernskikh komissii po Evreiskomu voprosu.* St. Petersburg, 1884.

Vishniak, Mark. "Anti-Semitism in Tsarist Russia." In *Essays on Anti-Semitism,* edited by Koppel S. Pinson, 79–110. New York, 1942.

Vital, David. *The Origins of Zionism.* Oxford, 1975.

Voitinskii, V. S., et al. *Iz arkhiva P. B. Akselroda, 1881–1896.* Berlin, [1924].

Von Laue, T. H. *Sergei Witte and the Industrialization of Russia.* New York, 1969.

Witte, S. Iu. *Detstvo. Tsarstvovaniia Aleksandra II i Aleksandra III. (1849–1894).* Vol. I of *Vospominaniia.* Edited by A. L. Sidorov, P. Sh. Ganelin, and B. V. Anan'ich. Moscow, 1960. Cited as Witte (I).

———. *Tsarstvovanie Nikolaia II. (1894–Okt., 1905).* Vol. II of *Vospominaniia.* Edited by A. L. Sidorov, V. I. Bovykin, and K. N. Tarnovskii. Moscow, 1960. Cited as Witte (II).

———. *Tsarstvovanie Nikolaia II. (17 Okt., 1905–1911).* Vol. III of *Vospominaniia.* Edited by A. L. Sidorov, I. V. Bestuzhev, and V. A. Emets. Moscow, 1960. Cited as Witte (III).

Yaney, George. *The Urge to Mobilize: Agrarian Reform in Russia, 1861–1930.* Urbana, Ill., 1982.

Yarmolinsky, Avrahm. *Road to Revolution.* New York, 1962.

Zacek, Judith Cohen. "Champion of the Past: Count D. A. Tolstoi as Minister of the Interior, 1882–1889." *Historian* 30 (May 1968): 412–38.

Zaionchkovskii, Petr Andreevich. "Aleksandr III i ego blizhaishee okruzhenie."
   *Voprosy istorii* 8 (1966): 130–46. Cited as Zaionchkovskii (I).
————. *Krizis samoderzhaviia na rubezhe 1870–1880-kh godov.* Moscow, 1964. Cited
   as Zaionchkovskii (II).
————. "Popytka sozyva zemskogo sobora i padenie ministerstva N. P. Ignat'eva."
   *Istoriia S.S.S.R.* 4 (September–October 1960): 126–39. Cited as Zaionchkov-
   skii (III).
————. *Rossiiskoe samoderzhavie v kontse XIX stoletiia.* Moscow, 1970. Cited as
   Zaionchkovskii (IV).
————. *The Russian Autocracy in Crisis.* Gulf Breeze, Fla., 1979. (Translation of
   *Krizis samoderzhaviia na rubezhe 1870–1880-kh godov.*)
Zaslavskii, D. "Kritika G. Ia. Krasnogo-Admona, *Materialy dlia istorii antievreiskikh
   pogromov v Rossii,* Vol. II." *Byloe* 23 (1924): 293–96.
Zipperstein, Steven J. *The Jews of Odessa. A Cultural History, 1794–1881.* Stanford,
   Calif., 1985.

# INDEX

Note: The place names appearing in the tables and maps are not included in this index.

# Pitt Series in Russian and East European Studies

*Jonathan Harris, Editor*